VISIONS OF COMPASSION

VISIONS OF COMPASSION

Western Scientists and
Tibetan Buddhists
Examine Human Nature

Edited by Richard J. Davidson &
Anne Harrington

OXFORD
UNIVERSITY PRESS

2002

OXFORD
UNIVERSITY PRESS

Oxford   New York
Athens   Auckland   Bangkok   Bogotá   Buenos Aires   Cape Town
Chennai   Dar es Salaam   Delhi   Florence   Hong Kong   Istanbul   Karachi
Kolkata   Kuala Lumpur   Madrid   Melbourne   Mexico City   Mumbai   Nairobi
Paris   São Paulo   Shanghai   Singapore   Taipei   Tokyo   Toronto   Warsaw

and associated companies in
Berlin   Ibadan

Library of Congress Cataloging-in-Publication Data
Visions of compassion: western scientists and Tibetan Buddhists examine
human nature / edited by Richard J. Davidson and Anne Harrington.
   p.   cm.
Includes bibliographical references and index.
ISBN 0-19-513043-X
1. Meditation (Buddhism)—Psychology.   2. Meditation (Buddhism)—
Physiological aspects.   3. Compassion (Buddhism)   4. Altruism.   5. Empathy.
6. Buddhism—China—Tibet.   I. Davidson, Richard J.   II. Harrington, Anne, 1960–
BQ7805 .S35 2001
294.3'375—dc21   2001021078

Title page and chapter openers: Lotus flower from Mādavela Rājamāhavihāra (Sri Lanka), fresco,
mid-eighteenth century. Reproduced from John Clifford Holt, The Religious World of Kīrti Śrī
(Oxford University Press, 1996). Used by permission of the author.

9 8 7 6 5 4 3 2 1

Printed in the United States of America
on acid-free paper

Preface

This book is about compassion: what it is, where it "fits" into our understandings of human nature, and what it could mean for science in particular to learn more about it. It is also a book about what could happen if Western biobehavioral science were to allow its thinking to be challenged by the interrogating voice of a fundamentally different cultural perspective: that of Tibetan Buddhism. While there is a modest research tradition in the Western behavioral sciences concerned with altruism, prosocial behavior, the development of sympathy, empathy, and so on, the dominant note of the biobehavioral sciences in the West has been tragic-machismo: We find our origins in ancestors we call "killer apes," ponder our potential for violence, explore the genetic and biochemical bases of our capacity for selfishness, depression, and anxiety. In contrast, Tibetan Buddhism has long celebrated the human potential for compassion, is dedicated to studying the scope, expression, and training of compassionate feeling and action, and sees compassion as a key to enduring happiness and, even more fundamentally, spiritual transformation. Given this, two questions immediately suggest themselves. (1) Why these differences? And (2), given our understandings of our points of difference and of overlap, what can we expect to learn from each other when we start to talk?

The idea of developing an edited volume devoted to these questions had its inspiration in a week-long conference entitled "Altruism, Ethics, and Compassion" that took place in October 1995 in Dharamsala, India. The participants in that meeting consisted of a small group of

Tibetan Buddhist monks, His Holiness, the XIV Dalai Lama—exiled political and spiritual leader of Tibet—and six leading Western scholars and scientists: a developmental psychologist (Nancy Eisenberg), a neuroscientist (Richard Davidson), a social psychologist (Ervin Staub), an economist (Robert Frank), a historian of science (Anne Harrington), and a philosopher of biology (Elliott Sober).

Each speaker was provided with an entire morning to present. The charge was to "locate" the topic at hand—"compassion"—within the theoretical framework of one's own discipline, and its empirical knowledge. The afternoon sessions, turned over wholly to discussion, then offered a further challenge: to see what might happen when a particular disciplinary understanding was subjected to the scrutiny of a radically unfamiliar cultural perspective, namely, Tibetan Buddhism. Underlying the entire process was an implicit question: were there ways that Western biobehavioral science and scholarship had an impoverished sense of human potential; failed to do justice to certain human emotions and behavior—like compassion—that were perhaps much better understood and honored within other cultural systems?

Structured around both the metaphor and the reality of dialogue, the book that has resulted from that 1995 meeting aims to be more than just a proceedings of a meeting, however extraordinary. Chapters are included here that address questions that emerged during the week but were not adequately resolved by its close. For example, in attendance at the Dharamsala meeting was a Western Tibetan scholar (Georges Dreyfus) who for many years lived as a monk and now teaches Tibetan studies in America. As the dialogues unfolded, many technical subtleties and linguistic ambiguities associated with differences in Tibetan and Western understandings of emotion came to the surface. Dreyfus was an energetic, clarifying voice in these exchanges, and we therefore asked him to write on this issue for this volume. His Holiness the Dalai Lama was also persuaded to contribute a chapter to this volume on his views on "human nature." It became clear over the course of the week that a certain understanding of essential human nature was coloring many of his interventions and comments, and a self-standing exposition of these seemed potentially very useful. To our knowledge, it is the most comprehensive statement of his views on this matter available in the published literature to date. The book opens with an unusual multi-authored chapter that describes an effort by one of us (RJD) and his colleagues to launch a research project on the psychophysiological effects of long-term meditation practice among Tibetan monks living in semi-isolation in the mountains around Dharamasala. With the encouragement and support of the Dalai Lama, and loaded down with laptop computers and various electrophysiological recording instruments, the researchers had hiked up the mountains behind the town, searching out the scattering of humble huts on the mountainside that they knew were occupied by the monks. The goal: to persuade these practitioners to participate in a study that would allow certain kinds of neurophysiological and cognitive data to be gathered on their mental abilities (especially emotional and attentional abilities). The scientists were interested in characterizing the kinds of shifts in mental functioning that one could hypothesize might result from spending a major portion of one's life in intensive meditation practice.

But the monks, while concerned to be helpful, somehow did not quite "get it." Instead they persevered with a series of questions that had not been part of the scientists' own original brief. In their practice, they said, one studied meditation in order to enhance one's capacity to practice compassion in the world. Was this also the intention of the work of these scientists? If not, what was the goal? Little by little, the back-and-forth of these conversations took on a dynamic that transcended the original recruitment goals. It began to provoke as well a process of reflection on all that might really be involved, tacitly and explicitly, in proposing an encounter between the tools and perspectives of Western experimental science and the tools and perspectives of traditional Tibetan Buddhism. The decision by one of us (RJD) to take the lead in organizing the 1995 meeting was, in a very real sense, born directly out of those somewhat destabilizing mountainside conversations.

Structurally, this book is organized in two parts. Part I draws on Buddhist studies, anthropology and history of science to bring into focus some of the cultural, historical, and metalinguistic challenges that face an effort such as this one. Part II shifts gears and moves the reader systematically through some of the best of what the Western (largely North American) biobehavioral and social scientific tradition has to say about altruism, ethics, empathy, and compassion, with the goal of seeing how the different elements bear up to cross-cultural scrutiny.

We round off each of the two parts of the book with two thematically organized series of conversations edited from transcripts of our actual exchanges in Dharamsala. The first of these is concerned with "Fundamental Questions" about compassion and its standing in human psychobiological functioning (as understood both by Tibetan Buddhism and by various disciplines in Western biobehavioral science). The second is concerned with "Pragmatic Extensions and Applications" of the understandings in question. While these dialogues can be read and understood on their own, they obviously cover a broad range of issues that were stimulated by the formal presentations in Dharamsala. Taken together, we think they also convey a sense of the intellectual intensity, the surprising moments of convergence, the frequent humor, the occasional tensions and misfirings, and the general feeling of the unexpected that characterized our efforts to talk across our differences about a topic that mattered greatly—albeit in different ways—to us all. On this level, if nothing else, they are offered as a record of a cross-cultural project-in-process, with progress made to date.

Contents

Contributors

RICHARD J. DAVIDSON, PH.D. William James and Vilas Professor of Psychology and Psychiatry, University of Wisconsin

GEORGES DREYFUS, PH.D. Associate Professor of Religion and Philosophy, Williams College

NANCY EISENBERG, PH.D. Regents' Professor of Psychology, Arizona State University

ROBERT FRANK, PH.D. Goldwin Smith Professor of Economics, Ethics, and Public Policy, Cornell University

TENZIN GYATSO. His Holiness, the XIVth Dalai Lama of Tibet

ANNE HARRINGTON, PH.D. Professor of the History of Science, Harvard University

ZARA HOUSHMAND, B.A. Editor, San Francisco, CA

CLIFFORD SARON, PH.D. Consultant, San Francisco, CA

ELLIOTT SOBER, PH.D. Vilas Professor of Philosophy, University of Wisconsin

ERVIN STAUB, PH.D. Professor of Psychology, University of Massachusetts, Amherst

Part One

HISTORICAL AND
PHILOSOPHICAL
BACKGROUND

I

Training the Mind: First Steps in a Cross-Cultural Collaboration in Neuroscientific Research

ZARA HOUSHMAND, ANNE HARRINGTON, CLIFFORD SARON, & RICHARD J. DAVIDSON

On the first southern slopes of the Himalayas, where the monsoon-soaked forest thins to shrub and meadow and rolling mist, a scattering of stone huts recedes up the mountain. The tidy tin-roofed shacks, set discretely apart from each other, see none of the workaday bustle of an Indian village, let alone the commotion of the town of Dharamsala a few hours' hike below. A gentle silence wraps the mountainside, punctuated only by the rustle of wind or the distant bleat of a goat.

Here some sixty or seventy Tibetan monks live in retreat, spending their days in intensive meditation and prayer, subsisting on a tiny stipend from the Dalai Lama's office and occasional offerings from the Tibetan refugee community. For some, a radical life change led them to Bhagsu Mountain; but many had completed up to twenty years of academic training in Buddhist philosophy and psychology as preparation for this commitment to intensive, long-term meditation. Some have now lived in retreat for as long as twenty-five years. For all, it is a privilege to be able to practice here free from distractions, whether those of a crowded monastery in India, a busy teaching schedule in the West, or a Chinese prison in Tibet.

But in September of 1992, ten of these monks agreed to accommodate an unusual disturbance in their daily routine. They met with a team of scientists to begin to plan a comprehensive study of the long-term effects of intensive meditation on cognitive and emotional processes. Not only did the scientists involved hope to construct the most ambitious empirical study of its kind to date, they also aimed to set a new conceptual standard for cross-cultural research in neuropsychology. For the first time, highly accomplished yogis were being invited to become involved, not just as subjects, but as collaborators in the research. They would be asked to provide insights both from the formal teachings of their own tradition and from their own direct experience of meditative practice to help shape the ultimate design of the experiments.[1]

Organized by the Mind and Life Institute and funded by the Fetzer Institute,[2] the original project had grown from seeds planted during a 1990 conference sponsored by Mind and Life, when the Dalai Lama met with scientists to discuss the effects of emotions on health.[3] The scientists who went on to form the research team were Richard Davidson, Clifford Saron, Gregory Simpson, and Francisco Varela, all trained variously in laboratory methods of exploring relationships between the human brain, cognition, emotions, and behavior. They were joined by Alan Wallace and José Cabezón, scholars of Tibetan Buddhism, who brought essential skills to meet the cross-cultural challenges of the project. In addition to their academic training in Buddhist studies, each possessed a priori Western scientific education, each was fluent in Tibetan, and each had first-hand experience as an ordained monk in the Tibetan tradition.

The focus of the proposed study was to be an assessment of the monks' mental abilities in four overlapping areas relevant to meditative practice: attention, visualization, linguistic processing, and emotional resilience. Conventionally, human psychological and behavioral capacities in the West have been regarded as relatively fixed, within a limited range of variation for the interplay of genetic endowment and environmental influence. Buddhism, in contrast, has seen the human mind as trainable and, within Tibetan culture, both traditional and contemporary accounts credit highly advanced practitioners with capacities that, at the very least, are beyond the normal range observed in subjects studied by normative Western science. What substance might there be to such claims? The goal was to bring standard scientific laboratory methods to the investigation of this question.

On one level, there was nothing new about the idea of using methods from the laboratory to investigate claims of unusual mental powers associated with meditative practice.[4] Since the 1930s, a number of studies had attempted to pin down one or another psychophysiological correlate of meditation, but by and large no coherent pattern had emerged from the results. The researchers believed that the variability here had likely been a function of several factors. First, different studies had looked at a range of different specific meditation practices, not all of which would be expected to cultivate identical mental capacities. In addition, with a few notable exceptions, previous studies had relied on subjects who were beginners, or only moderately experienced meditators. Buddhist psychology, however, insists that meditation is a slowly learned skill, with cumulative benefits. There is effectively a lifetime's difference in capacity between the beginner and the adept. To focus strictly on the skills of the former is equivalent to studying the cognitive, emotional, and motor skills involved in musical performance by looking strictly at, say, beginning piano students (or violin students, or choral singers), without considering either experimental data or first-hand reports from a range of experienced musicians.

Some of the problematic aspects of previous studies were explained— if not excused—by the cultural, geographical, and political barriers that have prevented Western scientists from gaining access to advanced practitioners in Tibet and other traditionally Buddhist societies. It is true that, over the past 40 years, certain practitioners from India and elsewhere had achieved prominence in the West, and some had also sought scientific validation of their techniques. By and large, however, the research associated with such individuals has had a relentless, self-promoting, "tainted" feel to it that made it a *prima facie* poor base on which to build.[5] Alternatively, looking to native Western practitioners—American Buddhists or European Buddhists—has also felt problematic. Buddhism is so recently established in countries like the United States that the researchers felt the capacities of even the most advanced Western practitioners would not afford comparison with those of, say, Tibetan yogis who have spent decades pursuing intensive practice within millennia-old established institutional contexts.

A final significant quarrel that the researchers had with previous efforts concerned the fact that those studies had been overwhelmingly and exclusively focused on the meditative state itself or its short-term effects, rather than its cumulative, long-term effects. For example, a typical experiment would involve measuring physiological changes immediately before, during, and after a subject's meditation session. The Buddhist contemplative tradition itself, however, points in a different direction than these studies had pursued. Buddhism teaches that although medita-tion requires formal periods of practice, its purpose is to acquire mental abilities that are valuable insofar as they manifest in everyday life. The long-term effects in question are mental traits that may have profound implications for mental health and education, and these are distinct from any more fleeting unusual mental states that are achieved during actual meditation practice, however intriguing such possible states might be.

Finally, for the researchers, there was a question of timing. In the study of both state and trait effects, the knowledge and technical re-sources of cognitive neuroscience have advanced substantively beyond what had been available during the previous heyday of research on med-itation. Most previous studies, for example, had tracked the immediate effects of meditation on nonspecific measures of brain activity, or on body temperature, metabolism levels, and perceptual sensitivity. Al-though such data might reveal global changes associated with some med-itation practices, they offered little understanding of the specific brain processes potentially affected by meditation practice. By the early 1990s, in contrast, developments in microcomputer technology had made it possible to imagine conducting field research on a remote mountainside in India using much more differentiated measures that were comparable to the best of the new laboratory-based instruments.

It was, in short, with both a fair amount of cautious optimism and a strong sense of the limitations of previous studies that the first Mind and Life research project took shape. The research team took on board the importance of a cross-cultural interdisciplinary approach—of listening to what experts with life-long experience in the field had to say, regard-less of whether they spoke the language of Western science. Perhaps a bit over-optimistically, they saw their task as clear: to find those practi-tioner-experts, to negotiate some common grounds for collaboration, and to design experiments that would maximally reveal the nature of their mental training and abilities. The Dalai Lama's interest in the proj-ect facilitated the critical first step toward these conversations by provid-ing unprecedented access to experienced meditators. He took the initia-tive of consulting personally with the Council for Religious and Cultural Affairs of the Tibetan government-in-exile to identify the most senior monks living in retreat on Bhagsu Mountain, and he provided that infor-mation to the scientists. Without his intervention, the effort would prob-ably have ground to a halt at the outset.

In preparation for their meetings with the monks, the team designed a number of experimental protocols, guided both by some practical considerations of available measurement tools and by a review of the types of practices in which the monks were likely to be engaged. The techniques of Tibetan Buddhist meditation that most intrigued them were, first, those intended to refine the mind's powers of attention, and second, those that aimed to regulate or retrain the practitioner's emotional responses to stressful external situations.

Attention is one of the most fundamental aspects of mental function, affecting every perception, every memory and internal representation we have. Attention is also the controlling mechanism of our conscious mind: a set of processes determining which parts of the external and internal worlds we are aware of at any given instant, and possibly even controlling mental representations that do not manifest consciously at the time. When these processes malfunction, the results are greatly disruptive, producing defects ranging from attention deficit disorder to schizophrenia. It is clear that these processes are essential for daily living and that attentional skills contribute vitally to education. But to what degree can attention itself be taught?[6]

In Buddhism, a variety of techniques are used to enhance the stability and clarity of attention, leading to a state known as meditative quiescence (or in Sanskrit, *shamatha*). The practice involves cultivating, in sequence, the mental qualities of relaxation, attentional stability, and attentional clarity. Relaxation is a necessary first step to counter the tensions that come with intense mental focus. It is induced by directing attention to one's breathing, as well as by establishing a context of trust and of altruistic motivation, which counters any stress related to personal ambition for the practice. Having reached a state of relaxation, the practitioner works on improving attentional stability, focusing attention at will continuously on a single object, whether physical or imagined, without the distraction of wandering thoughts. When the mind is stilled in this way, a sense of inner peace and calm arises, free from the agitation of incessant inner dialogue. Then, with the enhanced control that stability offers, one next cultivates attentional clarity. The goal at this stage is to perceive, or envision, the object of one's attention with increased vividness and acuity of detail, actively countering the tendency to dullness when attention rests on one object for a protracted period of time. In Tibetan Buddhism, the chosen object of attention is often visualization involving elaborately detailed mental imagery.

This type of practice, in one form or another, with or without a visualized component, is common to most schools of Buddhism throughout Asia and is found in non-Buddhist Asian contemplative traditions as well. As taught in a Buddhist context, the chief purpose of such practice is to make the mind a more serviceable tool: to apply one's improved attentional skills toward gaining insight into the nature of the mind and other aspects of the world of human experience. The state of meditative quiescence, which in advanced stages is accompanied by withdrawal of the physical senses, is also seen as beneficial in itself. Traditional Tibetan meditation manuals claim that, in addition to enhancing psychological health at any level of practice, the culmination of meditative quiescence—its accomplishment at the highest level of attentional skill—also brings about distinct, beneficial physiological changes.

The team's initial review of the traditional descriptions of meditative quiescence catalyzed a rich set of questions. Some concerned the state effects of the practice: What are the brain mechanisms of a profound state of sensory withdrawal? When a yogi in deep meditation is oblivious to external sounds, are early subcortical or "automatic" brain processes affected as well as cortical auditory processing? What happens to the brain's electrophysiology when attention is directed to one sense modality, such as visualization, to the exclusion of another, such as sound? How is the silencing of internal dialogue in meditative quiescence reflected in the activity of brain regions specialized for linguistic processing? Many other forms of meditation in Tibetan Buddhism involve contemplation guided by a verbal structure—do the patterns of brain activation change when a practitioner switches from meditative quiescence to such discursive forms of meditation?

Other questions focused on the long-term trait effects of the practice. Does the training in meditative quiescence result in improved attentional skills outside of meditation? How do the yogis compare with controls in their abilities to sustain attention for long periods, to redirect attention quickly, to discriminate between different types of stimuli, or to focus narrowly without distraction? Do these attentional skills extend to linguistic processing as well as visualization? Are the brain processes related to attention in yogis the same as in other individuals, only faster or more extreme, or does their training bring different processes into play? Might their exceptional visualization skills bring fresh insights to the existing research that explored the relationship between visual imagination and visual processing?

So far as the interest in attention was concerned, the questions that presented themselves, along with the hypotheses and experimental approaches, were grounded in current research in the West. The theme of attention had occupied science to the point that a large body of normative data was available, allowing comparisons of yogis with various control populations. Of course, it would also be necessary to test Tibetans of similar backgrounds who were not involved in intensive meditation to establish a more well-matched control group, but at least the territory had been well mapped.

By comparison, the second aspect of Buddhist practice that interested the scientists—the training of emotional responses—was more or less *terra incognita*. Although modern research has examined individual differences in patterns of emotional reactivity and the effects of emotions on cognitive tasks, very little research has explored the human capacity for self-regulation of emotion.[7]

Yet in Buddhism, emotional self-regulation is seen as indispensable to the spiritual path and receives a great deal of focused effort in a yogi's training. According to Buddhist psychology, pleasant stimuli naturally evoke desire and attachment, while unpleasant stimuli evoke aversion and hostility. Both of these emotional responses are deemed unwholesome. Equanimity and detachment are the preferred responses, insofar as they free the practitioner from looking to the perpetually changing circumstances of the external world as the source of happiness. But equanimity and detachment are not to be won at the expense of sympathy, compassion, affection, and good cheer—emotions that are altruistic rather than self-centered. All these traits are considered to be integral features of spiritual maturity, and specific exercises are practiced to cultivate them, as well as to reduce self-centered and turbulent responses.

Based on the team's understanding of Tibetan Buddhist theory and practice—for which they relied heavily on the input of their Tibetan scholar collaborators—many more experiments were eventually developed than the scientists could reasonably expect to ever implement. The plan then was to travel to India for preliminary meetings with the monks, in which the team hoped to establish good working relationships, clarify details of the specific practices of the practitioners, and get their feedback on the draft experimental designs. Based on that feedback, the scientists hoped then to choose the most suitable of the experiments and refine them. They would do more pilot studies in the United States, if necessary, and then return to India for a longer period of testing and data collection.

And this was, in bare fact, more or less what happened, although the experience proved far more complex and challenging than the optimism of the scientists had allowed, and it raised a range of unanticipated, if productive, new questions.

The initial meetings in India took place over a period of two weeks. The team met with each of the ten monks individually in their own huts for two sessions, each lasting up to three hours. Except for conversations with one monk who was fluent in English, the meetings were conducted in Tibetan, with Alan Wallace translating. During the first visit with each of the monks, the team introduced themselves and discussed the context of the project; on the second visit, the focus shifted to the specifics of the research. The scientists explained at the outset that their intent was to establish a collaborative relationship with each individual yogi, to become familiar with their practices, to share the ideas and techniques involved in the scientific research, and to address any concerns or qualms that the monks might have about participating in the study.

In fact, they had many. Although they welcomed the scientists warmly and were very interested in discussing the project, most were reluctant to participate in the testing. They questioned the scientists' goals and motives. They had doubts, very candidly expressed, about the premises of the research. And they were worried about the personal risks involved.

The first question was in many ways the easiest to address. For the monks, what mattered most was whether the project was altruistically motivated. Would the outcome be of benefit to others—help somehow to attenuate suffering? In other words, was it consonant with their own goals and commitments as dedicated Buddhist practitioners? If not, it would be a waste of their time to participate. Alan Wallace's involvement here was indispensable, as was José Cabezón's in a similar role later in the project. The presence of integral members of the team who not only spoke fluent Tibetan but had themselves been ordained as monks in the same tradition made all the difference. Not only were they able to engage easily with the monks and establish a friendly and trusting rapport, their own participation was a vital bridge: an authoritative testimony to the worthiness of the project and the values that both cultures shared. For their part, the scientists defended their own conviction that, if it proved possible to demonstrate that training could transform afflictive emotions or attentional skills, there would be huge potential benefits for healing and education in the Western world, where such mental qualities were often seen as intractable.

However, against the potential benefits, the monks had to weigh the risks of harm to themselves and disruption, if not setbacks, to their practice. Unfortunately, there was a bad history in their community of dealings with scientists. The monks were particularly disturbed by the stories of a colleague, Lobsang Tenzin, who had traveled to Boston to participate in another psychophysiological research project and had died just four months after returning. Whatever the relationship between the circumstances of his trip and the cause of his death, the two events were linked in the yogis' minds. Even without Tenzin's untimely death, his account[8] of the psychological distress and physical discomfort he had experienced in the laboratory seemed reason enough to these monks to decline what appeared to them to be a similar invitation.

Obviously, the researchers had failed to appreciate how even mundane procedures can become profoundly intrusive to monks from another cultural context, committed to an intensive contemplative lifestyle with few, if any, modern analogues in our own world. The human subject research guidelines that have become standard operating procedure in the West may not provide sufficient protection in studies that cross cultural boundaries. What does informed consent mean for a subject who lacks information that researchers take for granted? The missing knowledge may be as broad as a general understanding of the methods, goals, and role of science that is shared by both scientists and lay people in modern Western culture, or as particular as the stresses of international travel. Researchers working in a cultural context different from their own know they have an additional burden of communication; but what may be less clear is the extent to which no amount of communication, however empathic or patient, may always be able to guarantee genuinely informed and willing participation.

Indeed, communication itself can be intrusive if it is culturally inappropriate. An indication of this was the monks' unexpected resistance to disclosing the details of their specific practices to the Mind and Life team. This is a sensitive area, because many of the practices are traditionally held as secret, to be discussed only with one's teacher or perhaps with others who are similarly initiated. Likewise, it is almost unheard of for a monk to speak of his own accomplishment or progress in the practice. Thus, it turned out that very few of the monks were willing to describe their practices in detail during the initial round of meetings, and all denied having achieved any special spiritual progress. This was a disappointment, but the team felt that pressing for information beyond what was easily offered would be intrusive and disrespectful. Given the diversity of techniques that are taught in Tibetan Buddhism, the scientists had hoped to match specific practices with experimental protocols and stimuli to suit the different emphases in training. As it happened, many of the monks were more forthcoming about details of their practice on the second research trip to India, when José Cabezón worked alone with them. The key to their openness might have been the relative intimacy of meetings that were conducted one-on-one and entirely in Tibetan, without the presence of additional team members who required translation. Perhaps the later success in this area was also the result of trust developed slowly, in a relationship built over time.

Another form of intrusion that was of serious concern to the team was, ironically, the Dalai Lama's enthusiastic support for the project. Because of the hierarchy of the Tibetan monastic community and the monks' sense of personal devotion to the Dalai Lama, a mere suggestion from His Holiness could feel as compelling as an order. Any discomfort the monks felt as a result of being "summoned"—as they put it—to participate in a study would probably not be communicated to their teacher. In fact, when the Mind and Life team discussed the problem with Dalai Lama, he was unaware that the monks had negative perceptions of previous interactions with Western science. (He did, however, identify another related problem: the responsibility, and resulting anxiety, that the monks would feel to produce data that represented Tibetan Buddhism favorably.) Here again, the ethical guidelines that ensure voluntary participation in scientific studies in the West may be strained in translation to another culture. Assumptions about a person's ability to make decisions as a free agent are based on Western social structures and roles. In dealing with other cultures, the group came up against unanticipated requirements to be sensitive to the ways that authority and power may be exercised implicitly and may compromise the voluntary nature of participation.

Beyond the problems of intrusion and disruption of their practice, the monks had other concerns about the validity of scientific approaches to the study of the mind. In a manner reminiscent of the competitive formal debates that are typical of Tibetan monastic training, one of them challenged the scientists: How can the mind, which is formless and nonphysical in nature, be physically measured? Wouldn't any physical correlate of mind be of very limited utility? If scientists did not believe in reincarnation, which is so important to Buddhist philosophy, then how can they interpret the results they obtain in a way that takes the Buddhist context of the training into account? The scientists answered by stressing that they did not wish to attempt a comprehensive characterization of the mind or of Buddhist meditation as such, but rather to focus on a few domains where small improvements in the understanding of human capacities for change might have a large impact on Western thinking.

Ultimately, the success of cross-cultural research demands a humility that goes beyond sensitivity: It involves a willingness to grant alien notions the same respect as familiar ones. In this regard, a particularly telling moment arose later in the project. One of the monks was considering the team's request to attach electrodes to his body to record EEG. He accepted the explanation that the equipment would only measure electrical signals that were already present in his body, but he questioned how the procedure might affect his subtle energy body. The scientists had to admit their ignorance. Given that scientific measures have yet to confirm the existence of the subtle energy body, it would be dishonest to offer reassurance that the instrumentation would have no effect on it. Understandably, he declined to participate. The team could choose to experience such a moment merely as something that had frustrated their well-laid plans or instead as a moment of opportunity; perhaps one that even suggested new directions for inquiry. Often, the measures of success shifted as it became clear that the cross-cultural dialogue was a much larger project than could be embodied in starting or immediate research goals.

Implementing the ideal of scientists and yogis as collaborative partners required educating one another on fundamental issues. The monks' lack of familiarity with scientific knowledge and modern technology— particularly the older monks who had been educated in Tibet before the Chinese occupation—was the first obvious cultural chasm that had to be bridged. It turned out that, in spite of the monks' many reservations about participating in the project, most were very interested to learn about and respond to the scientists' approach to the study of mind, so different from their own.

The initial meetings thus encompassed hours of discussions about the Western neuroscientific approach to the study of the mind in general, as well as detailed discussions of attention and emotion. The conversations were greatly facilitated by a "show-and-tell" approach, with the scientists demonstrating prototype experiments on the actual equipment. As well as easing the burden of language, the demonstrations also began to familiarize the monks with technical aspects of the methodology and to dispel fears of handling the equipment.

The team had initially set up the EEG and other test equipment in a house at the approach to the mountain where the monks lived. The idea was, after the first visit to each of the monks in their own huts, to invite them down to the field lab for a demonstration of the experiments and, if they were willing, to participate in pilot testing of the prototypes. However, early in the meetings, one of the most senior yogis strongly advised bringing the equipment up to the monks' huts. He reasoned that the sudden change in climate and altitude would have an adverse effect on the monks' meditation. The scientists were happy to move their operations up the mountain, insofar as this would minimize disruption of the monks' routine. However, the seventy-five minute daily hike up the mountain limited what could reasonably be carried.

In general, the monks' responses to the demonstrations made "onsite" often showed an intellectual rigor and curiosity that belied their lack of science education. Independently, they proposed the concept of a control group, noting the importance of testing non-meditators for comparison. They pointed out the fallacy of assuming causality from correlations in the data. They suggested that individual differences would distort the results unless a large enough sample were tested. Such moments were gratifying to the scientists and seemed promising for the prospects of a true collaboration. They were reminded of the common ground they shared with an ancient tradition grounded in empirical examination of phenomena and rigorously logical dialectic debate.

But it was sobering to balance such moments of connection and familiarity with others where the monks' thinking seemed inaccessibly remote. A recommendation for a mantra practice that had the beneficial side effect of growing new teeth was easy to dismiss as superstition, but hard to reconcile with the stress that Buddhism places on critical thinking. There were other questions, such as how past life experiences might interact with individual differences and progress in training, that could neither be dismissed nor approached, but only held at a respectful distance until the dialogue had matured.

In the end, one of the most salient recurring themes of the conversations between the scientists and the monks was how to conceptualize and possibly measure the unfolding of compassion when it arises, since this was so central to the goals of the practices pursued by the monks and thus had been made one target for study in tests of emotional reactivity.

Many of the monks offered their own insights on the nature and expression of compassion. It is difficult to gauge how much they spoke from direct personal experience and how much they were articulating traditional teachings, but some degree of convergence of the two was certainly implied. One monk gave a remarkably eloquent discourse on the nature of compassion and its relationship to, and distinction from, sadness. He described compassion as being a state "beyond sadness," in which the heart is filled with a desire to help those suffering. In compassion, the sight or contemplation of suffering moves one to action. Sadness, which is passive in comparison, might act as a catalyst or trigger for compassion, but it is a separate and different quality of mind, and the two are not experienced simultaneously but sequentially. Sadness is not a necessary or essential component of compassion; compassion could be experienced with equanimity instead of sadness. In fact, the highest realization of compassion, known technically as "uncontrived spontaneous great compassion," is a direct and spontaneous reaction to suffering that does not involve sadness as an intermediate stage. Distinct facial expressions were also ascribed to sadness and compassion. Sadness appears "as if the face collapses," while compassion manifests as an intent focus on the other who is suffering, with an expression of affection and gentleness. These comments all suggested important new directions for the study of the expressive signs of compassion.

A procedure for generating compassion in meditation was then described minutely. The practice focuses on first observing one's own experience, noting which mental processes lead to suffering and which lead to well-being. The understanding gained in this way is then extended to others, by assuming a commonality of human experience: "As for myself, so for others." Buddhism distinguishes different categories of suffering. In the early stages of practice, one would not focus on blatant suffering, but rather on the more existential forms of suffering that exist even in pleasant circumstances, the suffering implied in the transience of all things. In this context, sadness is elicited as an effective way to motivate renunciation. One renounces the causes of suffering and generates a desire to emerge from the continuous round of suffering. This desire is then turned toward others: one assumes they also would wish to be free of suffering and experiences the urge to enable their release from suffering. And at this point the feeling is one of compassion, experienced with equanimity and a lack of attachment.

The theme of compassion felt equally for the perpetrator and the victim was then elaborated. As part of the larger project of cultivating compassion for all sentient beings, the meditator recognizes that the perpetrator is also a victim of his or her own delusions. The long-term effects of perpetrators' actions will bring suffering back on themselves, which is further cause for compassion.

The story of this early encounter between a team of modern neuroscientists and Tibetan Buddhism remains unfinished. Each of the scientists involved in the TTM project were deeply affected and moved by their participation and left persuaded that more dialogue was required in advance of more science; or, perhaps better, that the two activities needed to be developed in an intimate dialectic with each other.[9] In particular, the complexity of the process and the importance of cultivating a trusting relationship between the scientists and the subjects were clearly more involved and significant than the team had imagined at the outset. In this sense, some of the mental and emotional qualities emphasized by the Tibetan practitioners—altruistic motivation, clarity, and equanimity—could not be attributes that the scientific team simply studied in others; somehow, they would also need to find their due weight in the very process of designing and implementing new research protocols. It was a revelation that was partly unexpected, but in the end hardly unwelcome, even as full realization of the lessons learned remains a project for the future.

NOTES

The text of this chapter was largely written by Zara Houshmand. Portions were adapted from extensive field notes composed by Clifford Saron, who participated in the expedition recounted here. The argument itself was developed in collaboration with Anne Harrington and Richard Davidson, both of whom also reviewed and revised the final version.

1. Our ability to give appropriate credit for individual monks as collaborators in the project unfortunately conflicts with the ethical need to maintain anonymity so that individuals are not identified with their experimental results.

2. For more information on these organizations, see www.mindandlife.org and www.fetzer.org.

3. The results of that meeting were published in an edited volume by Daniel Goleman, *Healing Emotions: Conversations with the Dalai Lama on Mindfulness, Emotions, and Health*. Shambhala Press, 1997.

4. One of the more impressive recent efforts to review the field and provide a framework of "testable hypotheses" for the future is James Austin's *Zen and the Brain: Toward an Understanding of Meditation and Consciousness*. Cambridge, MA: Massachusetts Institute of Technology Press, 1998. For some individual examples of both representative and classical studies in this broad field, see the online database, *Trance Passages*, developed by Anne Harrington (www.trancescience.org). For an early presentation of a research agenda of testable hypotheses, see R. J. Davidson and D. J. Goleman (1977), "The role of

attention in meditation and hypnosis: A psychobiological perspective on transformations of consciousness." *International Journal of Clinical and Experimental Hypnosis*, 25, 291–309.

5. The best-known example of this genre of work is associated with the Maharishi Mahesh Yogi, who, in the late 1950s, introduced into the West the technique of so-called Transcendental Meditation (TM), a simplified form of Hindu meditative practice. Quickly developing a coterie of celebrity followers (including the Beatles), he and his supporting organizations also moved rapidly to facilitate the publication of a string of laboratory studies on the alleged physiological markers and physiological and psychological effects of the practice. In part, the Maharishi and his followers looked to these studies to buttress their claim that TM is not a religion but is grounded in the objective data of science. A 1978 New Jersey court disputed this claim and ruled TM to be, in fact, a religious practice. With this ruling, TM proponents lost their public funding and their right to teach TM in public institutions of education in the United States, though they now continue to teach the practice in the institutional framework of their own educational programs.

For a fuller analysis of the ways in which this movement has interfaced with the scientific community, see William Bainbridge, *Sociology of Religious Movements*. New York: Routledge, 1997, pp. 187–191. For a flavor of the style of scientific work associated with the movement, see www.alltm.org/research.html.

6. This was a question that William James asked in 1890 in the *Principles of Psychology*. He acknowledged that educating attention would be "the education par excellance" but was unaware of methods that could be used for such purposes.

7. See R. J. Davidson, D. C. Jackson and N. H. Kalin (In press), "Emotion, plasticity, context and regulation: Perspectives from affective neuroscience," *Psychological Bulletin*, for a review of modern research on this topic.

8. As well as circulating by word of mouth, the account was published in *Chö Yang, The Voice of Tibetan Religion and Culture*, vol. 3, Dharamsala.

9. The team did have the opportunity to do some data collection using some of the new protocols on three occasions in 1993 and 1994. This pilot work was carried out in the United States with senior Tibetan monks who were teaching in the West. One of these was among those first interviewed in India. Although none of the data from these experiments provides any conclusive or definitive evidence, they do offer some tantalizing clues. For example, in Dr. Davidson's laboratory, one monk agreed to have brain electrical activity recorded. Davidson had found in his other work (see his chapter in this volume) that a pattern of left prefrontal activation is associated with dispositional positive affect. The brain activity from this one monk showed a pattern of left prefrontal activation that was more intense than that seen in a normative sample of 175 other individuals who Davidson had tested over the years.

2

A Science of Compassion or a Compassionate Science? What Do We Expect from a Cross-Cultural Dialogue with Buddhism?

ANNE HARRINGTON

Knowledge without compassion is inhuman. Compassion without knowledge is ineffective.

—Victor Weisskopf

This chapter is a preliminary meditation about compassion and where it has "fit" historically into our scientific investigations of nature, including and especially human nature. Historians of science make their trade by telling stories about the past, but it is important to realize that this is done to analytic purpose: to get some clarity about how some aspect of science came to be the way it is, rather than some other way. A working assumption of much scholarship in the history of science is that events in the past are marked by greater or lesser degrees of contingency—of noninevitability. We believe that understanding the how's, where's, and why's of this contingency can make an important contribution to the project of understanding what kind of an entity science is and what kinds of truths it is in a position to provide us with. Historians of science are, in a sense, asking what it means to say that truth has a history. They ask how, if earlier generations had known different kinds of historical pressures as a society, if they had faced different kinds of intellectual and practical challenges, or if they had cherished different kinds of cultural values, certain of the questions we would be asking today as scientists, the ways in which we would be working and experimenting, might have been different.

Adopting an interrogatory stance of this sort appears as a liberating move in terms of our concerns here, because it implies that we can do more than just urge Western behavioral science to become more interested in compassion. We can actually try to see how past choices and pressures may have made compassion an elusive and complicated entity for research and study in the science we have today. We can then begin to sort out how necessary or persuasive these choices and pressures still feel—and can maybe, in this way, help open a road to a future history of science in which compassion has become a more central commitment.

Let us begin by first trying to create a feeling of mild surprise that the traditions of Western science and of Buddhism are not already rather closer together on this issue than they are, by recalling the extent to which our two traditions, in many other respects, have much in common. Both are deeply committed to inquiry and investigation, and, in their investigations, to probing beneath surface appearances. Both have a notion that certain levels of reality only become accessible through special techniques of investigation. Both traditions see knowledge as a hard-won product of prolonged training and day-to-day practice. And in an important sense, both traditions have also historically recognized the enormity of human suffering throughout the world and have felt moved to try to use the knowledge at their disposal as a means of alleviating this suffering.

Yet, by and large, they end up at very different places. Buddhism has historically sought a solution to suffering in inner transformation and a corresponding commitment to the highest ethical ideals, whereas science has sought a solution through knowledge that would ease the human estate through manipulation of the material world. Speaking only for the Western scientific side, the results have been, as we all know, both spectacular and morally ambiguous. Again, we all know about that: how the much-revered capacity of science to alleviate human suffering, perhaps particularly in medicine, exists side by side with a capacity to cause enormous human suffering—through the development of terrible weapons of mass destruction, for example, or through disruptions to natural balances in the world that no one really intended, but that seemed to be the price we have paid for using our knowledge to serve short-sighted, self-interested goals.

There have been other costs. While the process of coming to know reality in Buddhism seems to be associated with an expansive sense of liberation for its practitioners, a feeling of connectedness to cosmic and living processes, modern scientific practitioners often feel alienated from the very reality they seek to understand. The Nobel prize–winning physicist Steven Weinberg captured the paradox here when he said that "the more the universe seems comprehensible, the more it also seems pointless."[1] In this sense, I am moved to say that the world that comes into view through the focusing lens of science is, at its deepest explanatory level, one in which compassion is irrelevant. We understand ourselves to be emergent products of indifferent physiochemical process; and—though we have always admitted our capacity to experience and practice compassion—there is little in the stories we tell of our origins and emergence that is likely to incline us to see compassion as fundamental to our nature. Rather, (and especially since the mid-twentieth century) we have been much more inclined to see it as a curiosity; something we need to account for in terms of other factors that we do suppose to be more fundamental.

Compassion as "Thing Known" or, Where Is Compassion in the Sciences of Human Nature?

Let us see if we can probe the issues here a bit more deeply and in a more focused way. Let us begin by asking in particular whether there are certain things in the history of the life and mind sciences that can help us begin to understand better why it feels normal and appropriate for science to study human violence, but less common, even less respectable, for it to study human compassion. Did we just not yet fully "get around" to this problem yet, or are there deeper reasons for this relative paucity in our efforts? The answer I will explore in this chapter has two parts—one methodological and one metaphysical—but both of them concern how poorly compassion, as a phenomenon, "fits" into our modern understanding of what we think it means for science to study human beings as parts of nature.

Compassion is a human emotional and cognitive experience that does not happen to a single individual in isolation, but as a response to another sentient being. It is a process of external and internal reorientation that softens our sense of our individuality by bringing it into a felt relationship with the pain and needs of some other. We all know that such intimate experiences are the blood and flesh of a rich human life; yet the tradition of Western laboratory behavioral and brain science has been historically so attached to the idea of the autonomous "self" that it largely lacks effective and conceptually robust ways to study the transactions, the processes that may happen "inbetween" individual selves. Methodologically, we tend to study human life one mind and one brain at a time—and this is true even in subfields of behavioral science such as social psychology where one might otherwise hope for exceptions. And the closer we then get to the "hard" core of life and mind science—neurobiology, physiology—the more true this seems to be.

Sometimes we do notice that, as a result of our narrow focus on the autonomous self, we are unable to make good sense of phenomena that we actually would like to know more about, especially in the domain of medicine. One may think here of phenomena like the so-called "placebo effect," in which a patient with an illness may experience significant improvement even when no medication or so-called "active" treatment is given—just a compassionate interaction with the physician.[2] One may think here also of the work of researchers such as the psychiatrist David Spiegel that suggests that women with life-threatening illness significantly can increase the length of time that they live simply by meeting together in supportive groups and giving analytic focus to each other's pain.[3] Spiegel knows—or thinks he knows—that this therapy "works" but has struggled to develop a framework for studying *how* it might work. These examples give us a hint of what some of the conceptual, as well as practical, benefits might be in opening up our scientific thinking to interpersonal phenomena such as compassion as a serious force in human affairs.

But there will be other more basic work we will have to do first. Beyond the methodological challenges, another reason that the modern sciences of human behavior have not developed a systematic perspective on compassion is that these natural sciences are not really convinced that human beings are "naturally" compassionate. On the contrary, they tend to tell us that altruism and self-sacrifice are fragile, even slightly puzzling human qualities, that selfishness and a ready penchant toward violence—especially in men—are ingredients of our true estate, the historical burden of our natural heritage, against which we must perpetually struggle. Our basic pessimism here stands in intriguing contrast to the Buddhist tradition, in which (to quote here the words of His Holiness the Dalai Lama) we hear asserted that the "natural state" of humans is "gentleness."[4] We hear this asserted in spite of the fact that, since the late 1950s, Tibetan society has been a victim of cultural devastation, torture, and mass murder. Compare a claim like this with the comment made by another witness of cultural devastation and genocidal atrocities: the Nobel Peace Prize winner and Holocaust survivor Elie Wiesel. Wiesel does not seem to be a particularly bitter man, but his conclusion from the data of history has been that "Man is not human."

In short, we in the West look out at the world stage of history and find evidence that goodness is far from certain, that a great deal of our potential nature is set up to behave in inhuman ways. On some level, we believe in evil as a basic capacity always lying dormant within us, waiting for the right provocation to come out. We may also believe that education or moral training or other things can keep our darker sides under check, but, unlike Buddhism, we generally do not believe that we have the resources within us to purify and transform ourselves without help.

Who has taught us to think this way? Certainly our religious traditions, the Jewish and Christian traditions must take part of the responsibility for shaping our thinking here. The Christian tradition, for example, believes profoundly in compassion, but it also teaches that human beings are fundamentally flawed and can only be saved through the intervention of Christ, who alone possesses a compassion for our plight great enough to lift us out of our sinfulness. We are granted eternal life as a gift we could never deserve on our own.

Now the question one might ask is, what happened in the West in the late nineteenth century when science began to replace religion at least within the academy, as a dominant framework for understanding human nature? The answer is complicated. It would seem that the scientists who began to create understandings of human nature that would help set the tenor of research and question-asking up to our present may or may not have believed officially in a Christian God. Emotionally and morally it proved harder to shake off the Christian ethos in which so many of them had been raised. The result was a new message, informed by Christian-Judaic values, but with a twist. All the problems of human nature identified by the Christian tradition—all the propensity for violence, selfishness, evil—remained, but now it was not because of what had happened in the Garden of Eden or because the devil tempted our weak flesh, but because we were "natural," part of the natural order like the rocks and stars and amebas. We were left with the same problems, but the old solutions, the hopes that divine forces from the outside would be there to rescue us, had been taken away from us. At best, in the new natural world order that began to develop in the nineteenth century, it would be up to us to save ourselves from ourselves—and, while some despaired, others hoped that our human rationality, especially our science, might rescue us where we no longer could trust God to do so.

The naturalizing of the human mind meant not only that we must doubt our own capacity for compassion; it also meant that we must doubt that there was any larger compassionate principle operating in Reality as a whole. Buddhism speaks a great deal about the mother as the ultimate image of the compassionate being; but the new sciences of human nature that began to develop in the nineteenth century looked at its mother Nature and saw an indifferent, impersonal process that had not particularly wanted us to be born and would hardly shrug if we were to vanish. We learned that the apes were our brethren, indeed that we were part of the entire fabric of life on this planet. However, instead of this insight increasing our sense of connection with other sentient beings, it tended to threaten our continuing need to clarify our uniqueness and special worth in the drama of life. In practice, if not in theory—as seen, for example, in our willingness to perform experiments we would not contemplate performing on ourselves on animals—we reinstated categorical distinctions between our species and the rest of life.[5]

One of the best known—and still among the most moving—poems on the basically pitiless natural world into which we believed ourselves now to live was written in the immediate pre-Darwinian era by the English poet Alfred Lord Tennyson. In the poem, the narrator—who is in mourning because his best friend has died at a young age—stretches out feeble hands and begs Nature for some sign of a higher, compassionate principle at work in the endless rhythms of life, destruction, and suffering. But no sign is to be found. Instead, Nature's voice cries out to him over the cliffs and mountains: "A thousand types [of life] are gone; I care for nothing, all shall go. . . . I bring to life, I bring to death; the spirit does but mean the breath: I know no more."[6]

Of course, it was obvious, even to Victorians (perhaps even, in some way, especially to them), that individual human beings were capable of high moral behavior under the right circumstances—altruism, probably even deep compassion. The question was how this had come to be and how trustworthy and enduring it was, given what we now knew to be our "natures." Pioneering efforts were made, by Darwin and others, to understand the evolution of generous, altruistic behavior in terms of the survival of the group or the tribe. But even in these cases, the assumption generally was that individuals cared for one another in a group in order to compete better with other groups. Even in the finest acts of altruism, a more "fundamental" principle of competitiveness could be discerned.

Some people responded to these understandings by saying that if this was the natural way of the world, and if we are part of nature, then we needed to make Nature our teacher, follow her lead. If Nature lacks compassion because life is a struggle for survival in which the weak die and the strong survive, then this must be how we must become as well. We must embrace the evolutionary drama as it is and take every step to make sure that we end up among its victors. The nineteenth-century evolutionary philosopher Herbert Spencer became particularly identified with this view and especially well known for his conclusion that all forms of charity and welfare should be dismantled: The weak and stupid of the race had to be allowed to die so that the strong could prevail and the human race as a whole could progress toward greater perfection. He admitted that one needed to have the fortitude to follow the example of Nature and practice: "a stern discipline, which is a little cruel that it may be very kind." This kind of argument, often known as "social Darwinism," had some influence, especially in the young industrialist countries, where businessmen and others were learning various ways of growing rich at the expense of the less fortunate and able.[7] At the time, there was little if any awareness of the ironies inherent in the assumption that people had to be exhorted to follow their "true natures," that it would not necessarily be easy to persuade people to repress compassionate impulses in the face of suffering of another.

But a different answer also came out of this time—one that may even be more important for our understanding of why compassion today, as something we study and are concerned about is not a central part of our natural scientific tradition. The answer itself was motivated by what one could definitely consider to be a compassionate impulse. Thomas Henry Huxley, Darwin's close colleague and a committed evolutionist, declared that Nature might be all that Spencer had said—but because we had invented science, because we had evolved reason, we did not have to be natural anymore. We could oppose what he called "the ape and the tiger" principles of the jungle. We could build what he called "gardens of kindness" where the vulnerable members of our society—that Nature would have let die in a minute—could live in a garden with high fences that would keep back the cruelty of what Huxley called the "cosmic process."[8]

It was an interesting paradox: Science had disillusioned us of the hope that there was a moral order in the natural scheme of things, but science also provided a new kind of hope that rational application of our understandings of nature would allow us to create a moral order of our own. We could build shelters to protect ourselves and those we loved from the elements. We could develop medicines that would allow the weak to recover from diseases that should "naturally" have killed them. Huxley's was a vision of Nature improved on and humanized by science. His vision would be shared by many, to some extent or another, through the late nineteenth century. It would not be until the twentieth century—and especially not until the shock of World War I—that this vision would begin to be badly shaken; that we would begin to feel that we had perhaps missed something important in our understanding of science and its capacity unerringly to function in the service of human kindness. This is a point to which we will be returning in the second section of this chapter.

First, though, one more point on the present theme still needs to be made. Even in Huxley's own time, some people were not clear that he had sorted through the whole problem. They suggested perhaps not so much that Huxley was *wrong*, but more that he had not gone far enough. It was not enough to fight the "cosmic process" of nature outside in the world: We also needed to fight its continued presence inside of us. In other words, we may have evolved reason and science, but we were still descended from Nature, and we still bore the traces of our animal ancestors—what Huxley himself had called the "ape and tiger" within us. Darwin himself had spoken of the "devil baboon" inside the human mind and identified this as the origin of what moralists called "evil," of the terrible suffering caused by the brutality of human beings toward other human beings.[9] If science was going to help us create a more compassionate—or at least a more civilized— world by helping us to become more than natural, then we also needed to use all our ingenuity, all our scientific knowledge, to conquer this "devil baboon" in our minds.

When we have looked, we have discovered him everywhere. We have discovered him in criminals, in the mentally ill, in the supposedly "primitive" people of non-European countries. Sigmund Freud, the founder of psychoanalysis, found him in the animalistic impulses of the universal unconscious mind, and he developed a therapeutic technology that was, in part, designed to domesticate and manage those impulses— "where Id was, there Ego shall be." The current practices of psychiatric psychopharmacology, those that use medications to "manage" the destructive behaviors associated with some kinds of mental illness, continue this trend into our own time. In our secularized Judeo-Christian world that still perhaps believes in evil but has lost its faith in God, it has seemed for some time now that only science and rationality stand a chance of helping us transcend the harmful consequences of our own inadequate origins.

Compassion as "Knowing Eye," or Reintegrating Truth and Consequences

Yet most people who have absorbed the sobering lessons of the twentieth century—where two world wars saw science as frequently used for the purposes of human destruction as for the purposes of alleviating human suffering—are convinced that things are not quite that simple. Clearly, there was something naive in believing—as some once did—that progress in our capacity to manipulate the world would be accompanied by any inevitable progress in our capacity to direct our knowledge to worthy, compassionate ends.

Reflecting on this fact leads us to a new sort of question—one that perhaps can only be asked in the context of a cross-cultural venture such as this volume. What we want to ask is how far the act of imagining a "science of compassion"—which both the scientist and Buddhist contributors collectively are doing in this volume—could or should have implications for at least some of the heuristics of knowledge-seeking itself. Can we imagine a situation in which science is affected by any of the moral imperatives of the thing it is studying?

It is, of course, well known that the classical epistemology of science—the canonical mode of scientific seeing—is rooted in an ideal, not of compassion, but of dispassion. The head is supposed to record the world as it is, and the heart is supposed to stay out of the way. Only the head or even better, instruments constructed by the head, can neutrally register the facts of the world as they are: The heart is full of too many biases, emotions, and motivations. Historians of science sometimes call this idea the "view from nowhere." It is, in its own way, a noble vision.

And yet at the same time it is a vision that, empirically, has on some level clearly failed to deliver on its high ideals. I remember how shaken I personally was when, as an eighteen-year-old just beginning to study at Harvard, I had the opportunity to sit in an audience of students and listen to a group of physicists who had helped build the atom bomb. This was in the late 1970s, and Cold War tensions were quite high. I lived my life pretty much convinced that my days were numbered; that the big war could come any day, and I would burn in a nuclear apocalypse that I frequently previewed in nightmares. On that particular evening, I sat in the audience and listened to these physicists talk about how fascinating they had found the technical challenges of the project. They admitted how they continued to pursue the work even when it was clear that the original military justification—the fear that the Germans were also building a bomb—was not justified. It had in part become an end in itself. They then talked about how they had not really seen the moral and human implications of what they were doing until it was too late. This did not feel to me like clear seeing; it felt like constricted seeing, biased seeing. So with what kind of eyes—really—does science enable the world?

In 1946 *Time* magazine in the United States published a cover that can be described as follows. On the left was Albert Einstein, well known not only as a brilliant physicist but as a gentle pacifist. On the right was the piece of the secret of the universe that he was brilliant enough to discover: $E=mc^2$. That formula was then superimposed by the artist against another very familiar image: the mushroom cloud that ushered in our nuclear age. The message here is both troubling and powerful. Troubling, because as we move our eyes across these different images, there seems to be no choice, no responsibility. There is just tragic inevitability. After all, Einstein was a good man. After all, no one would want to stop the human quest for knowledge and understanding. The mushroom cloud appears, but these are tragic consequences caused by forces and people so remote they do not even appear in the image. Certainly, the processes associated with the activities of a neutral science itself are not to blame here, and so we have no choice but to contemplate the inevitability of our tragedy.

And here we may come back to compassion and whether it has any potential to function as a second "eye" for science; one that—rather than *undermining* the qualities we associate with dispassion, or the ability to see the world honestly—actually enlarges that ability. Whatever a compassionate science would be and could produce, at a minimum, it would surely be a science committed in its own way to what the Buddhists call "dependent arising": a science that did not believe that scientific truth was something that stood outside and beyond human affairs. It would be a science that would look unblinkingly at the fact that its search for truth has caused both good and evil and would ask, over and over, how the consequences of truth come to be. Is it really the case that science just discovers "truth" (e.g., E=mc^2) that obscure "others" then choose to use or misuse (by building atomic weapons), or are there ways that certain kinds of scientific questions harbor within themselves certain probable consequences in advance? In this understanding of science I am probing, science would no longer be the unexamined eye looking out and examining the rest of the world: Compassionately motivated seeing would help science look to understand the part it played in the causal chain of its human consequences, both good and evil. It would understand that the quest to understand nature would not be undermined by attempting to understand the ways in which its practices are also human.

I have reviewed two themes in this chapter that may, at first glance, appear to be distinct. In the first instance, I have asked questions about a relative absence of attention in the Western behavioral and biological sciences to the problem of human compassion—as a first step toward inviting us to imagine what an empirically enriched science of compassion might look like. In the second instance, I have asked questions about the ways in which the effort to imagine a science of compassion could or should be tempered by a concern with the compassionate goals of such a science; or, more generally, with a commitment to imagining what we could call a compassionate science.

A science of compassion versus a compassionate science. Again, the two agendas might appear to be logically distinct to us, but when we carry both concerns together into a cultural setting with a knowledge system that has undergone a different historical evolution than our own, we may wonder. A final brief story may serve to underscore this last point. When, in 1995, I first received the exotic invitation to attend a meeting on compassion with the Dalai Lama of Tibet, I told some of my historian colleagues and was a bit taken aback by the skepticism, if not cynicism, of the reactions: "Why would the Dalai Lama think he could learn anything about compassion from science? What does science know about compassion?"

On one level, there was a misunderstanding going on here. These colleagues were supposing that science was being invited, not to talk about compassion as an emotion and human behavior, but about what *it* "knew" itself about compassion—pragmatically and experientially. But even after the misunderstanding had been cleared up, there remained the questions that misunderstanding had inadvertently forced. What to make of such knowing skepticism in the first place? Why might science be thought an inadequate partner in any discussion with Buddhism about fostering compassion in the world? And how seriously should we take concerns about its possible deficiencies in this connection, especially given what I thought I was learning: namely, that Buddhism might actually insist that any vision of a science of compassion forged in the nexus of cross-cultural understanding must also explain how Western science will be changed and touched by the knowledge it wins for itself.

We were indeed being invited to go to Dharamsala in order to imagine together what a future science of compassion might look like; but I concluded that the disconnect between that intellectual project and the other ethical one might actually be more due to inadequacies in our own cultural imagination than to an inherent incoherence. And I wondered whether the challenge of being asked to exercise our familiar habits of thought in an unfamiliar cultural setting might stimulate us to think again about whether compassion was just going to be one more "thing" that we now hoped science would study. Perhaps instead we would conclude that what we wanted to know and how we aimed to learn about it had to be seen as parts of a larger common project—even if we could not yet envision all the details of the linkages.

NOTES

1. Steven Weinberg, *The First Three Minutes*, New York: Basic Books, 1993, p. 154.

2. This is not the only interpretation of the "active element" in the placebo effect, but it seems likely to be an important component of any comprehensive analysis. See Anne Harrington, ed., *The Placebo Effect: An Interdisciplinary Exploration*. Cambridge: Harvard University Press, 1997.

3. David Spiegel, Joan R. Bloom, Helena C. Kraemer, and Ellen Gottheil, "Effect of Psychosocial Treatment on Survival of Patients with Metastatic Breast Cancer," *The Lancet* (October 1989) pp. 888–891.

4. His Holiness the Dalai Lama has made this claim in numerous publications and public lectures.

5. On the other hand, science historian John Durant has called attention to ways in which the life sciences

> today do live with a certain undigested tension in their conclusions about the real implication of the Darwinian discovery of our relatedness to the rest of the animal world. Field-based ethological studies—perhaps particularly the "soft" narratives of ape social life associated with the work of (perhaps not irrelevantly) female primatologists like Jane Goodall—have fed an impulse, perhaps more in the popular culture than the scientific one, to identify emotionally with our nonhuman brethren. This impulse

coexists uneasily with the dominant perspective on animals that rules in brain science and other laboratory sciences, in which animals are probed for insights into the functioning of the mechanisms underlying their behaviors and modeled as information-processing and/or biological systems.

See John Durant, "Animal Awareness and Human Sensibility: Scientific and Social Dislocations in the Debate about Animal Suffering," in: A. Harrington, ed., *So Human a Brain*, Boston: Birkhauser, 1992, pp. 179–189.

6. Lord Alfred Tennyson, In Memoriam: A.H.H, 1850. The key passages here are stanzas 54–56.

7. Herbert H. Spencer. *Social Statics, or, the Conditions Essential to Human Happiness.* New York: Appleton & Co., 1882.

8. Thomas H. Huxley. (1893) Evolution and Ethics (with "Prolegomena" [1894]). In *Touchstone for Ethics, 1893–1943,* T. Huxley and J. Huxley. New York: Harper, 1947, pp. 38–112.

9. In the words of a young Darwin, written as notes to himself in his private "metaphysical" notebooks: "the mind of man is no more perfect than instincts of animals. . . .—Our descent, then, is the origin of our evil passions! —The Devil under form of Baboon is our grandfather." *Charles Darwin's Notebooks, 1836–1844,* P. H. Barrett, P. J. Gautrey, S. Herbert, D. Kohn, and S. Smith, eds. British Museum (Natural History), Cambridge University Press, 1985 (*notebook M*).

3

Is Compassion An Emotion? A Cross-Cultural Exploration of Mental Typologies

GEORGES DREYFUS

Over the years I have had quite a few opportunities to intepret the ideas of Tibetan teachers for Western audiences. In doing so, I have noticed that one of the questions often raised is whether or not compassion is an emotion. This question initially appears perfectly straightforward, and audiences expect a simple answer. The reality is quite different, however, and it turns out to be rather difficult to get a clear answer. The immediate reason for this is that there is, or I should say there was, no Tibetan word for our word *emotion*. I said "there was" because by now Tibetan teachers have been exposed to this question so many times that they have created a new word (*tshor myong*) to translate our *emotion*. It appears, however, that this neologism, which means literally "experience of feeling," is not very meaningful yet. It is only slowly gathering meaning and is not able to mediate between the traditional Tibetan Buddhist and the modern English contexts.

When audiences learn that there is no equivalent in classical Tibetan Buddhist typologies to the English *emotion* they are usually surprised. The concept of emotion is so basic to the way that we, speakers of a modern international language such as English, have of understanding ourselves that it is hard to conceive of its absence. We may imagine people who do not have exactly the same register of emotions that we have, but it seems hard to conceive of people who do not understand the concept of emotion, which seems basic to our being human. How can traditional Tibetan Buddhists be human like us if they do not understand a notion that we feel is so basic to our being human?

The immediate answer to this question is not particularly difficult. We need to realize it is a crude mistake to take the absence of the concept *emotion* in Tibetan Buddhist mental vocabulary or in Tibetan language as a sign that Tibetans do not have emotions. Traditional Tibetans may be different from us, but not as much as the absence of the concept of *emotion* in traditional Tibetan would suggest, for they do experience the mental states that we recognize as emotions. For example, Tibetan Buddhist typologies recognize particular mental states such as jealousy, anger and shame that we characterize as emotions. Thus, though traditional Tibetans may not have *emotions* (i.e., know the term *emotion*), they do have emotions and hence have experiences quite similar to ours, at least in most respects. The difference between us (speakers of modern English) and them (speakers of a language embedded in Buddhist tradition) is not a complete incommensurability but a more nuanced difference in mental vocabulary. It is this more subtle difference I wish to explore here in order to answer our basic question—whether compassion is an emotion.

In order to do so intelligently, we need to leave the crude level of discussion and involve ourselves in a more fine-tuned and difficult work of cross-cultural comparision of the mental typologies used by both sides. We will then be in a position to examine the question more appropriately and to understand the limits of the work of translation, realizing that although translation is necessary for any cross-cultural comparative work it may not be sufficient to achieve understanding.

Emotion and Mental Vocabulary

Though necessary, the comparison between modern and traditional Tibetan Buddhist mental idioms is not without difficulty. The modern concept of *emotion* is by far not as clear or univocal as one might expect. Although we have a certain intuitive understanding of what this term means, a more detailed analysis reveals important differences in the way it is used. For example, what is the relation between passion and emotion? Some have argued that there has been an evolution.[1] Whereas in the old days *emotion* designated a strong passion, nowadays *passion* refers to a strong emotion. This is not, however, the only or main difficulty, for it is the very nature of emotion that is hard to establish.

Several thinkers describe emotions as being mental phenomena. For instance, Plato in the *Republic* describes the mind as being divided into three parts: the reasoning, the desiring, and the emotive or affective parts. Others such as Williams James dispute that emotions are primarily mental. They notice that emotions involve bodily manifestations and argue that emotions are primarily physical. For James, emotions are the readings by the mind of bodily states. In recent years, both views of emotions (Plato's view of emotion as noncognitive and James's view of emotions as bodily states) have come under criticism from thinkers who take their inspiration from Aristotle's view that emotions play an important cognitive role. They help us to focus on particular aspects of a situation. Without them we could not function cognitively, argue these thinkers. For example, without emotion we would not be able to make any decision. We would be flooded by an enormous number of facts but be unable to choose among them. Such a decision cannot be made on purely rational ground since theoretically there is an infinite number of possibilities. It is the emotions that allow us to zero in on relevant facts and come to a decision. Thus, argue these thinkers, emotions play an essential cognitive role.

Whatever the truth of these arguments, which have considerable merit, they show that the understanding of emotion is far from simple. We have a certain intuitive grasp of how we use the concept of *emotion* primarily based on our grasp of a few prototypical situations that we clearly identify as involving emotions. But when we go further and require greater clarity and systematicity, we realize that we have several intuitions that are pulling apart, if not downright contradicting each other. For example, we feel that emotions concern our minds. Hence they seem mental, as Plato argued. But we also feel that emotions concern our bodies. Are they then physical, as suggested by James?

Thus, a little reflection shows that the concept of *emotion* is complex. It is not something we know directly by acquaintance, but something that we know through a description. This point is important and subtle, for since emotions exist in our mind, we are always tempted by the Cartesian fallacy, the illusory certainty that we know them directly in some self-evident way. This is not, however, the case, for emotions are enormously complicated. For one, the nature of particular emotions is difficult to capture, and we need the sensibility of great artists such as

Shakespeare, Stendhal, and Proust to show us their subtleties. Moreover, as we saw above, the very notion of emotion is difficult to determine and is to a certain extent, up for grabs. We have conflicting intuitions about the nature of emotions, and the different views (Plato's, James's, etc.) we mentioned above reflect these intuitions. Finally, and more important for our purpose here, the understanding of emotion depends on the conflicting mental typologies in which emotions are understood. For example, in Plato's typology of the mind, the concept of emotion acquires its meaning on the basis of its opposition to the other parts (intellectual and conative) of the mind. This shows once more that the understanding of emotion is far from immediate and requires an extended conceptual analysis. In particular, the concept of emotion cannot be tackled independently of an analysis of the whole mental vocabulary within which this term makes sense.

The embeddedness of the concept of emotion in a wider mental vocabulary has important consequence for our basic task, a cross-cultural exploration of whether our term *emotion* can apply to certain forms of Buddhist compassion. For if terms such as *emotion* make sense only within a certain mental typology, it seems that the best and safest way to tackle the question is to analyze the mental typologies involved on both sides of the comparison. This task is not, however, without difficulties. On the so-called Western side, there is, as we saw, little clarity or unanimity. There are several competing models difficult to reconcile. Furthermore, it is not the case that the situation on the Buddhist side differs, for this tradition has also several ways to understand the mind. The different understandings that Buddhist traditions have developed in the many centuries of the history of this tradition do not cohere into a single picture or theory of how Buddhists understand what we call *mind*. Nevertheless, it is possible to simplify our task by focusing on one model of the mind that is central to many Buddhist traditions. This model is found in the Abhidharma tradition. Here I focus on Tibetan views of the Abhidharma, complemented by ideas taken from Tibetan interpretations of Buddhist epistemology.

Mind and Mental Factors in the Abhidharma Tradition

To start this discussion, we must wonder just what we mean by *mind* in the Buddhist context. There is a term in the Indian and Tibetan Buddhist contexts, *jñā* (in Tibetan *shes*), which means to be aware or to cognize.

This is the term I use to translate the English *mind*. This term *jñā* is some-times translated by *knowledge,* but I think this translation is misleading since this word does not imply the truth entailed by "knowledge." Instead I understand *jñā,* and its equivalents such as *buddhi (blo)* and *saṃvitti (rig pa),*[2] to refer to something like a mental state, a mental episode, a cognition, a state of consciousness, or a moment of awareness understood as a phenomenological[3] entity that in most, if not all, cases apprehends an object that is thereby revealed to it.

Rather than being a general reservoir of information or a mechanism of the brain that produce thoughts and ideas, here a mind consists of in-dividual moments of awareness bearing upon their objects. Each mental episode gives rise to a following one, constituting a mental continuum or stream of awareness *(santāna, rgyud).* The mental episodes that compose such a stream of awareness take as their objects either real or fictional en-tities. This object-directedness character of mind has been called *inten-tionality* by some Western philosophers and has been proposed as a cri-terion for the mental. Brentano says:

> Every mental phenomenon is characterized by what the scholastics
> of the Middle Ages called the intentional (and also mental) non-
> existence (*Inexistenz*) of an object (*Gegenstand*), and what we
> would call, although not entirely in unambiguous terms, the refer-
> ence to a content, a direction upon an object (by which we are not
> to understand a reality in this case), or an immanent objectivity.[4]

According to Brentano, only mental phenomena are intentional; no physical phenomena manifest anything similar, and hence they are not conscious. Mind is characterized by being directed upon an object. All acts of awareness bear upon an object, regardless of whether this object exists or not. We cannot think, wish, or dread unless our mind is directed toward something that appears to it. Therefore, to be aware is for some-thing to appear to our mind.

A similar view of mind *(jñāna, shes pa)* as intentional is brought out by most Indian and Tibetan Buddhist epistemologists. For example, Dhar-makīrti (seventh century C.E.) says, "Apprehension of an object is the [defining] characteristic of awareness."[5] Tibetan epistemologists have elaborated this definition of awareness as "that which is clear and cog-nizes."[6] "Clear" *(gsal)* refers to the ability that mental states have of re-vealing things.[7] This clarity can be understood in several ways. Dharma-kīrti understands the clarity of mental states as their ability to represent external objects. He also understands clarity as being the ability of cognition to free itself from distortion in its apprehension of its object. For Dharmakīrti, there is a kind of natural fit between awareness and reality, but this fit is less actual than potential. The minds of all beings have the potential for reaching an unimpeded attunement to reality. Hence, they have clarity. To actualize this potential, beings need to free themselves from obstructions.

The word "cognize" (rig) in the definition of awareness describes the capacity of mental episodes to apprehend things that appear to them. For Dharmakīrti, however, objects that are directly apprehended by mental states are not external objects, but their representations. Some interpreters give a realist account according to which mental states apprehend external objects that appear to them. All agree, however, in describing mental states as having the ability to reveal objects that appear (snang) and that they apprehend ('dzin).[8] In this way, mental states cognize objects; hence they are intentional. They are also momentary, disappearing the next moment, making a place for other moments of awareness.

Contrary to the modern Western tradition of acute mind-body dualism, the Indian and Tibetan traditions are less concerned with this problem, although it is not unknown. The Materialists, for instance, reduce the mental to physical events. Most thinkers, however, refuse this reduction, arguing that the mental can neither be eliminated nor reduced. These views do not, however, necessarily amount to a classical mind-body dualism, for Indian philosophers often hold that the mental is partly material. For example, the Sāṃkhya metaphysics is based on the duality between material Nature and conscious Self.[9] The dichotomy is radical but does not coincide exactly with the modern Western mind-body divide.[10]

Buddhist thinkers do not explain our changing mental life in terms of a changeless self. Since they reject such a self, they see mental life as consisting of a succession of related intentional states of awareness constituting a stream or continuum of consciousness (santāna, rgyud). Such a stream is not material. Hence, Buddhists seem to come the closest among Indian philosophers to a mind-body dualism. Nevertheless, Buddhist philosophers partake of the general Indian reluctance to separate the material and the mental. Hence, they do not hold that the divide between the material and mental spheres is absolute. Moreover, Buddhist epistemologists do not believe in an ontology of substances, but argue that reality is made of things consisting of a succession of evanescent moments.

Thus, mental and material events interact in a constantly on-going and fluctuating process.

This general picture of the mind has broad acceptance in the Buddhist tradition. There are discussions of whether all mental states need to be intentional. For example, are yogic perceptions of the ultimate intentional? This is a difficult question on which Buddhist epistemologists appear to be sharply divided. Some argue that all mental states have an object because they are cognitive and hence, according to Western vocabulary, intentional. Others argue that this is true only of conventional or dualistic cognitions. Cognition of the ultimate does not bear on an object but is an unmediated awareness of the mind by itself, a kind of self-cognition. Opponents counter that such a self-cognition is a contradiction in terms. No mental state can apprehend itself, in the same way that nobody can climb on their own shoulder however flexible they are! Regardless of these differences, the Abhidharmico-epistemological model sketched earlier has broad acceptance and can be considered a good basis of discussion.

Within this view of the mind, there is an important, and for our comparative goal, crucial distinction between *citta* (*sems*) and *caita* (*sems byung*). These terms are often translated as *consciousness* and *mental factors*. But here again the translation is not without difficulty, for the term *consciousness* as used here in the context of translating Buddhist terminology has an unusual meaning. Instead of meaning a part of the mind involving self-awareness, *consciousness* here refers to the primary factor of any given mental state, the one responsible for the fact that the state has the clear and knowing quality discussed above. Every mental state is clear and cognizing inasmuch as it involves what we call here *consciousness*.

We may wonder, however, why make a distinction between a mental state and its primary factor, consciousness. What is gained by defining mental states as "clear and cognizing," and afterward by differentiating the mental state from its main factor, which is responsible for this clear and cognizing quality? The answer is that a mental state is not just a clear and cognizing phenomenon since its cognition of an object involves other factors. For example, a mental state comes together with a feeling tone. The object cognized either feels good, bad, or neutral. Similarly, the mental state involves a certain intention (not in the philosophical sense described above but in the colloquial sense of the term). This intention can be neutral but it is often not, involving either a positive or a negative (to be defined later) intention. Thus, the important distinction here is between those factors that qualify the cognition of the object and the mere fact that the mental state is aware of an object. The latter function of the mental state is described as *consciousness,* the former as *mental factors.* Mental factors are the elements in the mental state that make it into a full-blown cognition of an object, including its feeling tone, intention, and so forth.

One may be puzzled by the use of terms such as *consciousness* and *mental factors* to describe different functions of the mind. In the (so-called) Western context, these terms often designate separable entities; we have consciousness here and mental factors there. This is not, however, the way most Buddhist scholars have understood *citta* and *caita.* Mental terms in the Buddhist context are better taken as referring to processes rather than entities. When we use the terms *citta* and *caita* and their English equivalents, we are not referring to separable entities but to aspects of a single process of cognition. Consciousness and mental factors do not exist apart from each other. They are not even understandable apart from each other, but should be thought of in terms of the functions that are found in a single phenomenologically available mental state. One function, the primary one, is to cognize the object. The other is to qualify this cognition. We call here *consciousness* the first function and *mental factor* the second one.

Although both functions are necessary for any mental state to take place, this does not mean that all mental states have the same mental factors. Mental factors are manifold and can be present or absent in different mental states. There are, however, certain mental factors that are always present. Versions of the Abhidharma disagree on the number of these omnipresent mental factors. The version favored by Tibetans speaks of five omnipresent mental factors: feeling, recognition, intention, engagement, and contact. I will not discuss them here since they have been already well treated by others and are not directly relevant to our topic.[11] It will be sufficient to remember that the most important among these five are the two factors we have already discussed: feelings (*vedanā, tshor ba*) and intention (*cetanā, sems pa*). There is also recognition (*samjñā, 'du shes*), a factor that is at the basis of our capacity to make distinctions. This factor is difficult to understand, for it is involved not only in conceptual cognition, where the process of differentiation is obvious, but also in nonconceptual states where it is less so. Whatever the solution is to this problem, according to the Abhidharma, these five mental factors are present in all mental states. They are the obligatory functions that every state has.

Positive and Negative Factors

Besides the five omnipresent mental factors, other factors are also present, and this is where our discussion gets closer to an area where the term *emotion* becomes relevant. One of the primary distinctions among the many other mental factors is based on whether these factors are virtuous (*kuśala, dge ba*), nonvirtuous, or neutral. This is in fact the most important distinction among mental factors, since the main purpose of discussing mental factors is to differentiate the positive from the negative ones. The whole system is established in order to support such a distinction, which is crucial for Buddhist practice. The question is then: How is this distinction drawn? What distinguishes virtuous from other mental factors? The response to this question is bound to be complex, for it involves the notion of karma and its result, one of the most complicated doctrines in the Buddhist tradition. In short, actions are defined as virtuous in relation to their positive karmic results. The Indian teacher Vasubandhu states:

> A good (*kuśala*) act is salvific because it brings about pleasant retribution and in consequence protects from suffering for a certain time (this is the impure good act); or because it leads to the attainment of Nirvāṇa, and, in consequence, protects definitively from suffering (this is the pure good act).[12]

Actions are virtuous because they correspond to the type of action that produces a good result. This result can be of several types. It can be a good rebirth or it can be Arhathood or Buddhahood. In all cases, the good result is brought about by the virtuous action.

This definition of virtue raises a number of problems. For how are we supposed to evaluate the result of a given action? In many cases, recognized Buddhist virtues fail to bring immediate positive results. In other cases, there may be several contradictory results. If one answers, as Buddhist traditions do, that the result that matters only concerns the long term, the problem remains, for how do we know which result is produced by which action? How do we know that a result produced five lifetimes after a particular action is the result of that action? The short answer to these complicated epistemological problems is that we do not know. To decide which action produces positive effects, we must rely on the testimony of an enlightened person as found in a scripture.

Thus, in final analysis, it is the scriptural tradition that decides what counts as virtuous. The relation between a particular action and its particular effects is not directly relevant to our determining whether an action is virtuous.

A similar difficulty affects the distinction between virtuous and nonvirtuous mental factors. In general, a mental factor is determined as virtuous in relation to its karmic results, but here again such a determination is not immediate. The relationship between a particular attitude and its karmic result is so remote that it is impossible to understand for ordinary minds. Since it is important for Buddhist practice that we be able to distinguish virtuous and nonvirtuous mental factors, we need other more practical ways of determining the virtuous nature of a mental factor. The Buddhist traditions answer this need by providing a list of virtuous and nonvirtuous mental factors. For example, the Tibetan tradition usually enumerates eleven virtuous factors such as faith, detachment, wisdom, nonhatred (i.e., loving-kindness), nonharmfulness (i.e., compassion), and so forth. Similarly, a list of twenty-eight nonvirtuous mental factors such as hatred, attachment, ignorance, pride, jealousy, and so forth, is provided. Finally, there are a few mental factors that are neither virtuous, nor nonvirtuous, nor omnipresent, such as attention, concentration, aspiration, investigation, and the like.

These lists are important in the context of Buddhist practice, for they provide guidance, recommending certain attitudes and disallowing others. These lists are not, however, exhaustive. Many mental factors are not mentioned. Thus, the need for criteria to distinguish virtuous from nonvirtuous factors remains. Moreover, a question remains: How are these lists established?

There are several ways to answer this question. One is that these lists are established by the tradition, which is the repository of moral knowledge and hence in charge of establishing moral distinctions. Such an answer is not, however, very informative. In particular, it does not help when we are facing a type of action that is not described or when we are in doubt about which description to apply to a particular action. Hence, experienced teachers usually try to give other more empirically minded and less dogmatic answers. Their answers often focus on experientially available distinctions between types of mental state. For example, one way of differentiating virtuous from nonvirtuous mental factors can be put in this way. The mental states that tend to enhance the peace of the mind are virtuous. They are factors such as faith and loving-kindness which, by their very presence in the mind, bring it to a state of calm and poise. In this state, we feel good and at peace with ourselves. We do not feel pulled here and there but feel well balanced. Quite different is the experience we have with nonvirtuous factors. Whenever they arise they disturb the mind. We feel then restless, disturbed, unable to remain quiet, and compelled to move. These factors are called *kleśa* (nyong mongs), a term that can be translated in a variety of ways: *passion, affliction, delusion, negative mental factors, negative emotions,* and so forth.

As some of these translations indicate, these afflictions bear a close connection to our concept of *emotion.* This connection is confirmed by the fact that many of the negative mental states such as anger or jealousy are obviously emotions. We could then wonder what is the difference betweentween the Buddhist term of *kleśa* and our concept of *emotion?* Is *kleśa* an equivalent of *emotion?* Have we not found here what we were looking for, a translation of *emotion?*

Are There Positive Emotions?

The answer to this question is bound to be both important and complex because it is going to determine the role of emotion in Buddhist practice. Are Buddhists committed to the eradication of emotions as they are often represented in the Western imagination? They are certainly committed to the eradication of negative mental factors. Moreover, we cannot but notice that many, perhaps the majority of mental states we call *emotion,* are included in the list of negative mental factors. So it is clear that Buddhist practice, as it is understood by the Abhidharma tradition, is committed to the elimination of a great deal of what we label *emotion.* Nevertheless, two points must be noticed.

First, not all negative mental factors are emotions. Attachment or desire, for example, may not qualify as an emotion. Plato thought of desire as different from emotion. Desire is not affective but conative—that is, pertaining to the inclination to act purposefully. For Plato, desire is not a passive reaction to events, as emotions tend to be, but an active attempt to modify the world. We may decide, however, to disagree with Plato's description of emotions as passive and include desire among emotions. Buddhists might be sympathetic to this move, because for them the fact that a mental factor disturbs the mind and compels it is what makes it negative. But even if we include desire in emotions, there are negative mental factors that clearly do not fit this category. Ignorance, for example, can hardly be described as an emotion. Thus, *kleśa* and *emotion* do not correspond completely.

Second, equating afflictions and emotions is not possible for it would presuppose that all emotions are negative. This is not, I would argue, the case, and in this respect the translation *negative emotion* for afflictions is important, if not necessarily exact. The term suggests that there are positive emotions and that only negative ones are to be abandoned. This suggestion is important, though it is slightly misleading since, as we just noticed, a great deal of what we call *emotions* is to be abandoned on the Buddhist path. Nevertheless, it remains that not all emotions are to be eliminated. For example, what Buddhists describe as loving-kindness, the wishing well to other beings, is, at least in its most common forms, what we would describe as an emotion in English. It is an affective response to a situation that also involves somatic factors. When we feel moved by loving-kindness, our heart is swelling, our eyes are wet, and so on. Hence, it seems clear that at a certain level loving-kindness is an emotion. And so is compassion, the wishing that others be free from suffering.

Thus it would seem that our inquiry has reached a clear answer. There are positive emotions in Buddhist tradition, and compassion, at least in certain forms, is an emotion. This is so despite the fact that Buddhists do not recognize *emotion* as a category and that no Buddhist category can be mapped onto *emotion*. Although many negative mental factors are emotions, not all are. Similarly, not all positive mental factors are emotions. Wisdom, for example, is certainly not an emotion. Moreover, although Buddhist loving-kindness and compassion can be emotions, they are not necessarily so, or at least not immediately so. Let me elaborate this point, which goes to the heart of whether compassion is an emotion.

Compassion and loving-kindness are mental factors included in the list of eleven virtuous mental factors. As such they exist at least potentially in the mind of every human being and, from a Buddhist point of view, in every sentient being. But the compassion that exists naturally in humans is limited. It is underdeveloped, weak, and partial. We may feel compassion only toward certain beings whereas we feel rather hostile toward others. This is quite different from the compassion developed by the Buddhist path. Such a compassion is stronger and less limited. This is particularly true for the bodhisattvas (beings seeking to become buddha for the sake of helping others), who extend their compassion to all sentient beings. The possibility of cultivating compassion, an essential aspect of Buddhist practice from a normative point of view, raises an interesting question. Is compassion, throughout its cultivation on the path, an emotion, or is it transformed into a mental state that is so different from what we mean by *emotion* that it cannot be included in this category?

The answer to this question is difficult. There is in the Buddhist tradition a distinction between bodhisattvas who are beginners and those who are more advanced. Both types intensively cultivate compassion, but only the former seem to exhibit the kind of psychological and somatic characterstics that we usually associate with emotions. Beginning bodhisattvas are often described as being overwhelmed by compassion. They can be deeply moved by compassion and sometimes cry. From our point of view, it seems quite clear that they experience compassion as an emotion accompanied by the somatic signs associated with emotions. Such an emotion is positive in that it does not disturb the peace of the mind, but it does arouse the mind. When bodhisattvas progress, however, their compassion seems to change. It is less clearly emotional in the usual sense of the word. Such a compassion is described as being equanimous. It is very strong, even stronger than that of beginning bodhisattvas, but it is more balanced and does not lead to the kind of emotional outburst mentioned previously.

Is such compassion still an emotion? Certainly not in the immediate or usual sense of the word. It may then be tempting to decide quickly that such a compassion is not an emotion. We have to be careful, however, for we have to remember that the concept of *emotion* is far from immediate. A negative answer is certainly defensible. We may want to say that a fully equanimous compassion is not an emotion. But it is important to realize that this is not the only possible or even feasible answer, for we could argue that to answer this question we need to extend the concept of *emotion*. Emotions are not just immediate responses but can be cultivated, transformed, and enhanced, as suggested by Aristotle. If we follow this view of emotions, which may be appropriate here given that we are facing a phenomenon that is not usually considered in normal use an *emotion,* we may want to say that the compassion of more advanced bodhisattvas is an emotion. It is the enhancement of the earlier more immitately emotional compassion of beginning bodhisattvas and as such it is still an emotion.

Even then, however, the category of positive mental factors would not map onto that of positive emotion. Thus, our assertion that Buddhist typologies do not recognize the concept of *emotion* stands. There is no Buddhist category that can be used to translate our concept of *emotion,* and similarly our concept of *emotion* is difficult to use to translate

Buddhist terminology. The Buddhist (Abhidharmic) way of cutting the pie of the mind is different from the Western typologies in which the concept of *emotion* appears. The mental typologies or classifications used by both sides are incommensurable. This does not mean, however, that the experiences on both sides are so. The experiences of traditional Buddhist practitioners can be translated through "our" modern English categories. We can discuss, for example, whether compassion is an emotion. This may be a difficult task that involves more than the mechanical application of a predefined notion. We may have to expand the concept of emotion to accommodate the levels of compassion as described by Buddhist traditions. We may also refrain from such an expansion and decide that the more equanimous levels of compassion as described by Buddhist traditions are not emotions after all. Whatever we decide, it is clear that there is no incommensurability here. We are able to understand Buddhist experiences by applying modern English terms. We are also able to have intelligible discussions about such an application despite the fact that our translations remain problematic.

NOTES

1. A. Baier, "What Emotions Are About?" *Philosophical Perspectives* 4 (1990): 1–29.

2. Those are accepted as equivalent by the Buddhists. Other Indian schools have each their own mental vocabulary. All agree, however, on the understanding of mental terms as designating fleeting, cognizing of states or processes rather than as mechanisms.

3. The investigation of phenomena in accordance with the way in which they appear to the precritical mind involved in common daily affairs.

4. F. Brentano, "The Distinction between Mental and Material Phenomena," in R. M. Chisholm, ed., *Realism and the Background of Philosophy*, Atascadero, CA: Ridgeview, 1960, 39–61, 50. The concept of intentional inexistence relates to a complex of ontological issues pertaining to the type of existence attributed to mental objects, which need not detain us any further.

5. *rnam shes yul 'dzin pa yi chos/ (viṣayagrahaṇaṃ dharmo vijñānasya).* Dharmakīrti, *Commentary,* II.206.c

6. *gsal shing rig pa/* Napper, *Mind,* Tibetan Text, 1.3.

7. Several Tibetan scholars interpret clarity as the observable nonmaterial nature of the mind that phenomenologically differentiates it from other observables.

8. Both appearance and apprehension can be correct or incorrect. There is no suggestion here of a given distorted by subjective apprehension as in some Naiyāyikas who hold that a sense-cognition is always factual but can be dis-

torted by thought. We will discuss a similar problem in relation to Dignāga's definition of perception.

9. The Sāṃkhya view is, however, monistic in its understanding of Nature, which is the universal substratum of all phenomena other than Self. A mental episode is seen as complex, involving two factors: the permanent and knowing Self and the mental organ made of subtle matter and composed by elements such as *buddhi, manas,* etc. The mental event comes about through the conjunction of these two heterogeneous factors. To greatly simplify, we could say that, for the Sāṃkhya, the content of the mental event is provided by the mental organs and the factor of awareness by the immobile Self. The Self illuminates the mental content, making it part of the field of consciousness.

10. The views of other schools differ. For example, the Nyāya does not accept the dualism of Nature and Self. Instead, it holds that there is a plurality of entities falling in the six or seven categories we examined earlier. According to this analyis, a mental event is the momentary property of the permanent Self and is enabled by the mental organ and other various conditions. Here again, we notice the reluctance of Hindu philosophers to boil down mental episodes to a single factor. This is partly due to their view that mental life involves a permanent Self. Since it also involves changes, it cannot be reduced to this single motionless factor; hence, the complicated analysis provided by the different schools.

11. See, for example, Napper, *Mind,* 144.

12. L. de la Vallee Poussin, trans., *L' Abhidharmakoça de Vasubandhu,* Bruxelles: Institut Belge des Hautes Etudes Chinoises, 1971, III.106.

4

Kindness and Cruelty in Evolution

ELLIOTT SOBER

Human beings are capable of both kindness and cruelty. Are these two capacities equally part of human nature? Or is just one of them natural for us, with the other being an unnatural deviation from what is in our nature?

To address these questions, we must clarify what we mean by "human nature" and by the word "natural." These terms are often used in a way that is misleading. For example, when someone says that homosexuality is "unnatural," what is he or she saying? I suggest that the remark merely reports the fact that the speaker disapproves of homosexuality. The word "unnatural" misleadingly suggests that it is somehow a biological fact that homosexuality is wrong. There is no such biological fact. What a biologist can report is that homosexual behavior is found in nature—both in our species and in others—just as heterosexual behavior is found in nature. For this reason, I suggest that we use the term "natural" to mean *found in nature*. If someone wants to use the term in some other way, we should demand that the meaning of the term be explained. The word "natural" should not be used to allow a claim about ethics to masquerade as a discovery made by natural science.[1]

A consequence of this way of understanding the word "natural" is that cruelty and kindness are both natural; both are found in nature. This is

46

not to deny that kindness is good and cruelty is bad. However, these ethical ideas are not derivable from biological facts about what is natural.

In this chapter, I want to discuss how one important part of biology—the theory of evolution—regards the concepts of kindness and cruelty. If both are found in nature, what does evolutionary theory tell us to expect about their distribution? Does the theory predict that a person will have the ultimate aim of advancing his or her well-being and will care about the well-being of others only to the extent that this promotes self-interest? This view about motivation is called *psychological egoism.* If evolutionary theory says that individuals will care about others, who should we expect those others to be? Does the theory predict that I will care about my family, my relatives, my community, my nation, my species? What does the theory say concerning whether human beings will care about the well-being of all sentient beings? How large is the *circle of compassion* that surrounds an individual (Singer 1981)? Similarly, if cruelty is found in nature, on whom should we expect it to be focused? If people are sometimes cruel to others, who should we expect those others to be?

Although I will explore these questions from the point of view of the theory of evolution, I want to emphasize that human beings do many things that are not predicted by the theory of evolution. Of course, if the theory is true, then everything we do must be *consistent* with that theory. In the same way, everything we do must be *consistent* with physical laws about gravitation. But this does not mean that gravitation is able to explain everything we do; the same goes for evolution.

So I am *not* going to try to develop a complete scientific picture of kindness and cruelty. That would be an enormous undertaking. Since the scientific study of human beings includes more than evolutionary theory, an evolutionary perspective on the questions I'll pose can provide only a partial view. However, this partial view is important, since evolutionary considerations provide a baseline for identifying the changes that non-evolutionary processes have effected on the human mind. To see how far human beings have transcended the constraints of their evolutionary past, we first must assess what that evolutionary inheritance is.

Darwin's Two-Part Theory

Even though Darwin published the *On the Origin of Species* in 1859, his theory, in its basic outline, is still the standard view among biologists today. Thus, in examining Darwin's ideas, we are not merely describing the old ideas of a great nineteenth-century scientist. In many ways, we are investigating the influential ideas of an intellectual contemporary.

Darwin's theory of evolution has two parts. The first component is the *tree of life hypothesis*. This says that all life currently found on earth traces back to a common ancestor. If we consider any two human beings alive today, those two individuals will have an ancestor in common—a grandparent or a great-grandparent or a great-great-grandparent, etc.— if we go back a sufficient number of generations into the past. The same is true if we consider a human being and a monkey, though here we need to trace the lines of descent still farther into the past. And the same holds for human beings and their relationship to dogs, snakes, fish, frogs, insects, plants, and bacteria. Just as the members of a human family can be depicted on a *family tree*, so all living things now on earth can be located at the tips of a *phylogenetic tree* like the one shown in Figure 4.1, whose interior nodes represent common ancestors.

The tree of life hypothesis not only makes a claim about *genealogy*; in addition, it has implications about the *characteristics* that different organisms will have. Why is the human spinal column structured as it is? The arrangement is puzzling; although it allows us to walk upright, it also guarantees that we will have a lot of back pain. The answer is that our backbones and the backbones of other primates are similar. We inherited this structure from the common ancestor we share with apes and monkeys. Many of the imperfections that we see in living things can be understood in this way. Why do human fetuses have gill slits, which disappear as they develop? Gill slits do the fetus no good; rather, they are vestiges of traits found in our ancestors. Human beings and present-day fish have a common ancestor, and this ancestor had gill slits. The trait is still useful for fish, but in human beings it is retained as a useless residue of our evolutionary past.

A descendant organism will retain some traits that its ancestors possessed, but it also will exhibit novel characteristics. The similarity of descendant and ancestor bears witness to their genealogical relatedness; but even when the descendant has a novel trait, the evidence of relatedness is still there to be seen. This is because novel characteristics are *modifications* of earlier forms. Our spinal structure isn't exactly like that of apes and monkeys. It has been modified to permit upright gait. Still, we can see in this novel trait the vestiges of the ancestry we share with creatures that walk on all fours. New traits appear in evolution, but on closer inspection they can be found to resemble old ones in many respects. This is why Darwin defined *evolution* as "descent with modification."

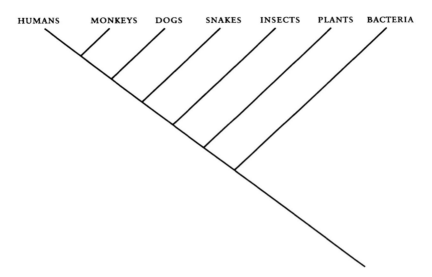

HUMANS   MONKEYS   DOGS   SNAKES   INSECTS   PLANTS   BACTERIA

FIGURE 4.1   Human beings are phylogenetically related to all living things, though we are more closely related to some organisms than others.

If new traits evolve out of old ones in the tree of life, what is the causal mechanism that explains why novelties appear? This is the second part of Darwin's theory—that *natural selection* is the principal (though not exclusive) explanation of life's diversity. Selection is a process that causes traits that help individual organisms to survive and reproduce to become common in a population. Consider, as a simple example, the process depicted in Figure 4.2. The zebras in a population all run slow. Then, a mutation arises in the genes found in a zebra; this mutation lengthens the leg bone that the zebra develops and thus allows the animal to run a bit faster. This fast zebra does better at evading predators than the other zebras in the population. As a result, this fast zebra has more offspring than the average slow zebra. Assuming that running speed is an inherited trait—that fast parents have fast offspring and slow parents have slow offspring—the effect on the next generation is that the trait of running fast will increase in frequency. If this process continues for many generations, the advantageous trait will continue to increase in frequency and eventually will reach 100% representation. Natural selection has "made over" the population, transforming it from a population in which everyone runs slow to a population in which everyone runs fast.

Let's be clear about what this selection process involves. First, the organisms must *vary*. If all the animals run slow or all run fast, there can be

START	S	S	S	S	S	S	S	S	S	S
THEN A MUTATION ARISES	(F)	S	S	S	S	S	S	S	S	S
THE MUTATION SPREADS	(F)	(F)	(F)	S	S	S	S	S	S	S
AND SPREADS	(F)	(F)	(F)	(F)	(F)	(F)	(F)	(F)	S	S
FINISH	(F)	(F)	(F)	(F)	(F)	(F)	(F)	(F)	(F)	(F)

FIGURE 4.2   The trait of running fast (F) replaces the trait of running slow (S) after the former trait appears as a mutation in a population of slow zebras.

no natural selection on running speed; there will be no variants to select *among*. Second, the variation must make a difference in the organisms' chances of surviving and reproducing. If fast zebras do exactly as well as slow ones in evading predators and in other tasks that matter, then there will be no selective advantage in having one trait rather than the other. Thus, selection requires that there be variation in *fitness*, by which biologists mean an organism's ability to survive and be reproductively successful. Third, the trait of interest must be *inherited*. It is crucial that offspring resemble their parents, if the trait is to increase in frequency. These conditions are what makes evolution by natural selection possible.

Darwin never used the expression "survival of the fittest" to describe this process; that label was suggested by Herbert Spencer. It is nonetheless a serviceable phrase, as long as "fittest" is understood to mean the fittest of the *available* variants. There is no assumption that the range of variation will include all traits that are *conceivable*. The theory may predict that zebras will run fast rather than slow; it does not predict that they will evolve machine guns with which to repel lion attacks (Krebs & Davies, 1981).

Darwin used the phrase "struggle for existence" to describe what he had in mind, and his clarification of this phrase is still important. He says in the *Origin* that he uses this phrase "in a large and metaphorical sense." Two dogs may struggle against each other for a piece of meat; but it also is true that two plants at the edge of a dessert may struggle against the drought. The difference between these examples concerns whether there is a resource in short supply. For the dogs, one of them gets the meat if and only if the other does not. No such rule applies to the plants in Darwin's example; how one plant fares does not materially affect how the other one does.

It is tempting to mark the distinction that Darwin is describing by saying that the two dogs *compete* with each other but the two plants do not. However, this way of putting things is potentially misleading. It certainly would be a mistake to think that the two plants are *cooperating* rather than *competing*. In fact, from the point of view of the theory of natural selection, the two processes are basically the same. The dog that is better able to get the meat is fitter; the plant that is better able to survive the drought is fitter. Both the dogs and the plants are involved in "struggles for existence," even though the dogs struggle *with each other* while the plants struggle *against the drought*. The important point is that both processes involve a competition of individuals with each other; the trait that evolves is the one that allows one organism to do better than the other.

The fact that we predict which trait will evolve in a selection process by comparing their fitnesses has an important implication, which we can see by returning to the example of zebra running speed. In the scenario I described, the population is initially composed of zebras who run at a speed of m miles per hour. A novel mutation then arises, which allows the organism in which it occurs to run faster—at a speed of $m + b$. The trait that evolves is the running speed of $m + b$. Notice that the zebras at the end of the process run faster than the zebras did before the process began. If the lions that prey on zebras haven't simultaneously evolved the ability to run faster, then the selection process in the zebra herd has improved the fitness of the individuals in the population.

Now let's consider a slightly different sequence of events. As before, the zebras initially run at a speed of m. Then a mutation arises that makes the zebra in which it occurs run slower—at a rate of $m - c_1$, say— but makes the other zebras in the population run even slower—at a rate of $m - c_1 - c_2$. Since it is better to run at a speed of $m - c_1$ than to run at a speed of $m - c_1 - c_2$, the novel mutation will evolve. After this trait sweeps to 100%, the zebras in the population are less fit than the zebras were before the process began. The zebras at the end of the process run at a speed of $m - c_1$, whereas their speed at the beginning was m. Selection has reduced the average level of fitness in the population.

When natural selection acts on the individual organisms in a single population, there is no fundamental difference between these two examples. In both cases, the fitter trait is the one that evolves. A trait that helps the individual that possesses it, but not other individuals, is structurally just like a trait that hurts the individual that possesses it, but hurts others even more.

It might be pointed out that these two examples differ in an important respect. If the zebras in a population all run slower than they did before, the herd stands a greater risk of going extinct. In contrast, if the zebras all run faster than they did initially, this will help the group avoid extinction. The point is correct, but it does not affect what one should say about a process of natural selection in which individuals compete against each other in the confines of a single population. It is quite possible for the selection process to carry the entire population straight to extinction. What is guaranteed is that the fitter of the two traits will be the one that evolves; the effect of this on the welfare of the group is irrelevant.

The Units of Selection Problem—A Brief History

Darwin usually conceived of natural selection in the way I just described—as a competition among the individuals in a single population. However, on a few occasions Darwin departed from this pattern. His discussion in *The Descent of Man* of human morality is the clearest case in which he deployed an alternative formulation. Here is the problem that Darwin addressed:

> It is extremely doubtful whether the offspring of the more sympathetic and benevolent parents, or of those which were the most faithful to their comrades, would be reared in greater numbers than the children of selfish and treacherous parents of the same tribe. He who was ready to sacrifice his life, as many a savage has been, rather than betray his comrades, would often leave no offspring to inherit his noble nature. The bravest men, who were always willing to come to the front in war, and who freely risked their lives for others would on average perish in larger numbers than other men. (p. 163)

If altruistic self-sacrifice is *disadvantageous* to the individual altruist, how could the characteristic evolve? Darwin answers:

It must not be forgotten that although a high standard of morality gives but a slight or no advantage to each individual man and his children over the other men of the same tribe, yet that an advancement in the standard of morality and an increase in the number of well-endowed men will certainly give an immense advantage to one tribe over another. (p. 166)

Darwin is appealing to the process of *group selection*. Groups of altruists do better than groups of selfish individuals, so altruism can evolve, even though selfish individuals do better than altruists in the same group.

Although Darwin occasionally invoked the hypothesis of group selection to explain the existence of traits that benefit the group but are deleterious to the individual, his basic approach was almost always that traits evolve because they benefit the individuals that have them. Darwin's successors were less restrained. After evolutionary theory was integrated with population genetics in the 1930s in the so-called Modern Synthesis, characteristics found in nature were frequently explained by describing the group advantage they provide. Why are species genetically diverse? Because this helps them avoid extinction when the environment changes (Dobzhansky, 1937). Why do so many groups have dominance hierarchies? Because this reduces within-group conflict and helps the group be more productive (Allee et al., 1949). Why do individuals reduce their food intake and produce fewer offspring than they could? Because this prevents the population from over-exploiting its resources and crashing to extinction (Wynne Edwards, 1962). Many biologists happily invoked these group-level explanations, while at the same time explaining running speed, camouflage, and disease immunity in terms of the individual advantages they provide. Biologists simply chose the level of explanation that they found more intuitive, appealing to individual benefits on Mondays, Wednesdays, and Fridays, and to group benefits on Tuesdays, Thursdays, and Saturdays.

All this changed in 1966 when G. C. Williams published a devastating critique of the hypothesis of group selection in his book *Adaptation and Natural Selection*. Williams touched a nerve and his vigorous rejection of adaptations that exist for the good of the group quickly spread through the evolution community and became the received view. For the next decade, group selection was something of a dirty word in biology; it was the sort of thing that well-trained biologists were expected *not* to mention, except perhaps to dismiss with disdain. Matters are now rather different, in that biologists increasingly recognize that group selection can be thought about rigorously and that important biological adaptations are to be explained in terms of it. Indeed, Williams (1992) himself has recently come around to this point of view. The naive group selectionism of the past has been replaced by a more sophisticated body of theory and evidence.

During the dark days when group selection was regarded as beyond the pale, biologists began to devise theories that are able to explain how traits that diminish the fitness of the individuals that have them, but enhance the fitness of others, can evolve. Many biologists were loathe to think of those theories as "theories of group selection," but, in retrospect, that is exactly what they are (Sober & Wilson, 1998). In any event, whether group selection has been vindicated or consigned to the rubbish heap of history is not of fundamental importance for our purposes. What is important is that biologists now universally acknowledge that altruism can evolve and actually has done so. The picture of nature as thoroughly red in tooth and claw is one-sided. It is no more adequate than the rosy picture that everything is sweetness and light. Kindness *and* cruelty both have their place in nature, and evolutionary biology helps explain why.

How Can Altruism Evolve?

Darwin's idea—that altruism can evolve by a process of group selection—seems paradoxical. How can altruism increase in frequency, if altruists always do worse than the selfish individuals who live in the same group? Darwin did not explain the idea in any detail. In fact, it was only fairly recently that a rigorous answer to this question has been available. The key is to have altruists live with altruists and selfish individuals live with selfish individuals. To see how this solves the problem, let us imagine that there are a number of groups, each consisting of two individuals who interact in some way that affects their fitness. If groups contain only two individuals, then there are three types of groups—a group can contain two selfish individuals, one altruistic and one selfish individual, or two altruists. How fit are the individuals who live in these groups? Let's represent fitness by numbers; these might be numbers of offspring, or (if we multiply them by 0.1) probabilities of surviving to reproductive age:

	Composition of the group		
	A,A	A,S	S,S
Fitness of individuals	3	1,4	2

Altruists who live together enjoy the fruits of cooperation, each obtaining a score of 3; selfish individuals who pair with each other do worse, each obtaining a score of 2. And when an altruist and a selfish individual pair, the selfish individual exploits the altruist. The selfish individual gains a benefit from the altruist; the altruist in the pair gives something away and gets nothing in return. So, in such mixed groups, altruists receive a score of 1 and selfish individuals a score of 4.

Notice that if selfish individuals always live with altruists (and vice versa), then selfish individuals have a fitness of 4 and altruists have a fitness value of 1. On the other hand, if altruists always live with altruists and selfish individuals always live with selfish individuals, then the fitness of the average altruist is 3 and the fitness of the average selfish individual is 2. So altruists are fitter than selfish individuals when like lives with like, but the reverse is true when like lives with *unlike*. What do these fitness differences mean? As explained earlier, when evolution is guided by natural selection, fitter traits increase in frequency and less fit traits decline. This means that we have identified one circumstance in which altruism will evolve and replace selfishness, and a different circumstance in which precisely the opposite will occur. The important point is this: *for altruism to evolve, it is crucial that altruists tend to interact with other altruists.* This means that if we are to understand how altruism can evolve, we can't think of evolution as occurring within the confines of a single group in which everybody interacts with everybody else. Rather, we must think of a "metapopulation"—a group of groups; individuals interacting with those in their own group, but not with individuals in other groups.

I now want to give this idea a more general formulation, one that will cover the case of evolution within a single group and also the case of evolution in a metapopulation of groups. Suppose that an altruist increases the fitness of each of the other individuals in the same group by b units and that the altruistic behavior costs the altruist c units of fitness. Selfish individuals make no altruistic donations, so they incur no cost.

If the organisms we are considering live in a single population in which there are n altruists, then the fitnesses of the two traits are:

Fitness of the average selfish individual $= x + bn$
Fitness of the average altruist $= x - c + b(n - 1)$

Here "x" denotes the "baseline fitness" that individuals have apart from whether they make donations or receive them. A selfish individual receives n donations and pays no cost; an altruist pays a cost and receives donations from the $n - 1$ *other* altruists in the group. It follows from these fitness values that

    (1)   When individuals interact in a single group, the average selfish individual is fitter than the average altruist if and only if $c + b > 0$.

If the benefit really is a benefit ($b > 0$) and the cost really is a cost ($c > 0$), then altruism cannot evolve when organisms interact with each other in the confines of a single group.

Now let's use the same representation of the fitness consequences of altruism and selfishness to describe the fitnesses of individuals in the three types of groups that exist when groups contain just two individuals:

	Composition of the group		
	A,A	A,S	S,S
Fitness of individuals	$x + b - c$	$x - c, x + b$	x

Two simple conclusions follow from these fitness values:

    (2a)   If individuals interact in pairs and individuals always pair with individuals *unlike* themselves, then the average selfish individual is fitter than the average altruist if and only if $c + b > 0$.

    (2b)   If individuals interact in pairs and like always pairs withlike, then the average selfish individual is fitter than the average altruist if and only if $c > b$.

Notice that (1) and (2a) state the same criterion for determining which trait is fitter. In contrast, (2b) states a different criterion entirely. If like always pairs with like and $b > c$, then altruism will have the higher fitness. If the altruist's donation helps the recipient more than the donation reduces the fitness of the donor, altruism can evolve.

Proposition (2b) describes an extreme—when like *always* pairs with like. This isn't necessary for altruism to evolve. A fully general account of the circumstances under which altruism evolves must describe the *degree* to which like associates with like. How might this quantity be measured? I won't go into the mathematical details, but will merely mention three benchmarks.[2] When like always pairs with like, their degree of association has the value 1. When individuals pair at random, their degree of association has the value 0. And when individuals always pair with individuals unlike themselves, their degree of association has the value −1. The evolution of altruism depends not just on the degree of association, but on the magnitudes of the costs and benefits involved. These considerations come together in the following formula:

(3)   When individuals interact in pairs, the average altruist is fitter than the average selfish individual if and only if the degree to which like associates with like exceeds the ratio c/b.

Proposition (3) is restricted to the case in which groups are of size two, but the principle can be generalized. Group selection makes it possible for altruism to evolve. Although selfish individuals do better than altruists within the same group, groups in which altruism is common do better than groups in which altruism is rare. This is the two-level process that Darwin described.

If the evolution of altruism requires that altruists interact preferentially with each other, how might this be achieved in nature? One very important mechanism that causes like to live with like is to have kin live with kin (Hamilton 1964); genetic relatives tend to resemble each other. For example, if each female wasp has her own nest, then newly hatched wasps that occupy the same nest will be siblings. If siblings interact with each other before dispersing, that will help altruistic behaviors to evolve. Nests that contain altruists will do better than nests that do not, even though the altruists in a nest do worse than the selfish individuals in the same nest. This process does not require individual wasps to *think* about which individuals they will help. If a wasp helps those with whom it lives, it will end up helping its brothers and sisters.

Other mechanisms for getting altruists to interact preferentially with other altruists require more in the way of mental abilities. For example, if individuals can recognize the traits of others and choose those with whom they interact, this can help altruism to evolve. Every individual does best by interacting with altruists; if individuals choose those with whom they associate, then altruists will pair with each other, leaving selfish individuals to pair up or to go it alone. An interesting example of this selective association has recently been documented in the guppy. When a large, predatory fish approaches a school of guppies, one of them may venture out to inspect the intruder. This "scout" is behaving altruistically; it incurs a risk and provides a benefit to the other guppies in the school, who observe whether the predator goes after the scout. Dugatkin and Alfieri (1991) found in experiments that guppies choose to associate with other guppies whom they have seen engage in scouting behavior.

The Circle of Compassion

The concepts of altruism and selfishness that are used in evolutionary biology describe the fitness effects of a behavior, not the psychological motives, if any, that cause the behavior. A mindless organism can be altruistic or selfish in the evolutionary senses of those terms. Conversely, an individual who genuinely cares about the welfare of others can fail to produce behaviors that are evolutionarily altruistic. The most obvious example of this type is parental care. If parents love their children and help their children for purely selfless reasons, it may still be true that parents who take good care of their children are more reproductively successful than parents who do not. If so, parental care is not altruistic in the evolutionary sense; parental care enhances the parent's fitness rather than reducing it. Evolutionary altruism does not entail the existence of altruistic psychological motives, and the existence of altruistic psychological motives does not entail that the resulting behavior is evolutionarily altruistic.

Having drawn this logical distinction between the evolutionary and the psychological concepts, we nonetheless must recognize that they are often connected in important ways. Human beings help others (and themselves as well) because of the desires they have. If these helping behaviors are the result of evolution by natural selection, what kinds of desires can we expect people to have? To whom should we expect individuals to be kind, and to whom should we expect them to be cruel?

The idea that parents care about their children is entirely at home within an evolutionary framework. If loving one's children leads one to take better care of them, then natural selection can be expected to lead parents to love their children. This doesn't mean that the theory predicts that all parents will love their children, nor that all will love them to the same degree. Child abuse and child neglect are familiar phenomena. My point is that it is not alien to the evolutionary point of view to expect parents, usually, to love their children, when they live in environments that are relevantly similar to the ones in which our habits of parental care evolved.

However, evolutionary theory does *not* predict that parents will be prepared to engage in limitless self-sacrifice for their children. In fact, biologists have recently explored the idea that parents and children face *conflicts of interest* (Trivers 1974; Haig 1993). From the point of view of survival and reproductive success, a mother does best by having the largest number of viable, fertile offspring that she can. Of course, there is inevitably a trade-off between number and "quality" of offspring; a mother can spread her resources thinly among more offspring, or devote more of her resources to a smaller number. Theoretically, there is an "optimal clutch size" (Lack, 1954) that represents the parent's best way of satisfying these conflicting *desiderata*. From the point of view of the mother's child, however, matters are different. A child, beginning its life as a fetus in utero and continuing past birth through the period of dependence that we call childhood, does best by grabbing as much in the way of resources as it can from its parents. Actually, the optimal strategy for a child is a bit more complicated than this, in view of the fact that the child may receive help from its siblings and also in view of the fact that the child will someday be a parent whose children may behave toward it the way it behaves toward its parents. Nonetheless, after these details are taken into account, it remains true that the theoretical optimum in care giving for a mother and the theoretical optimum in care received for a child are not identical. This is especially clear once we realize that half the child's genes come from its father; if females frequently have children with more than one male, then a gene from the father may evolve that causes fetuses to extract more resources from the mother than would be in the mother's best reproductive interest. Of course, mothers can be expected to evolve characteristics that resist this sort of exploitation. Seen in this way, the mother-child relationship is the setting for an arms race, in which each side evolves strategies and counterstrategies in response to the other.

This theoretical prediction is verified by a number of observations. For example, human fetuses secrete a substance called *human placental lactogen* (hPL); this interferes with maternal insulin and thereby allows the mother's glucose levels to rise, thus providing the fetus with more nutrition. The mother responds by secreting more insulin, which causes the fetus to secrete even more hPL. This arms race would not occur if the adaptive interests of mother and child were identical. A similar point of view applies to the fact that up to 78 percent of fertilized eggs fail to be implanted or are aborted early in pregnancy. Mothers have evolved the ability to detect defective fetuses and cut their losses; an important cue that they attend to is whether the fetus secretes human chorionic gonadotropin (hCG). Although this strategy makes sense from the mother's point of view, it obviously does not work to the advantage of the fetus. Other examples could be described, but the basic point should now be clear: even the mother/child pair is, from an evolutionary point of view, not one that we should expect to be perfectly harmonious and cooperative. Parental care is to be expected, but we also expect it to be circumscribed in important respects (Haig, 1993; Nesse & Williams, 1994).

If we widen the circle a bit, from concern for one's offspring to concern for one's genetic relatives, it is again to be expected that human beings will feel compassion. If individuals who care about their kin tend to help them, then the evolution of altruistic behaviors directed towards kin can be expected to bring in its wake the evolution of kind feelings towards those relatives. As Darwin's example about morality illustrates, if human beings evolve under the influence of group selection in which the groups were composed of genetic relatives, then we expect individuals to care about the other individuals in their own "tribe."

What about helping behavior directed toward *non*relatives? Here it is important to remember that associating with genetic relatives is just one method for getting similar individuals to interact with each other. If nonrelatives associate with each other in various cooperative undertakings (e.g., hunting and gathering), then altruistic behaviors will have an opportunity to evolve, provided that altruists are able to associate with altruists. Thus, when modern human beings come together in voluntary associations, it will not be surprising, from an evolutionary point of view, if they often care about each other and help each other. Once again, I am not talking about limitless self-sacrifice. As proposition (3) implies, it is a precondition on the evolution of altruism that the benefits received by others must exceed the cost to the donor. Evolutionary theory does not predict that human beings will be prepared to die to make someone smile. However, something like the reverse—being prepared to smile to save someone's life—is hardly alien to the evolutionary outlook.

If we extend the circle still farther, we encounter a kind of compassion that poses more of a problem for evolutionary theory. First, there is caring about the well-being of all human beings, even total strangers. Second, there is concern for the well-being of organisms in other species. Could either of these be the product of evolution by natural selection?

Let's begin answering this question by returning to a point I made in connection with the example of zebra running speed. I pointed out that what matters in natural selection is *comparative* fitness. If one zebra runs faster than another, the one that runs faster has the advantage in evading predators. I mentioned two ways in which a mutant zebra might be faster than the other zebras in the population. The mutant may be faster because it has an adaptation that causes it to run faster than any zebra did before. Alternatively, the mutant may be faster because it has some adaptation that causes the other zebras to slow down. Either way, the mutant zebra wins. In individual selection, helping one's self and hurting others are equivalent—both will evolve as long as they are fitter than the available alternative traits.

A similar point holds when we consider the process of group selection. Altruism evolves under group selection because altruism helps the group to do better. The crucial point is not that altruists help the group to do better than it would have done without such individuals; what matters is that groups that contain altruists do better than groups that do not. From the point of view of group selection, helping one's own group and hurting other groups are equivalent. When groups compete against other groups, what will evolve is within-group niceness *and* between-group nastiness. Group selection cannot be expected to produce universal benevolence.

Individual selection involves competition, but so does group selection. *All* selection processes have this property. The basic pattern is that the traits that evolve under natural selection—individual or group—have *differential* effects; they benefit some individuals or groups, *but not others*.

We now can make the puzzle about extended compassion more precise. What sort of selection process could cause extended compassion to become more common, once a mutation has allowed the characteristic to make its appearance? What might cause the trait to spread? If individuals who have extended compassion do better at surviving and reproducing than individuals who do not, then the trait will evolve by individual selection. If groups of human beings who have extended compassion do better than groups that do not, then the trait will evolve by group selection. However, how can either of these claims be true, since *limited* compassion seems to do better than *extended* compassion? If one individual feels extended compassion, and a second feels limited compassion (perhaps just toward self and offspring), it is hard to see why the first individual will do better than the second. Similarly, if the members of one group feel extended compassion, while the members of a second group feel compassion only toward members of their own group, then group selection will favor limited compassion over extended

compassion. It is not puzzling why *some* compassion should evolve and replace the trait of having no compassion at all; what is puzzling is how *extended* compassion could evolve and replace *limited* compassion.

Adaptation and Side Effect

Our blood is red because hemoglobin happens to be red. The hemoglobin molecule evolved because it is good at transporting oxygen, not because there was an advantage in having red blood. The color of our blood is not an adaptation for anything. Rather, it is a side effect of the process of natural selection.

The concept of evolutionary side effect has an important application to the units of the selection problem. When the running speed in a population of zebras improves as a result of individual competition, the group may end up better off; after all, a fast herd is less likely to go extinct than a slow one. However, in this instance running speed does not evolve *because* this trait benefits the group. The benefit to the group is *fortuitous*; the trait evolves because it benefits individuals, not groups of individuals. The benefit to the group is a *side effect* of the selection process, not a cause of the trait's evolution.

The idea of evolutionary side effect may be the key to understanding why human beings are able to experience extended compassion. It isn't that this ability evolved because it was beneficial to the individual or to the group of individuals in which it arose. Rather, the idea is that the ability to feel extended compassion is a byproduct of selection for some other suite of traits. But which other suite of traits?

To understand how red blood can evolve even though blood color has no adaptive function, we must understand the idea of *correlation of characters*. Having red blood and having blood that contains hemoglobin are traits that are correlated. If other molecules confer different colors on the blood, then there will be a statistical association between blood color and the presence of different molecules. Given this correlation, if selection favors the hemoglobin molecule, selection will cause the correlated character to evolve as well. Red blood gets selected, but there is no selection *for* having red blood (Sober, 1984). If blood color had evolved independently of the molecule that transports oxygen, there would be no particular reason to expect our blood to be red. However, when the characters are *nonindependent* (i.e., correlated), the evolution of one brings with it the evolution of the other.

The proposal I wish to consider is that the ability to feel extended compassion is correlated with the ability to feel compassion toward close relatives, including one's offspring. I argued in the previous section that feeling compassion toward one's children and one's other relatives could easily have been selectively advantageous. The present conjecture is that the psychological capacities that underwrite this advantageous trait have side-effects. Individuals well attuned to the suffering of those near and dear have circles of compassion that potentially extend quite far afield.

There is some evidence for this conjecture about our evolutionary past based on human beings who live here and now. Oliner and Oliner (1988) studied Christians who helped save Jews from the Nazis during World War II; the authors compared these individuals with a control group of individuals who did not help, but who resembled the helpers in terms of education, occupation, and other measures. The Oliners found that helpers tended to have closer relationships with their parents than the nonhelpers did. Similarly, Rosenhan (1970) studied individuals who participated in the civil rights movement in the American South during the 1960s. He found that the individuals who participated the most tended to be more than usually close with their parents. In both these cases, we find an association between helping and having a close relationship with one's parents. It wouldn't be surprising if there also were an association between helping others and loving one's children.

The claim I am defending is not that all people experience extended compassion, and that they do so to the same degree. Plainly, there is a great deal of variation among human beings; all too frequently, it appears that extended compassion is more a possibility than an actuality. Of course, the same is true of compassion directed toward children and close relatives. What evolution has ensured is that human beings frequently develop feelings of love toward their children. A spin-off consequence of this evolutionary event is that human beings are inclined, in suitable circumstances, to feel compassion toward nonrelatives. When your own baby cries, this elicits the desire to help; but the sound that other babies produce is much the same as the sound that comes from your own daughter or son. There was an adaptive advantage in the fact that parents are moved by the cries of their children; a side effect of this evolutionary event is that we are moved by the cries of any baby. The fact that extended compassion confers no adaptive benefit of its own does not mean that it has no evolutionary explanation.

An analog of the kind of argument I am advancing is provided by the dispute that Darwin had with the co-discoverer of the theory of evolution by natural selection, Alfred Russel Wallace, concerning how human intelligence should be explained (Gould, 1980). Wallace maintained that natural selection cannot explain mental abilities that provide no help in surviving and reproducing. A keen eye is useful in hunting, but why should natural selection favor the ability to write symphonies or invent scientific theories? Wallace thought that natural selection can explain practical skills, not "higher" abilities. Darwin countered with the suggestion that the separation of "practical" and "higher" abilities is an illusion; the same mental abilities that helped our ancestors survive and reproduce now allow us to pursue intellectual activities that have no practical benefits at all.

It is important to notice that Darwin's argument does not require that our ancestors actually engaged in artistic and scientific activity. These activities emerged only later, when human beings found themselves in novel circumstances. In similar fashion, it is not required by the explanation I am suggesting for the capacity to experience extended compassion that our ancestors actually felt extended compassion and acted on it. Perhaps this ability was unexpressed ancestrally. Maybe it was a potentiality that flowered only later, when suitable circumstances arose. Just as science and art are latecomers in human evolutionary history, perhaps the full expression of compassion is something that will emerge more in the future than it has in the past. Evolution has made this possible; whether, and to what extent, possibility transforms into actuality, remains to be seen.

NOTES

1. In Sober (1994), I argue that the Aristotelian ideas of "natural state" and "deviation from type" have been rejected by contemporary genetics and evolutionary theory.

2. The relevant measure of the degree of association between two individuals is the difference between two conditional probabilities: Pr (your partner is an altruist | you are an altruist) − Pr(your partner is an altruist | you are selfish). See Sober (1993, section 4.6) for an elementary explanation.

REFERENCES

Allee, W., Emerson, O., Park, T., & Schmidt, K. (1949). *Principles of Animal Ecology*. Philadelphia: W. B. Saunders.
Dobzhansky, T. (1937). *Genetics and the Origin of Species*. New York: Columbia University Press.

Dugatkin, L. & Alfieri, M. (1991). "Guppie and the Tit for Tat Strategy: Preference Based on Past Interaction." *Behavior Ecology and Sociobiology* 28: 243–246.

Gould, S. (1980). *The Panda's Thumb*. New York: Norton.

Krebs, J., & Davies, N. (1981). *An Introduction to Behavioral Ecology*. Sunderland, MA: Sinauer.

Lack, D. (1954). *The Optimal Regulation of Animal Numbers*. Oxford: Oxford University Press.

Haig, D. (1993): "Genetic Conflicts in Human Pregnancy." *Quarterly Review of Biology* 68: 495–532.

Hamilton, W. (1964). "The Genetical Theory of Social Behavior, I and II." *Journal of Theoretical Biology* 7: 1–52.

Nesse, R., & Williams, G. (1994). *Why We Get Sick—The New Science of Darwinian Medicine*. New York: Random House.

Oliner, S. P., & Oliner, P. M. (1988). *The Altruistic Personality: Rescuers of Jews in Nazi Europe*. New York: Free Press.

Rosenhan, D. L. (1970). "The Natural Socialization of Altruistic Autonomy." In J. Macauley and L. Berkowitz (eds.), *Altruism and Helping Behavior*. New York: Academic Press, pp. 251–268.

Singer, P. (1981). *The Expanding Circle—Ethics and Sociobiology*. New York: Farrar, Strauss, and Giroux.

Sober, E. (1984). *The Nature of Selection*. Cambridge, MA: MIT Press.

Sober, E. (1993). *Philosophy of Biology*. Boulder, CO: Westview Press.

Sober, E. (1994). "Evolution, Population Thinking, and Essentialism." In *From a Biological Point of View*. Cambridge: Cambridge University Press.

Sober, E., & Wilson, D. (1998). *Unto Others: The Evolution and Psychology of Unselfish Behavior*. Cambridge, MA: Harvard University Press.

Trivers, R. (1974). "Parent-Offspring Conflict." *American Zoologist* 14: 249–264.

Williams, G. C. (1966). *Adaptation and Natural Selection*. Princeton, NJ: Princeton University Press.

Williams, G. (1992). *Natural Selection—Domains, Levels, and Challenges*. Oxford: Oxford University Press.

Wynne Edwards, V. (1962). *Animal Dispersion in Relation to Social Behavior*. Edinburgh: Oliver and Boyd.

5

Understanding Our Fundamental Nature

HIS HOLINESS THE DALAI LAMA

If we look at history, we find a specific set of assumptions about basic human nature behind the dominant ideology or world view of a given civilization. Each culture was characterized by a high degree of homogeneity, and the dominant world view of a given society often represented the standpoint of a particular religion. Today the situation is totally different. Contemporary secular culture holds no universally defined concept of fundamental human nature. A clear consensus is lacking.

Regardless of its actual content, such a consensus is essential. Without this, a society can have no genuine foundation for ethics. For any system of ethics presupposes certain basic characteristics of the human psyche—characteristics such as a sense of responsibility, individual identity, freedom of choice, a degree of knowledge pertaining to a given situation, and so on. In other words, ethics is by definition based on assumptions about our basic nature. And to a large extent, the particular values of a given culture are determined by its understanding of human nature.

I believe that a basic confusion concerning our fundamental nature lies at the heart of our current moral crisis; we have seriously lost touch with this fundamental humanity. I am not suggesting that our search for solutions to society's current crisis of meaning needs to involve a restoration of old world views based on religious faith. Any workable solution must be based on a clear recognition of present realities—of our time, our culture, and current scientific knowledge.

The importance of developing a clearly defined, viable conception of human nature cannot be underestimated. Ultimately, how we act and behave in relation to our fellow humans and the world depends on how we perceive ourselves. We tend to frame our conception of ourselves in terms of a variety of different characteristics—gender, race, nationality, social status, and so forth. For example, I am a human being, a man, a monk, a Tibetan, and the Dalai Lama. Our expectations of others and our behavior toward them also differ according to the situation in which we find ourselves. At a political meeting, for example, people tend to relate to one another as ideological colleagues or opponents. This is quite natural. But the way we relate to one another is also generally informed by our understanding of human nature. If we think of our nature as essentially compassionate and cooperative rather than violent and competitive, we will tend to behave in certain ways, as well as expecting similar tendencies from others. In contrast, if destructive traits such as aggression and selfishness dominate our fundamental view of human nature, we will incline in the opposite way. Furthermore, if we lack coherence in our own understanding of what we are, this confusion is bound to permeate our perception of others too.

Generally speaking, a viable conception of human nature must contain certain key elements. It must be situated within a wider understanding of the nature of existence in general, the universe at large. It must recognize the determining features that make each of us individual members of the human family. In other words, the theory must be able to tell us what it means to be a human being. The theory must also be able to suggest comprehensive diagnoses at moments when society at large face serious challenges. Finally, it must be able to recommend viable solutions or prescriptions for overcoming these crises. We must consider whether current theories meet these criteria.

Among the theories today that shape the secular conception of human nature is the idea that the universe and everything in it are ultimately the product of pure chance. Evolutionary theory is vaguely credited with being able to account, somehow, for every aspect of our existence. This goes hand in hand with the view that nature has built within us survival mechanisms, such that our fundamental instinct is to pursue our own self-interests. The powerful political ideals of individualism further reinforce this outlook. Individual liberties, self-determination, freedom, and self-fulfillment have become the key values that govern our interaction with others. On the metaphysical level, there is an unspoken consensus that science is the final arbitrator of what *exists* and what *does not*. This seems to go along with the view, despite the wishes and dreams of many, that to exist means to exist in a corporeal body. In this view, this life is our only life, and death represents the final nonexistence of the person. Other factors also influence the secular conception of human nature, not least the decline in religious faith. The resulting view, held perhaps by the majority, is that no set of values can be universally acceptable and applicable.

Even if an absolute foundation of ethics is logically untenable, we cannot infer that no ethical principles are universally binding. We must not confuse tolerance and openness of mind with trivial relativism. Surely there must be a way to demonstrate that hatred of people of different skin color, or different race, or gender, or faith, is wrong. No society can claim to have a healthy value system so long as it cannot adjudicate between Hitler's fascism and Mahatma Gandhi's principle of nonviolence. I, for one, believe that human nature itself provides the criteria by which we can judge the ethical nature of diverse values. If, as a society, we have a healthy understanding of our compassionate nature, we can judge the ethics of a value simply on the basis of whether or not it genuinely resonates with this fundamental nature.

Furthermore, it is mistaken to think that because religion is a matter for individual conscience there can be no basis for a universal system of ethics. Religious belief is clearly not a precondition for ethical behavior. Although religious belief certainly *can* provide the necessary basis for such a system, it is not indispensable. Indeed, I hold the opposite view— that it is both possible and desirable to justify ethical values without reference to any set of transcendental or metaphysical concepts. In fact, I would argue that the inability to distinguish between religion and ethics has caused considerable damage, and the sooner we dispel it, the better it will be for humanity's future. I believe that it is possible to establish a coherent, viable ethical value system without the notion of objective, absolute truth.

I propose a system of ethics that is based on a genuine appreciation of the nature of our human existence. I believe that at the most fundamental level our nature is compassionate, and that cooperation, not conflict, lies at the heart of the basic principles that govern our human existence. A genuine recognition and appreciation of this fundamental nature will have profound ethical implications for both the individual and society.

I base these premises on the simple observation that all sentient beings demonstrate certain basic tendencies. All desire happiness; none desire suffering. Everyone—even animals—appreciates affection. All living beings incline toward peace and harmony. All creatures prefer resting and quietness to bloody encounter.

If our most fundamental aspiration is to seek happiness, this says something very profound about our basic nature. As I see it, happiness is intimately connected with love: By desiring happiness we also seek love. We express our quest for happiness through the language of love. Love not only allows us to access our compassionate nature, it enables others to relate to us at the most human level. In contrast, suffering is closely linked to hostility and anger, for the full realization of hostility's goal is the destruction of the object of your wrath. By instinctually shunning suffering, we also express our dislike of destructive traits such as hostility, anger, and hatred. This is clearly manifested in our natural mind state: When we see death, destruction, or decay, we feel uncomfortable; whereas we feel pleasant and assured when we see life, color, and growth.

Then there is the fact that we all appreciate truthfulness. Everyone, no matter how simple or ignorant—even very small children—experiences displeasure on discovering deceit. I would argue that telling the truth comes more easily than telling lies. Telling lies requires a degree of sophistication; it entails an ability to anticipate the effects of one's action. I would be surprised if we could perceive such artificiality in any animal species. To me this indicates a certain innate disposition toward justice and honesty, beyond what we understand as religious or conventional morality.

Finally, there is the human impulse to create beauty. We can see the celebration of beauty in all cultures. Often it is through the expression and appreciation of beauty that we unlock the compassionate potential in the human heart. Most of us have had at least one profound aesthetic experience, be it the sight of an exquisite temple interior, a sculpture of amazing grace, a painting of real beauty, listening to a profoundly moving piece of music or an eloquent speech, and so on. There is a certain spontaneity in such experiences that directly touches the profound reality of the human heart. Someone once suggested that the reason the communist Chinese have destroyed so many monasteries in Tibet is not just because they contained the cultural heart of the Tibetan people, but because the monasteries were extremely beautiful. The Chinese must have sensed that, if allowed, the beauty of these cultural artifacts could function as a confirmation of the fundamental humanness and preciousness of the Tibetan people, thus awakening the compassionate potential in the hearts of the occupying forces. I think there is some truth in this observation. Any theory of human nature, no matter how scientific, cannot be considered complete so long as it cannot account for these positive fundamental qualities of the human mind.

I must admit at the outset that I have no illusion of possessing any conclusive "proofs" by means of which my proposition—*that basic human nature is compassionate*—can be logically deduced. All my arguments are suggestive at best, for the nature of the claim does not lend itself to fool-proof, deductive reasoning. I must also state here another important caveat. By arguing for a specific conception of our fundamental nature, I do not mean to imply that there is some static, unchanging, absolute entity called "human nature." Any reification of a concept, even one related to a positive characterization of our fundamental nature, is potentially harmful, for it breeds intolerance and a tendency toward dogmatism. All too often, the rhetoric of human nature is used to justify actions and characteristics on the grounds that they are inevitable and unchangeable. Marxist revolution justified its excessive use of force and the destruction of existing social order on the grounds that by doing so it enabled the full exploration of the potentials inherent in human beings. Slavery was justified in the past by assigning to the black people a clearly distinct identity and characteristics. This was also true of the Nazis' treatment of the Jewish people. What I am arguing for is not a hard position, but a certain basic orientation, a way of being and relating to others and to the world that is characterized in positive terms of reference.

Personally, I find that an analysis of the basic pattern of human existence provides a most compelling illustration of this fundamental goodness of humanity. If we look carefully, with discernment, we find that affection plays a central role in our life. Right from our earliest moment, through our mature life, and, of course, finally at the time of death, we are heavily dependent on the affection of others. At every important stage in our life, it is human affection that nurtures us, sustains us, and comforts us. It is as if the thread that runs through our entire life is the thread of affection. When we first come into the world, we are totally dependent on the care and affection of others, especially our mother. Without such care, we cannot survive. If our very survival both as individuals and as a species depends on others' care and affection, it is hard to see how hostility and violence could be the fundamental characteristics of human nature. We see the profound relationship between mother and child summed up in the first act of an infant on entering the world, which is to suckle at its mother's breast What more perfect lesson in love could there be, beyond this complete dependence matched by total acceptance and devotion? When a mother's love and affection for her child are total and unimpeded, even her milk flows more freely. In contrast, if she is agitated and in a state of emotional turbulence, the flow of milk through her nipples is disrupted. To me, the image of a mother breastfeeding a baby is the most potent symbol of human love.

The human need for love and affection does not cease once a child is weaned. According to many eminent medical scientists and biologists, the first few weeks immediately after birth are the most critical period for the rapid development of the brain of a newborn child. The child's brain increases in size most rapidly during the first few months of life. Interestingly, one of the most crucial factors ensuring healthy brain development during this period is simple bodily contact with the mother or mother-surrogate. Through constant physical touch the baby is assured of warmth, love, care, and protection.

Sadly, not all children are fortunate in this regard. A growing body of scientific evidence suggests that the quality of care and affection that children receive as they grow up has a direct bearing on their mental and emotional development. It is widely believed that children brought up in a stable, affectionate family environment are generally healthier, mentally and emotionally, than those whose lives are troubled by constant discord and unhappiness within the home. We often find that those children who are deprived of the elixir of love have difficulty developing such vital human characteristics as trust, warmth, generosity, patience, tolerance, and a sense of responsibility. If they are not shown gentleness, they may grow up unaware of their own innate gentleness. Instead, they tend to withdraw in self-defense or become aggressive in their demands for attention—or they may even adopt these strategies successively out of sheer desperation. Yet even the most violent and agitated child—or adult—must once have been nurtured by somebody. We can imagine such an individual benefiting from being surrounded by loving, caring people. Despite their fractiousness, there is a high probability that they will still be capable of responding to affection.

Thus the need for and appreciation of human affection can be regarded as a continuum at work in all who have experienced it. Some studies even suggest that a mother's own mental and emotional state affects the unborn child when she is pregnant. If she is constantly assailed by psychological and emotional disturbances—by fear, depression, or anxiety, for example—her child may suffer as a result. This implies that our need for the affection of others begins even before our birth, and it continues until our death.

Our need for others' love and care as adults is, of course, most apparent when we grow old or fall ill. In such times, our physical capacity is reduced to the point where once again we become totally dependent on others, whether they be family, friends, or health-care professionals. Even in materially developed nations, where care is bought for money rather than sought within the family, it is still true that affection is crucial. As anyone who has ever fallen ill will testify, it is of immense benefit if the person or persons looking after us show affection rather than a cold, purely clinical disposition. When we are shown affection, we respond with greater comfort and trust. This serves the healing process itself, a fact that is increasingly recognized in modern medical practice. Indeed, anyone who has ever been for a medical checkup knows what a difference it makes if the doctor relates to us with warm, human feelings. I myself am much more reassured when he or she smiles than by the quality of the apparatus or the number of formal degrees he or she may possess.

It is not only when we are young and helpless or old and dependent that we appreciate others' affection. It may seem that we have no particular need for others' care when we are young, healthy, or financially independent. It may even seem a virtue to do without it, but this is a mere illusion. We all need friends. Indeed, the quality of our lives directly reflects the love we receive from others. Modern society encourages us to strive for total autonomy, but it is obvious that we will always be dependent on others for affection, companionship, and comfort. We also know that a life bereft of these precious ingredients must be a miserable one, no matter how fulfilled in other ways. We should not underestimate the emotional and psychological impact of such deprivation: It is no coincidence that the lives of most criminals turn out to have been lonely and lacking in love.

Throughout our lives, human beings seem to possess both an innate need for and appreciation of others' affection, as if this tendency were embedded in our cells. Take, for example, my responses to a poor person on whom I depend for nothing, whose opinion will make no difference to me, someone who can bring no influence to bear on me. Such a person stands in a very different relationship to me than someone who does have the power to influence me, perhaps through a financial component in the relationship. Still, when that poor person smiles at me with affection, with the genuine smile that is a spontaneous expression of a joyous heart, I am touched. I feel happy and assured. Why should a smile cause me to feel happy? Why should I feel unhappy when this person's response to me is negative, in spite of the fact that there is nothing he or she can do that will make a material difference to me? The only possible answer is that a human smile touches something fundamental in me: my desire to receive affection.

An important support for my thesis that human beings are fundamentally compassionate is our natural ability to connect spontaneously and deeply with the suffering of others. Ethnicity, culture, geography, and religion make no difference so far as this inherent capacity for empathy is concerned. An Eskimo from Greenland, a nomad from the vast plateau of Tibet, a broker from Wall Street in New York, all share this basic characteristic. For most of us, when we confront the sight of suffering—for example, a child crying, a man in agony, people dying of starvation—our immediate visceral reaction is sympathy. Often we feel as if we ourselves are undergoing this suffering. There is a certain spontaneity and directness in our natural reaction. It touches us profoundly as human beings. Such a reaction may seem inexplicable from a strictly rational point of view, but it indicates a profound interconnectedness among all living beings.

We see further evidence for this human instinct for generosity and affection in the behavior of small children. When infants from diverse ethnic and cultural backgrounds meet, they often do not stop to consider their differences. They immediately get on with the much more important business of play. There is nothing new in this; yet all too often people condescendingly dismiss such observations by saying that one cannot draw conclusions from the behavior of children who are, by definition, ignorant of the ways of the world. I, for one, am reminded that we supposedly worldly adults have a lot to learn from innocent children whenever I visit one of the Pestalozzi Childrens' Villages where some of the Tibetan refugee children have been educated since the early 1960s. In these villages, children live and play together, children who come from nations and societies that are traditionally at war and where hatred of each other is overtly encouraged from an early age.

Another powerful indication of our fundamentally compassionate nature is found in the intimate connection observed between certain psychological and emotional states and their effect on the physical well being of the individual. We learn from our own personal experience, as well as from scientific studies, that many of the psychological and emotional states normally characterized as unwholesome contribute to high blood pressure, heart diseases, cancer, and various other physical disorders. Anger and hostility can lead to illness and premature death. Scientists are also beginning to consider negative emotional states as a factor in accident-proneness. In contrast, many of the emotions we perceive as wholesome—compassion, love, affection, and so on—enhance a person's physical well-being. The very constitution of our body is such that compassion and related emotions are conducive to the healthy continuation of life itself.

I was interested to learn at a previous Mind and Life Conference of a study[1] focusing on the possible benefits to patients suffering severe cancer of sharing their experiences with one another on a deep emotional level. The scientists organized two groups of patients. The members of one group were required to return to the hospital once a week to meet together and talk about their cancer. The other group was required only to go in for regular individual checkups. It was found that the members of the first group became very close, very caring about one another and about each others' problems and anxieties. They exchanged ideas and advice. At the same time, they clearly drew strength from supporting one another and from being able to share in the hopes and pains of their companions. At the end of 10 years, it was found that those patients who belonged to the support group had twice the life expectancy of those who did not.

From the same source I heard of another study where, in examining thirty- six candidates for major breast cancer surgery, doctors sought to discover whether there was any psychological factor common to long-term survivors. Sadly, after 7 years, twenty-four of the women had died. The doctors then looked to see what, if anything, distinguished the twelve survivors from the others. Comparing their records, they found that the only discernible difference was that the survivors all spoke of a sense of joy in their lives. Most impressively, the doctors found that this avowal of joy was an even more accurate predictor of survival than the number of sites to which the cancer had spread, usually considered the strongest predictor.

The exciting thing about these scientific findings is not that they tell us anything totally unexpected, but rather that they corroborate the vast body of knowledge about the human constitution accumulated over countless generations in various ancient cultures. For example, the traditional Tibetan medical system speaks a great deal about our destructive tendencies and their negative consequences for health. These studies demonstrate the empirical fact that the human body responds to our mental and emotional states. Taken at face value, these findings support the contention that not only receiving but also giving care and affection suits our nature. They indicate that we humans have an innate, not learned, disposition toward affection, care, gentleness, and positive mental and emotional states.

Just as compassion appears to be at the root of our basic nature so too is cooperation the fundamental principle at work in nature. Species survive in dependence on one another. Viewed from up close, we may get the impression that chaos and competition are the main forces at work. A jungle does not look ordered to a human eye that is accustomed to well-kept lawns and orchards, and the struggle between predator and prey can seem tragic. Yet seen from a distance, it is clear that the whole is finely balanced, harmonious, in equilibrium. Only when this balance is disturbed do we see signs of degeneration. On the larger scale of our ecosphere, this manifests as desertification, acid rain, and crop pestilence.

It appears that plants and animal species cooperate not of their own volition, but because they act in accordance with biological imperative. We humans may not be under such strict biological compulsion. It is true that we must cooperate with nature herself in order to grow food—and we must cooperate with one another to distribute this food (even though the explicit motive for doing so may be commercial). It is also true that our species is propagated through cooperation. There are hardly any areas of our lives where others' help is not needed. Furthermore, we fulfill our humanity when we participate in the culture, language, traditions, and institutions of our human community, all of which presuppose cooperation insofar as they are communal activities. Clearly too, the extent to which we cooperate with one another will determine our fate as a species, especially at this critical time in humankind's history. Yet, as humans we have a degree of choice in the matter that is not manifestly available to animals, so far as we can judge, and still less to plants.

To all this, one might object in the following manner: Although we need to cooperate with others in order to thrive, and although we need the care and affection of others for our own existence, we can in fact survive without expressing these qualities ourselves. Although we need to receive others' affection, this does not prove that we ourselves are fundamentally disposed toward giving affection.

I believe, however, that there is compelling circumstantial evidence to support my case. Often we have an opportunity for insight into the deeper nature of the human spirit when people are exposed to situations requiring an immediate response. When we ourselves or others are threatened, our instinct is to reach out, both in the expectation of receiving help and, crucially, to offer it. As we know from personal experience, most of us have within us a natural capacity to empathize with others' pain and suffering. If human beings were not fundamentally self-giving, fundamentally generous, such feelings and actions would be inexplicable. To say that there is no rational explanation for these phenomena is no better than saying that they are mysterious. What else but a bedrock of compassion and instinctive care could explain the empathy of one human being for another who suffers?

By arguing for a positive description of our fundamental nature, I do not mean to deny the naturalness of our more destructive traits. Anger, aggression, lust, selfishness, and jealousy are integral aspects of our emotional life. Of course, to a large degree what we are is an expression of our characteristics as a biological species. In other words, our "fundamental nature" is bound to be embodied in our biology. As social beings, we share with various other life forms many of the biological factors that drive our interactions with others and the world. However, I do not think that a biological description of what we are can be exhaustive. Often in our enthusiasm to perceive every aspect of existence within the current scientific paradigm, there is a tendency to read too much into the biological affinity between humans and animals. It is crucial to reflect on, and understand, both our similarities to and differences from the animals.

There are powerful positive forces that differentiate our life from animal life. As human beings, we have the capacity to be self-aware and relate to our experiences across time. This faculty enables us to respond to a given situation not purely in biological terms, but also in psychological and cognitive terms. Ours is perhaps the only life form on earth that can view the process of the entire universe as a whole and weigh short- and long-term consequences of our actions. We are gifted with a special faculty, our unique intelligence and imagination, that can intervene even in humanity's own destiny if we so desire. Appreciation of this point is critical, because our intelligence and capacity for reason and calculation also make us potentially the most destructive life form on earth. Not only do we humans exploit other species for our own interests, we are also capable of destroying members of our own species.

So relying on reason alone is dangerous. Look where our "reason" and "intelligence" have brought us! Reason in itself is blind to the considerations of deeper moral questions; we need qualities of the heart to counterbalance the force of our intelligence. It is our basic humanity that must guide our intelligence in the positive direction. The key to genuine peace lies in each of us reconnecting with the power of our mother's love, the affection that nurtured us when we were all children.

I once saw a black-and-white photograph taken during the First World War of an English soldier giving water to an injured Turkish soldier, an enemy! For me, this represented something very profound. In battle the two sides were shooting to kill, operating for that time under the label of "enemies." However, once the battle ended, they had the space to reconnect with their basic human feelings. On that level, of course, the injured Turkish soldier was just another human being. There was nothing unusual in the Englishman naturally responding to the urgent need of an injured man. He was acting spontaneously out of his compassionate potential.

We each possess this wonderful capacity to transcend the limitations of self-centeredness through acts of compassion and love. We must never forget that as human beings we are ultimately free agents. We are not just determined by purely physical laws; we are free to act according to our will and to deeply held principles. The very concept of responsibility, which is essential for understanding our moral life, presupposes free will. I base my approach to ethics on the assumption that, as human beings, we do have choices. Moreover, I assume that through effort we *can* and *do* change.

Perhaps the most vocal objections to my thesis may come from those who believe that the process of evolution itself entails, even depends on, aggression and selfishness. This notion is sloganized in the phrase "survival of the fittest," which is commonly understood to mean that in nature the strong survive and the weak do not (strength embracing not only physical might but also cunning). To my mind, nature is best understood as a process—as an organic, interdependently sustained whole, which, when analyzed, comprises infinite symbiotic relationships. It is impossible that the flora and fauna of our planet could have survived otherwise, let alone prospered as they have.

This is not to say that aggression and competition are not natural characteristics of the human mind. Nor does it signify that they are inherently negative. There is nothing wrong with being aggressive under appropriate circumstances—in sport, for example. Nor is strength, or even the aspiration to increase strength, necessarily negative. It depends on one's motivation. Competing simply to ensure the attainment of one's own goals is not negative. This is very different from competition where the primary concern is to prevent others from fulfilling their aspirations. I believe that the relationship between cunning and the evolutionary

notion of survival of the fittest is misconceived. For cunning is, by definition, a function of the imaginative faculty, and this, so far as we can tell,
is exclusive to human beings. We have a manifestly strong ability to anticipate a course of events. Assigning this faculty to other creatures is
nothing more than anthropomorphism.

The popular notion of the survival of the fittest definitely reflects
certain assumptions. Even the meaning of the word "fittest" is often
wrongly construed. In the context of evolution, it surely means "most
suitable" rather than "most able." It is hard to judge why most people
assume the latter meaning, but I think they do so mainly because it both
suits and justifies our present materialistic and individualistic culture.
Given the way that modern society functions, there are grounds for supposing that aggression and selfishness can provide greater prospects for
human survival at the individual level. But this is a reflection of the way
we humans order our affairs, not of the workings of nature. I don't think
there is really anything in evolutionary biology that would irrefutably
contradict my contention that caring and cooperation are the fundamental characteristics of human nature.

What, then, might be the significance of accepting such a positive picture of fundamental human nature? At the least, it will challenge the influential belief that somehow, biologically, we are destined to be selfish,
aggressive, and violent. The prevailing atmosphere in modern society encourages us to compete with one another and, in consequence, to be
aggressive. In a way, this may be a function of the progress of the modern
industrial ethos. In ancient times, people lived in low-density, rural communities in a way that was explicitly dependent on nature, but today this
is rarely the case. So-called primitive conditions may have fostered people's cooperative instincts, but today's densely populated urban areas
actually seem more conducive to aggressive behavior. Yet it would be
wrong to attribute this to human beings' fundamental nature. Significantly, all the world's religions agree that, while this aggressive potential
certainly exists, it can be controlled through spiritual discipline.

To say that human nature is fundamentally compassionate implies a
general principle that, by definition, must be applicable to each individual human being. What, then, are we to make of those people whose lives
seemingly are wholly given over to violence and aggression? What of
Hitler and his plan to exterminate the entire Jewish race? What of Stalin
and his pogroms? What of Pol Pot, the architect of the Killing Fields?
What of Chairman Mao, the man I once knew and admired, and the bar-

barous insanity of the Cultural Revolution? And what about the murderers who apparently kill for pleasure?

I admit that I can think of no single explanation to account for the monstrous acts of these people. However, one important factor that must be considered here is the role of intelligence or, better still, the imaginative faculty (the very characteristic that distinguishes human beings from animals). For it is imagination that enables us to conceive a vision and find ways of making it real. These people each carried out their schemes in accordance with a vision, albeit a perverted one. And it is clear that, although their aims may have been to seek satisfaction and fulfillment as they conceived it, their real motives were born of hatred. Even as a vision based on proper motivation can lead to wonders, when one's motivation is divorced from basic human feeling, its potential for destruction cannot be overestimated.

What we see in such extraordinary cases as these, of people directly responsible for the deaths of so many, represents the catastrophic consequence of a deep submergence of their basic human nature. I do not mean to suggest that the capacity to be moved by human affection has totally ceased to exist in them. Except perhaps in the most extreme cases, we know that even the most ruthless characters appreciate being shown affection.

How does this submergence come about? Here we must acknowledge that such people do not come from nowhere but from within society's prevailing social and cultural conditions. Such cases occur within the context of the whole of society, of which each of us is also a member. It is a mistake, therefore, to concentrate solely on the individual. So, while we tend to regard the behavior of these people as something essentially isolated, we ourselves as members of the human community must take our share of the responsibility for tolerating the conditions under which such disintegration of the human personality can take place. Each of us, as members of society, must ensure that conditions do not permit such negative, destructive characters to reach any position of influence or power within the human community.

If we all reflect deeply, we will find that our common humanity is precisely the universal principle that can bind us all together peacefully. None of us wants discord; we all desire harmony. When we recognize that our nature is basically compassionate and cooperative, it becomes clear that it is natural to behave in conformity with this basic disposition. It is also in our best interest to do so. We must also recognize that, as human beings, we are free agents capable of determining the course of our own destiny. With a will to change, confidence in our own positive potential, and a basic outlook on life that respects the profound interdependence of all things, we *can* and *must* secure a firm grounding for fundamental ethical principles. By living a way of life that expresses our basic goodness, we fulfill our humanity and give our actions dignity, worth, and meaning. Indeed, when we understand human nature correctly, we have within our grasp the foundation of a universal ethic.

NOTE

1. David Spiegel's study at Stanford as reported in *Healing Emotions* (D. Goleman, ed. Boston: Shambala), pp. 42–43.

Dialogues, Part I: Fundamental Questions

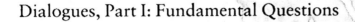

1. Why have the biobehavioral sciences neglected compassion?
2. Is scientific knowledge neutral?
3. Is human nature fundamentally compassionate?
4. Or is compassion fragile?
5. Are we as "naturally" competitive as we are cooperative?
6. Where does compassion come from?
7. What is the relationship between happiness and compassion?
8. How do we "see" and recognize compassion in others?

These conversations were edited and, in places, reordered, to enhance thematic coherence. All portions of the dialogue that appear under the name of the Dalai Lama are his own thoughts but are rendered here largely in the words of his translators, José Cabezon and Thubten Jinpa, since, for these complex conversations, he chose—with only occasional exceptions—to speak in Tibetan.

1. Why Have the Biobehavioral Sciences Neglected Compassion?

ANNE HARRINGTON   We talk about the similarities between Buddhists and scientists both wishing to know reality objectively. Yet I am struck by the fact that, historically, the more deeply our sciences have probed reality, the less relevant concepts like "compassion" become. Behind altruism is strategizing for genetic fitness; behind consciousness is meaningless material process. In contrast, when one employs Buddhist methods of exploring reality, one apparently arrives at a very different reality than ours: a cosmos in which compassion is basic, serves as a dominant framework for the dramas of life, and in which beings are all connected and not in struggle. So my reflections here begin by asking: How do we understand this difference? Here are two different approaches that say they are both seeking objective reality, but they don't find the same cosmic reality as a result of their methods.

DALAI LAMA   I wonder whether the mainstream understanding that has emerged through the scientific approach, of human nature as aggressive, selfish, and heartless, will be the final standpoint of science. Maybe it's too early to say. Has science stopped evolving? [Yours] is a particular viewpoint based on a certain stage of history and evolution in human knowledge. . . . In particular, I feel that science has not yet paid enough attention to the internal world [of consciousness] compared to the external. So maybe there is still a lot of ground to cover.

ELLIOTT SOBER   With respect to the question about what science will become, it's important to bear in mind that psychology as a science is a hundred years old in the West. One hundred years ago, philosophy and psychology were not separate disciplines. Psychology became an experimental, empirical subject only very recently. . . . And for about thirty years of that hundred-year period, the reigning ideology in psychology was behaviorism, which avoided thinking about the mind. You would describe environmental circumstances and behavior, but never think about mental activity. So we are right at the initial birth of serious scientific inquiry into the nature of the mind. It's not over; it's barely begun.

ERVIN STAUB   Even in that context, we who study altruism are not quite as atypical as Anne described us. Until about the 1960s, it's true that people had not done research on altruism, empathy, and compassion, or anything related. But since the 1960s there has been a lot of research on these topics in the United States, Europe, Japan, and other places. The word "compassion" has not been used in connection with empathy or sympathy. But altruism, helping behavior, caring—all these things have been the subject of a fair amount of attention in the last thirty years or so, and that does give us hope that there is room to expand and to go further.

RICHARD DAVIDSON   To some extent, as psychology has become an empirical science, it has been incorporated into the general area of biomedicine, which is very much focused on disease. Some of the bias toward negative emotion, and the excessive study of the negative in contrast to the positive, is a reflection of the general orientation of medicine itself toward disease in contrast to health. If you ask physicians for the definition of health, they most often describe it as the absence of disease. There really is no medicine of health, and there is just emerging now a psychology of positive emotional states. As we all have said, we're really at the beginning of this empirical effort. We need to change the balance. More people are beginning to understand that a focus on health and positive emotion may have important practical consequences in addition to its theoretical interest.

DALAI LAMA   Perhaps there is another factor here. My understanding of Western psychology is that it seems to be quite action-oriented. It looks at how psychological states manifest in behavior, such as aggression or violence. . . . And the fact is, when you look at behavioral expressions of strong emotions like anger and hostility, they are so striking. The resulting behavior is so noticeable. Whereas the [behavioral] manifestations of compassion may not be striking.

ERVIN STAUB   Another way of making this point, perhaps, is to say that violence is a negative force that impacts you. It's an act of commission. Whereas, when somebody acts altruistically, it's often an act of omission, simply the absence of something. People are very much impacted by the presence of a force, but they don't respond to the absence of something.

ELLIOTT SOBER   Well, on the other hand, we all know that positive emotion motivates us to act. Love makes us take care of children. I don't think any scientists, or ordinary people, believe that only negative emotions produce behavior. We all know that the positive ones are motivators too. It's a puzzle why the science of psychology hasn't focused on them. Richie's suggestion about the dominance of the medical model may be true very recently, but if you look back to the first half of the twentieth century, psychology was not really part of medicine.

2. Is Scientific Knowledge Neutral?

ERVIN STAUB   Anne raised another question concerning how scientists operate in the world. For example, she described the atomic scientists who had done research to develop the atomic bomb, and then continued busily with it even when the need was not immediate, because that was their life. In the same way, so-called Nazi scientists did horrible experiments. Science is represented as value-free, but we cannot expect that scientists will be different from other human beings. If Nazi culture propagates the idea that anything can be done to certain devalued human beings, then Nazi scientists, being part of their culture, tragically are going to do the same thing.

DALAI LAMA   So the argument here is that what we perceive and do in science is to a large extent conditioned by our culture and beliefs. The issue remains whether knowledge in itself can be seen as neutral. From the Buddhist point of view, knowledge in itself can be neutral. For example, although the fundamental aspiration in Buddhism is to seek enlightenment and perfection, to overcome the negative tendencies of the human mind and enhance the positive potential, Buddhism would not discourage exploring and understanding the mechanisms of the negative processes. Spiritual endeavor in Buddhism involves understanding the negative processes and taking a stand against them consciously and knowingly, rather than giving in to them or merely wishing them away.

ANNE HARRINGTON   I think we are still in dialogue about how to understand science simultaneously as a process that engages neutral truth and as something that is human. As a metaphor, I think of the Hindu religion, where there are many gods, all different dimensions of one higher reality that stands above any particular attributes. Human beings reach up and choose the different gods—the different faces of reality—that are necessary for the particular needs they have at that time. Perhaps science's encounter with reality is a little bit like the Hindu's encounter with the thousands of gods that represent the different faces of ultimate reality. It doesn't mean that there isn't an ultimate reality, but that we engage it through our motivations and needs.

If we could imagine climbing out of some imagined box of human history, there might be a place outside the box where all knowledge would be neutral. But my point is that we access knowledge only from inside the box. The moment knowledge becomes part of human history, all our motivations and needs and values become inevitably tangled with it. I don't disagree that knowledge can be neutral, but think perhaps wholly neutral knowledge is not accessible to us as human beings.

ADAM ENGLE   Maybe to a Buddha knowledge is neutral. But people who have obscurations bring those obscurations to the knowledge and tilt it one way or another.

ANNE HARRINGTON   The Buddha's view is a view from nowhere.

JOSÉ CABEZÓN   Or a view from everywhere.

ADAM ENGLE   And so from a Buddhist point of view, as His Holiness says, knowledge is neutral.

ANNE HARRINGTON   But we—most of us, at least—are not Buddhas.

DALAI LAMA   My point is that, in Buddhism, we make distinctions between scholarship and goodness. The ideal is for an individual to evolve to the point where scholarship doesn't take him too far into intellectualism, and goodness doesn't take him too far into just feeling good with no basis or substance. We say knowledge is neutral, but we also say that people need something to balance the knowledge component.

3. Is Human Nature Fundamentally Compassionate?

RICHARD DAVIDSON   Your Holiness, there is a world view common in the West that holds that there is a conflict between reason and passion, or emotion, where a cauldron of negative emotions is held down by our rational processes. The Buddhist view is apparently very different, where the assumption is that basic human nature is one of compassion: We may be hindered by ignorance [that keeps us from realizing our compassionate nature], but the goal is to peel away the layers of ignorance and then arrive at the compassion at our core. These two views of human nature are very different. Can you perhaps describe the Buddhist perspective in more detail, so that we can learn more about it and also understand what you make of these two very different conceptions of human nature?

DALAI LAMA   Approaching the question of human nature from the classical Buddhist point of view, one accepts that the natural state of a sentient being includes forces that are both positive and negative. Although much of my thinking is informed by Buddhist ideas, particularly the fundamental Buddhist tenet that all sentient beings have a seed of enlightenment, a potential for perfection, when I say that I believe human nature to be fundamentally good and compassionate, I base this belief more on empirical observation. For example, when I look at the basic pattern of human existence, from the time of our birth until death, I see affection and compassion playing the dominant role in the emotions.

One of the central premises of this belief in the fundamentally compassionate nature of human beings is that our basic instinct is to seek happiness. That is so deeply embedded, one could say it is our innate disposition. If you examine the nature of this disposition and also examine the mechanisms or the causal factors that give rise to happiness, you find that compassion, affection, and love are almost inextricably linked with this quest for happiness. It is love, affection, and the feeling of connectedness that bring joy and happiness.

Anger arises more as a reaction when this basic project of seeking happiness is hindered. When suffering or adverse situations get in the way of fulfilling this basic aspiration, then we react in a more aggressive, violent way. Although anger, violence, and aggression are a natural part of our mind, in some sense they are on a different level. One could say they are secondary levels of emotion. (Perhaps we ought to make a distinction between aggression and violence as reactions or behavioral characteristics, whereas anger and hostility are motivational or emotional states.)

For myself, I find this consideration most convincing: If you examine the nature of your own physical well being, somehow the wholesome emotions like affection, love, and compassion seem to create a sense of calmness and composure within your mind, which is also very conducive to better health; whereas strong emotions like anger and hostility lead to a kind of a turbulence within your mind that is not conducive to your physical wellbeing. So it seems as if, within the natural state, the constitution of the body itself is closer to emotions like love and affection.

ELLIOTT SOBER   A neutral way to describe human beings is that they have the capacity to be cruel and also to be kind. Whether we end up one way or the other is merely a consequence of our experiences, but neither is more intrinsic to human nature. They're both there.

THUBTEN JINPA   In China, this was also a big question for Chinese philosophers. Some claimed that human nature was evil. Some claimed that human nature was good; some claimed it was neither; and some claimed it was both.

ANNE HARRINGTON   That's where we are. [*Laughter*]

ELLIOTT SOBOR   But if I understood what you were saying, Your Holiness, the Buddhist picture is that both possibilities exist, but one is more fundamental, more part of human nature. The other is not part of human nature.

DALAI LAMA   No, it is part of human nature. The picture is a bit more complicated. According to Buddhist psychology, consciousness in itself is neutral. It's neither wholesome nor unwholesome, neither positive nor negative. Of course, it has the potential to be both, one way or another. Within each of us there is a possibility toward negative actions and a possibility toward positive actions. However, if you compare between these two different possibilities or potentials, it seems to be true that the more positive dispositions like compassion, affection, and love have a much more dominant influence on the natural state of a person's mind than the opposites like anger, hostility, and aggression. Generally speaking, the affectionate side is much more dominant; the person is not always angry, not always hostile.

ELLIOTT SOBER   Does dominant mean that the one occurs more often than the other?

DALAI LAMA   Not only that, but also in Buddhism there is a belief that the positive or wholesome emotions have more grounding.

ELLIOTT SOBER   But surely it varies from person to person whether one happens more often than the other. There are some people who are probably unhappy more often than happy, or angry more often than content.

DALAI LAMA   Of course, it will differ from individual to individual. But even in the case of someone we consider evil or some negative person, if you examine that person's life, especially in the early stage, that person has been nurtured by someone else's affection and love, be it the mother or someone acting as a mother. The nurturing through love and affection has been there right at the start, so it has a much more powerful effect on that person's nature. This is the process through which every human being grows up.

I am arguing for a particular picture of human nature in which affection or compassion is seen as a more fundamental disposition or state. The question then is, how do we account for all of the aggressive tendencies, the competitiveness, and the violence that we see in the world? All of these behavioral characteristics may have more to do with pressures of a particular time and environment. For example, look at the life of an animal. Their needs are quite simple, and they have a very simple life. They may shelter themselves in a cave. They kill another animal for their survival out of necessity. In order to fulfill their simple needs, they have simple behavioral characteristics.

If you compare that to a human being, human beings are gifted with the faculty of intelligence and imagination. As society has become more and more advanced and also as population increases, there is a greater degree of competition for scarce resources. Also, as societies become more advanced, what we perceive as our needs becomes more complicated. We tend to make our requirements broader. At the beginning, human life and the human community were simpler. There was no need for much competition. Perhaps at that time they were less aggressive. Even today in societies and cultures in remote areas that are not so industrialized, life is less tense, less anxious, more "laid back."

As far as human affection is concerned, today's human beings are the same, on a basic level, as in earlier times. But now all the external conditions are such that, unless we make more aggressive efforts, there is a danger of losing one's ground. Many of our current aggressive and competitive instincts may not necessarily be fundamental or innate. They may have more to do with pressures of a particular lifestyle, particular environmental, and material conditions.

In fact, I wonder if there is even a felt or experiential difference between wholesome states like affection and unwholesome states like anger. Anger is almost a reaction. You need a condition that triggers it. Whereas affection does not necessarily need an external condition to trigger it. And when you experience anger, you can have such an experience even against your wishes. You may not want to be angry, but you can't help it, you feel angry. But you wouldn't say that one feels affection without wanting to feel affection.

ELLIOTT SOBER   Well, I'm not sure. An example: You think someone has done something very wrong, but you find yourself liking them anyway. The positive emotion happens in spite of some rational voice in the back of your mind saying you shouldn't like this person. Take the example of laughter: Sometimes we laugh at a joke even though we know it's inappropriate to laugh or it's a sick joke. And laughter, I guess, is a positive emotion. We censor ourselves all the time, don't we?

ANNE HARRINGTON   We make judgments about our feelings.

ELLIOTT SOBER   We've discussed different views about human nature, and I understand your view that one needs to take an empirical approach: look at the evidence of how human beings behave in different circumstances and ground the view of human nature on that. Suppose we were able to do that somehow and actually know by observation what human nature is. In Western biology, one would take that set of facts and seek an evolutionary explanation for them. The inquiry would not end with a description of how human beings behave; it would then ask why human beings are inclined to behave the way they do. Is there an analogous process in Buddhist philosophy, where one first observes the patterns of human behavior, and then seeks an explanation? Supposing the Buddhist view that human nature is fundamentally good is correct. Is there an explanation offered why our species ended up this way? Could it have been otherwise?

DALAI LAMA   We need to make a distinction between the Buddhist position and my own views on human nature. My approach has been to argue for a certain conception of human nature based on empirical observations of the pattern of human existence, because I am concerned to communicate this idea to people without any recourse to Buddhist beliefs. This is an important point here. If there is any metaphysical premise on which I base my belief, then it is perhaps this claim that our fundamental instinct is to seek happiness. That could be taken as an empirical statement or as a metaphysical statement. Other than that, there is no further metaphysical foundation. My own view is very much based on empirical observation of how human life begins, how we depend so much on others' affection throughout our lives, especially at particular points, and how even physiologically we respond to affection. All of these are the grounds on which my conviction is based that basic human nature is good. This is not a specifically Buddhist approach.

4. Or Is Compassion Fragile?

RICHARD DAVIDSON   If, as Your Holiness asserts, compassion and caring are so basic, why are they also so fragile? Why is it so easy to perturb those qualities?

DALAI LAMA   Well, I do not fully agree that compassion and caring are so fragile. Perhaps we just pay less attention to compassion and caring; we reinforce it less. Whereas in some sense, we fully embrace hostility and anger in an emotional state, fueling and reinforcing it. If we were to give the same amount of energy, attention, and reinforcement to compassion and caring, they would definitely be stronger.

Sometimes human beings even use reason to justify thinking that anger and hostility are useful: "It makes me face challenges. It protects me and makes me feel strong, whereas compassion and caring make me vulnerable and weak." Sometimes we go to that extent to try to justify it.

This may not be a conclusive point, but one could argue that compassion is stronger because you can have anger motivated by compassion, but you cannot have compassion motivated by anger. Rationally speaking, the sense of urgency, spontaneity, and immediacy with which one can act out of anger can also be motivated by compassion or certain other emotions without giving in to anger. Compassion gives a sense of determination and commitment, and then intelligence, the understanding of the situation, gives guidance. In that way, one can have that same intensity, immediacy, and spontaneity. Yet the beneficial acts that are motivated by compassion and a sense of caring cannot be achieved through anger with other means.

ERVIN STAUB   Your Holiness, you mentioned that Buddhists see many things contextually, which makes a lot of sense to me. I was wondering, when monks go through monastic training and practices to develop a deep sense of compassion, how does that transfer into complex settings where there are many more elements in life that impact them than in a relatively protected monastery?

DALAI LAMA   It depends very much on the level of realization of the person, the level of compassion that was cultivated. If the level is quite high and stable, then even exposure to complex situations will not destroy that compassion. On the other hand, if the person is at an early stage of the compassion practice, a more complex environment will be much more challenging, and the person will be less able to deal with it compassionately. At the initial stage, before you have reached a stage of stability, it is much more effective to avoid the situation rather than trying to confront and deal with it. Until you get to the point where it is stabilized, you are much more vulnerable to external conditions.

Given this idea, according to Buddhist thinking, if a person who has attained stability in his or her compassion training continues to stay in seclusion, that person is not really doing anything with compassion. That person should now be out, running around like a mad dog, actively engaged in acts of compassion.

ROBERT LIVINGSTON   Some of the lower animals have a capacity for empathy that's quite striking. For example, I took care of a gorilla that had been wounded in Africa and taken to Yale. I nursed his wounds and I fed and cared for him from the time he was two months old until he was one year. One day I had a bad scratch on my arm from a cat. He saw that, and he was immediately concerned. So he took my arm, and he looked at it very carefully. He looked up in my face, he sniffed it, and looked in my face again. He turned my hand around and did everything he could to examine it carefully. He was obviously transmitting his love, affection, concern, and empathy.

DALAI LAMA   Probably this was a gorilla with a very strong disposition toward compassion carried from his previous life. [*Laughter*]

5. Are We as "Naturally" Competitive as We Are Cooperative?

ERVIN STAUB   Bob, you made an important assumption about human nature in your talk: that people in social situations want a relative advantage. You suggested that this was a result of biological evolution. You didn't elaborate on it, but it's a very important statement, especially because at first glance it seems so true. However, I think it is possible that capitalist Western culture and American culture actually can explain a lot of your data. For example, there have been experiments with children playing a game where they can increase their relative advantage even by taking a loss. It's similar to the prisoner's dilemma. Mexican-American children tend to be much more cooperative and don't try to increase their relative advantage. For Anglo-Saxon American children, their goal seems to be to increase their relative advantage. So do we really know how much of this is human nature and how much is human culture?

ROBERT FRANK   Several things lead me to believe that there is at least some common core component of human nature that cares about relative position, although I would immediately say that culture can modify it in many ways. After all, we are incredibly flexible animals and we can learn to deflect our attention to think in different ways.

There are some interesting biochemical effects observed by Michael McGuire and his collaborators. Your position in a dominance hierarchy affects the concentration of certain neurotransmitters in the brain. In particular he has found that a high status, dominant animal has a higher concentration of metabolites of the neurotransmitter serotonin in its cerebrospinal fluid. We know that the higher concentration of serotonin is a result, not a cause, of its high status because when the high-status animal is taken from the troupe, its serotonin level goes down. A new animal becomes dominant in the troupe and its serotonin level goes up as a result. Apparently, these increases in serotonin levels are experienced as pleasurable occurrences. It's a reinforcing mechanism.

McGuire and his colleagues have examined human populations as well on a small scale. They find that the leaders of athletic teams have higher serotonin than the nonleaders. The leaders of fraternities have higher concentrations than the nonleaders. So there is something basic in our biochemistry that cares about rank. How we translate that concern into the rules of culture obviously leaves a great deal of room to work. It's difficult to imagine that there could have been any animal that was completely indifferent to its rank, since rank was such a critical determinant of whether it got the resources it needed to survive. If there is a famine, typically it is the individuals of high rank who survive. I don't know the extent to which this can be modified by culture.

I know that we also have countervailing impulses. We are compassionate people. We sympathize with the distress of others. Your Holiness made the point earlier that some people prefer neither advantage nor disadvantage. Of course, I might prefer an advantage in the abstract because it provides security for me. And yet, if I am close to you and you are in a disadvantaged position, I feel your pain as a result of that. So, I'll sacrifice my advantage to avoid that sense of distress at your disadvantage. It's a very complicated mix of things. I would be very surprised if research taught us in the future that this was a purely cultural phenomenon, but I don't know the extent to which it can be modified.

ELLIOTT SOBER   In certain situations, the desire for equality may coexist with the desire for relative advantage. This is probably not a specifically Western finding, but in the ultimatum game, dividing a resource in half would be regarded as fair. If there is a prize that only one person can get, we decide who gets it by tossing a coin, or drawing straws, or some lottery in which each individual has the same chance. That's a process in which people have equal entitlements. So coexisting with this idea of relative advantage having biological roots, I think certain aspects of the importance we place on fairness and equality also have a biological origin.

ANNE HARRINGTON   Anthropologists often use observations from hunter-gatherer societies as a window onto our supposedly more fundamental human nature, because we believe that for most of our history we lived in such small groups. I've read a little bit about a hunter-gatherer society living in the Kalahari desert, who lay a tremendous amount of emphasis on ensuring that nobody in the society becomes too arrogant. If somebody comes home from hunting with an exceptionally large kill, a lot of joking goes on: "Oh what a skinny, silly, little thing you've brought back." A lot of humor is used to make sure that nobody gets too proud, and the meat is then distributed. I wonder whether it's only in agricultural societies, or societies where possessions begin to be accumulated, that these new considerations start to become important. If we are tempted to say that this is how we are "naturally," then maybe we should look at how these competitive tendencies actually play out in a hunter-gatherer society, where they don't seem in fact to be that pronounced.

ROBERT FRANK   On the contrary, the most compelling reason to care about rank actually does derive from the ancestral environment. Most primitive groups, and even many current societies, are polygamous. A man can take several wives, and this is a very powerful force in the selection of characteristics. If you are a male, having low rank in such a society is almost a disaster in terms of having your genes present in the next generation. You are completely frozen out of the genetic sweepstakes. If you have high rank, you will do quite well under those circumstances. So the idea that an individual organism wouldn't care about rank under those conditions would be very strange.

RICHARD DAVIDSON   The idea of relative rank is also very important in the explanation of the relationship between social class and health. It turns out that across the entire continuum of social class there is a linear relationship with health status. It's not just that the individuals at the low end of the social class continuum have poor access to health care, but if you look at each gradation, even between middle income and upper middle income, there are improvements in objective measures of health. The explanation offered for that concerns relative rank: It can have significant health consequences in addition.

DALAI LAMA   Of course, there are different types of competition, and sometimes competition is good and positive. But wouldn't you say that anxious competition, trying to get oneself in a better position than the other, is harmful to one's health?

RICHARD DAVIDSON   Yes, I think that competition that arises as a function of comparisons among people in different positions in the hierarchy is bad for one's health.

ELLIOTT SOBER   And so one's health would be improved by policies that lessened the consequences of differences in rank.

6. Where Does Compassion Come From?

RICHARD DAVIDSON   If competition can have negative health consequences, perhaps we can also explore the possibility that many, if not all forms of compassionate experience have biological consequences—that is, affect our physiology in ways that may be beneficial. There is initial experimental evidence that certain types of positive emotion in general may actually improve the immune system. Certain types of positive emotion may also enable us to recover more quickly from a stressful event. And certain types of positive emotion have beneficial effects on our sleep and on our autonomic nervous system, our heart, our blood pressure. These biological changes may actually be advantageous in an evolutionary sense. Regardless of whom we express compassion for, be it distant relatives or even viruses, the experience of compassion may produce biological benefits for the person who is expressing it. This is a different way of seeing the possible role of biological change that may be promoted by compassion and similar states.

ERVIN STAUB   There is actual evidence related to the benefits of altruism, or observing altruism. David McClelland did a study where students observed a movie of Mother Teresa helping children in India. Afterwards they found that one aspect of their immune function improved as a result of watching that movie. I did a study using a questionnaire published in the magazine *Psychology Today* that was returned by 7,000 people. People who reported more helping and more caring values also reported having a greater sense of well being in the world. Now, you don't know which way it goes. It could be that people who have a greater sense of well being will be more generous as a result. But I think it probably goes both ways.

ELLIOTT SOBER   Still, one important distinction that needs to be drawn is the difference between the current usefulness of a characteristic and the historical explanation of why the characteristic evolved. Suppose it turns out to be true that forms of compassion expressed for all sentient beings have good health consequences for us in many different ways. It's a separate question whether those benefits are part of the explanation for why that capacity evolved. The evolutionary explanation would require that some of the individuals in ancestral populations felt compassion for all sentient beings, and others did not. There was variation in the population, and the ones who felt compassion for all sentient beings did better at surviving and reproducing than the ones who did not, and so the characteristic has evolved. Now, are you suggesting that?

RICHARD DAVIDSON   I'm inviting that as a possibility.

ANNE HARRINGTON   From a Buddhist perspective, would a person who felt compassion for all sentient beings be less likely to marry, have a family, and reproduce, than a person who did not? Would a person who felt compassion for all sentient beings prefer to become a celibate monk so that he could more likely serve all of humanity? According to evolutionary theory, there would be selective disadvantages to experiencing compassion of that sort.

DALAI LAMA   There would be no difference.

ANNE HARRINGTON   If you marry and have children, are you not more apt to be attached to your children and to your spouse than to the rest of humanity, and in that sense fail to have true compassion and equanimity for all sentient beings?

DALAI LAMA   If you look at the historical evolution of Buddhism, both the Mahayana and also the Theravada tradition acknowledge both lay and monastic practitioners. Especially in the Mahayana system, there is a lot of discussion about Bodhisattvas, Buddhas-to-be at very high levels of spiritual realization, who are lay practitioners. So much so that the Theravada traditions have criticized the Mahayana as sometimes having a higher regard for lay Bodhisattvas than for fully ordained monks and nuns.

ANNE HARRINGTON   And these are people who would have families and children as well?

DALAI LAMA   Of course. There is even a reference in one of the scriptures that Bodhisattvas who have high levels of spiritual realization can skillfully utilize afflictive emotions like desire and attachment for positive purposes. It is said there that the Bodhisattvas will utilize desires to produce thousands of children. [*Laughter*] Whether it's true is questionable, but there is such a reference.

LUIGI LUISI   I would like to point out the possible discrepancy between the Buddhist view and the view that Elliott has been presenting. According to Elliott's presentation, compassion, and love in general, is actually a product of evolution. It's a quality which emerged because of a mechanical interaction between the genes and the environment. Compassion, love, and the mind itself are things that developed at a particular time: mind, according to modern science, is only one hundred thousand years old. This is certainly at variance with the Buddhist view, as I understand it, according to which each moment of mind is preceded by another, without beginning. I would like to ask His Holiness what he thinks about this contrast between the evolutionary view of mind versus a view of "mind without beginning."

DALAI LAMA   What has become clear over the years is that one fundamental way in which Buddhism diverges from science as it exists now is in our understandings of the continuum of consciousness itself. In Buddhism there is an understanding that the actual continuum of the mind itself is not confined to a single lifetime. An individual carries habits that are formed in his or her previous lifetimes, characteristics that would be transmitted through the continuum of consciousness and would predispose a person in different ways.

Here again it is important to remember that when Buddhism talks about consciousness, we are not talking about one single entity, a thing called consciousness. We are talking about a dynamic process. There are many different levels of subtleties.

LUIGI LUISI   Was there any consciousness before men existed?

DALAI LAMA   Of course. Before the formation of this present universe, there was another universe. There were sentient beings elsewhere. Given that basic Buddhist cosmology, if somehow it is proven that there was only one Big Bang at the beginning of the universe, then this is really going to challenge many of the Buddhist assumptions. But if, on the other hand, the Big Bang theory of the origin of the universe does not preclude the possibilities of many Big Bangs, then it will be much closer to the Buddhist understanding.

So according to Buddhism, the continuum of consciousness is beginningless, and it's endless as well. One of the main premises that argues for this infinite continuum is that any event or thing must have a continuum, a preceding moment, as its cause. It must have a cause that is not just circumstantial conditions, but a material cause, something that turns into it. It is argued that if you observe a phenomenon changing, it points to the fact that it is subject to causes and conditions and therefore cannot arise spontaneously without a cause. So anything that is a product, which clearly shows that it has been caused by certain conditions, must have an earlier continuum.

The cause must be concordant with the effect, unlike circumstantial conditions which could be varied. Let us take the example of an emotional state. It could have many circumstantial conditions, including physical conditions and other people's behavior and actions. However, if you were to trace the actual continuum of that conscious state, of that mental event in my own mind, then you have to look inside me, not outside. It has to be traced to its material cause: Each mental event arises out of the mind's prior state; each moment is caused by an earlier moment.

When you follow this line of reasoning, you get to a point where you have to say that either consciousness occurred randomly out of nowhere, or it must have a metaphysical cause. Buddhism solves this by arguing for a beginningless continuum. And this teleological explanation makes it possible also for Buddhists to accept and explain empirical accounts of people recollecting their past lives.

7. What Is the Relationship between Happiness and Compassion?

ANNE HARRINGTON   I want to ask Your Holiness about the relationship between seeking happiness and altruistic compassionate feeling, both of which you have stated are fundamental inclinations of human nature.

But it seems to me that state of happiness is not always or obviously an altruistic state. One might say that's often a very self-oriented state. So is the argument that the instinct to seek happiness facilitates compassionate behavior? It seems to me that something in addition is needed if seeking happiness is to lead us to be altruistic and compassionate.

DALAI LAMA   Perhaps there's a slight problem with language here. The Tibetan word for compassion is *tsewa*, which need not necessarily imply that it is directed to someone else. One can have that feeling toward oneself as well. When you say that someone should be compassionate, there is no connotation that you should totally disregard your self-interest. Compassion, or *tsewa*, as it is understood in the Tibetan tradition, is a state of mind or way of being where you extend how you relate to yourself toward others as well. Whatever or whoever the object of your affection, you wish it to be free of suffering. It's a state of wishing that the object of your compassion be free of suffering.

ANNE HARRINGTON   And that object may be yourself as well.

DALAI LAMA   Yourself first, and then in a more advanced way the aspiration will embrace others. In a way, high levels of compassion are nothing but an advanced state of that self-interest. That's why it is hard for people who have a strong sense of self-hatred to have genuine compassion toward others. There is no anchor, no basis to start from.

Having said that, there is specific training in Buddhist meditation aimed at enhancing the compassionate disposition. The meditator is encouraged to develop an outlook where he or she disregards his or her own self-interest and pursues the well-being of others. But here the aim is to develop a deep conviction of the negative consequences of excessive self-absorption or self-cherishing. You are trying to counter a way of thinking where your self-centeredness is so strong that you are totally oblivious to others' well-being. You are countering that self-centeredness, not the pursuit of self-interest.

RICHARD DAVIDSON   Do those training procedures imply that compassion requires this kind of cultivation, or are those sensibilities present from the very beginning?

DALAI LAMA   Generally speaking, there is the understanding in Buddhist psychology that for something to be cultivated by training, the seed must be there. If there is no seed or potential, then you cannot cultivate something afresh. Compassion is an example.

ERVIN STAUB   Where does that seed come from?

DALAI LAMA   A mysterious source. [*Laughter*] According to Buddhist tradition, the continuum of consciousness of an individual is without beginning.

ERVIN STAUB   Then everybody would have that seed, so the seed is there for everyone. Therefore, that kind of consciousness can be cultivated in everyone.

DALAI LAMA   That's true. All sentient beings have Buddha nature. Because of that, Buddhism believes that all sentient beings, not just human beings, have this potential for perfection, the seed for enlightenment.

ROBERT LIVINGSTON   With your Holiness's permission, I might bring to our attention the fact that the baby is born with capacities to render satisfaction to other people. For example, by the time he is born the baby has, built into his brain, the capacity to recognize faces. He turns to those faces, fixes on them, and responds to them by being activated. Moreover, he has an olfactory system: It is only developed to about 5 percent of what it will be when he is an adult, but it is devoted, as are the taste buds, to seeking the smell of the breast and the taste of milk. The baby therefore will swarm around on the mother's body to find the breast, to find the nipple, to fix on it with his mouth, and the gaze at the mother's face and knead the breast, giving her satisfaction as well as relieving her of the tension of the milk in her breast. Within a few days, and fully by seven weeks, the child has learned to make motions with its own face which it recognizes in the mother's face, imitating her gestures, such as pursing his lips, rolling his eyes, raising his eyebrows, opening his mouth, and making simple utterances. And these are very, very rewarding to the mother or caregiver. I think they represent some kind of embedding of altruism or the contribution to another person's satisfaction.

Another example is the kinds of self-stimulation that an animal undertakes in areas where endogenous opiates operate. These are molecules manufactured by the body that have an effect on brain centers similar to the effect of opium. They are very tranquilizing and calming, providing a sense of well-being, satisfaction, happiness, being rid of troubles, and so forth. The capacity to emit these endogenous opiates probably plays a role in an individual's commitment to creating an atmosphere within himself and toward others that is loving, compassionate, and altruistic. A lot of it is built in.

NANCY EISENBERG   There is further evidence that social contact re-
leases these opiates. There's a lot of evidence that young infants are very
much tuned to human stimuli and that contact has positive effects on
the infant. There's also evidence, you might be interested to know, that
by one to two years of age, children show sympathetic reactions to
other people in their environment. It's not there at birth. They cry at the
sounds of other infants, but it's not clear that this is sympathy; it's probably an innate response to certain stimuli. At six months of age, they
tend to look at somebody but not respond emotionally. By one to two
years of age you see evidence in many children of not only responding
emotionally but sometimes even of behaviors such as approaching,
touching, and calming. So by one to two years of age we see clear evidence of the ability to feel others' emotions and to deal with them.

ROBERT FRANK   There is also good evidence that children up to a certain age ignore a playmate who has been hurt. Then suddenly a natural
capacity emerges, in children in Israel, Russia, the United States, Swe-
den, whether they've been raised by two parents or one parent, or in a
group. When a playmate gets hurt the child comes and pats, hugs, and
helps. Before that age the response isn't there. But even in the nursery
when one child starts to cry the other children are likely to join in and
cry also. [*Laughter*]

DALAI LAMA   There's a Tibetan expression that when you look at
someone who is crying, you feel like crying; when you look at someone
who's laughing, you feel like laughing. Sometimes we also say that if
somebody yawns, I feel like yawning, too. [*Laughter*]

8. How Do We "See" and Recognize Compassion
in Others?

RICHARD DAVIDSON   We are just starting to examine in empirical psychology the extent to which the assumption that there is only one facial
expression for positive emotion is correct. If we looked more closely,
compassion, for example, may be reflected in subtle behavior that we
have not yet examined. I would be very interested in Your Holiness's
understanding of this.

NANCY EISENBERG   Actually, we have looked at that, and in fact compassion appears not as a distinct facial expression, but as intense inter-

est in the other person. Often the eyebrows move down and forward, and the body leans forward toward the other person. When people show this kind of reaction of deep interest, they are more likely to help.

ROBERT FRANK You should see, Richie, whether people recognize a look of serenity. There seems to be such an expression in experience.

DALAI LAMA In some of the Buddhist texts, there are descriptions of certain external signs shown by people affected by compassion. There are also a lot of expressions listed in Tibetan texts that have to do with visualizations of deities. There are lists that talk about nine moods or twelve moods. I wonder if we should ask good artists how they portray these expressions or moods.

ANNE HARRINGTON It seems to me that our tendency in this meeting is to worry a great deal about whether or not emotions like empathy and compassion translate into actual helping behavior. But in Bob's story about the gorilla, the gorilla didn't actually help. He just looked empathically at Bob and looked at the scratch. But, nevertheless, we would probably say that there was something valuable and special about that interaction between the gorilla and Bob.

So I wonder if, by focusing on such a practical way of thinking about empathy and compassion, we are overlooking an opportunity for a richer understanding of the role that compassion serves in human life. And Bob Frank gave us a model for thinking about what that might be in his talk: by emphasizing that emotion is not just something that compels us to action; it's a language. It's a way we communicate with one another. We know that people communicate with one another as an end in itself all the time. We don't simply talk to each other to exchange practical information. We have a cup of tea and we talk, and we're enriched and made happy by that. I think in some ways, knowing that a person is compassionately watching your suffering, bearing witness, is helpful in itself even if no action results. It might be nice if we could widen our understanding of that.

ROBERT FRANK It's not that the gorilla didn't help. He didn't take some action, but he did help.

DALAI LAMA Wouldn't you say that the gorilla looking intently at Bob's eyes is an action?

ROBERT FRANK Of course it's an action.

DALAI LAMA   It must give so much feeling to the person.

ANNE HARRINGTON   It mirrors back that you're not alone.

RICHARD DAVIDSON   I think that this issue is really central. In Bob's talk he emphasized the communication of character: How does another person know whether the individual with whom they are interacting is trustworthy or compassionate? It leads to the question of how is compassion conveyed. How do we exhibit compassion or more effectively communicate that we care about justice? Are there any tell-tale signs? In Bob's model, the communication of these qualities is absolutely critical for cooperative interactions to develop and evolve. I wonder if Your Holiness could comment on that?

DALAI LAMA   There are discussions about this in Buddhist texts. We say that by seeing smoke you can infer fire. Similarly, by seeing certain external signs of behavior, you can infer the compassionate nature of a Bodhisattva.

Normally it is quite difficult to infer the level of compassion of someone when you are observing in a normal situation. But sometimes you do have situations where a clear picture of the person emerges. For example, we can detect the courage of a person only when that person is exposed to a challenging situation. Similarly in the case of compassion: when a person confronts a situation that would demand a compassionate action, that's when we can infer compassion. It is through constant examination and observation that you can begin to get a sense of the character of the person.

There is a Tibetan text where the author, quoting from an Indian text, gives the analogy of looking for fish in the lake. When the water is still, although the fish are there, they may be hiding. But when there is a wave sometimes you can see a fish jumping. Similarly if you wait and observe a person constantly, then you will find opportunities to detect certain characteristics of that person.

On the other hand, there's a tradition in Buddhism that one shouldn't try to apprehend the qualities of others because they are impossible to discern with complete accuracy.

RICHARD DAVIDSON   In psychology, the idea of presenting a challenge to a person and then observing his response is very important in our research. There are many examples of being able to detect the characteristics of a person only when she or he is confronted with a challenge. For example, certain kinds of cardiovascular changes in response to stress, where the heart behaves abnormally, can only be seen when we actually challenge the person, and not in the resting state. So we have to develop situations that elicit compassion in the laboratory to measure the extent to which people display this characteristic.

DALAI LAMA   It's because of these considerations that Buddhist teachings say that enemies are so crucial. Enemies provide you with that challenge, that opportunity.

RICHARD DAVIDSON   So we should invite our enemies to the laboratory. [*Laughter*]

THUBTEN JINPA   And maybe to the conferences. We can start throwing the microphones around. [*Laughter*]

Part Two

SOCIAL, BEHAVIORAL, AND
BIOLOGICAL EXPLORATIONS OF
ALTRUISM, COMPASSION, AND
RELATED CONSTRUCTS

6

Toward a Biology of Positive Affect
and Compassion

RICHARD J. DAVIDSON

The seeds that gave rise to the meeting from which this book emerged and to this chapter in particular have their origins in the late 1960s and early 1970s. It was toward the end of the 1960s that I began to develop an interest in altered states of consciousness and meditation. It was the possibility of altered *traits* of consciousness that was particularly appealing to me. Altered traits implied the transformation of consciousness and personality in an enduring fashion to foster increased well-being. As a graduate student at Harvard in the early 1970s, I immersed myself in psychology and neuroscience with the firm idea that science could be brought to bear on the study of qualities of mind in which I was most interested, those that held the potential for human betterment. I also felt the acute lack of experiential learning in my formal graduate training and so arranged things so that I could pursue my interest in the practice of meditation along with my intellectual learning. After my second year of graduate school, I traveled to Asia for several months during which time I had my first experience in an intensive meditation retreat. This retreat in Buddhist mindfulness meditation was my first serious introduction to the power of the contemplative practice to alter mental habits, including those of an emotional nature. One of the practices that we learned at this retreat involves focusing on the happiness of oneself and of others and generating compassion toward those with whom we may have had conflicts and those who are less fortunate. I became convinced at the time that the contemplative traditions of the East had something meaningful to offer us in the West and that this dialogue and synthesis could occur without sacrificing the scientific method that I held to and continue to believe in so strongly.

Now, about 20 years after this formative experience, the opportunity to go back to India and continue this dialogue with His Holiness the Dalai Lama has been an honor and privilege and has helped me to renew my commitment to bring these worlds together. This chapter mostly presents a view from modern affective neuroscience of how we can approach the construct of compassion and bring it into the scientific lexicon. It necessarily reviews prior data and theory that provide a foundation for the present project but does not focus explicitly on this topic, for there has been virtually no research to draw on. Thus, the reader coming at this without much background in affective neuroscience will likely be surprised by the technical nature of the discussion and the fact that it veers quite far from what I would ideally wish to consider. However, given the paucity of knowledge in the area, this discussion should necessarily be regarded as a mere beginning. It is my hope that this and similar efforts will catalyze more serious and widely shared attention on this important issue. The cultivation of compassion and happiness is one of the most important applied projects in the biobehavioral sciences, yet our research efforts to date, with a few notable exceptions (see, e.g, Ryff & Singer, 1998), have focused on negative affect and disease.

Over the past decade, major strides have been made in our understanding of the neural circuitry associated with negative emotion as well as disorders of emotion such as depression and anxiety (see Davidson & Irwin, 1999; Davidson, Putnam, & Larson, 2000, for recent reviews). The new knowledge about these topics has been derived from a confluence of two major developments. One is the large number of studies at the animal level that have helped to clarify both the circuitry and molecular mechanisms underlying aversive learning (see, e.g., LeDoux, 1996). These findings have provided a useful model for aspects of human emotion and psychopathology. The second major development is the use of functional neuroimaging technologies to study the neural circuitry associated with emotion in humans. These techniques have enabled direct tests in humans of hypotheses developed on the basis of the animal evidence.

Comparably less attention has been devoted to the analysis of positive affect. Moreover, attention has been directed at a variety of different forms of negative affect—different discrete negative emotions such as fear, disgust, and anger and different affective traits such as anxiety, depression, and hostility. In the sphere of positive affect, there is little systematic differentiation. While the complete explanation of this disparity has not been satisfactorily provided, it is apparent that the increased differentiation among negative compared with positive emotions is at least in part a function of the larger number of discrete facial expressions of negative emotions compared with positive emotions. In fact, there is no systematic evidence for different facial signs of positive affect reliably differentiating among types of positive affect (Ekman, 1993). However, recent evidence suggests that there are universal gestures that may reliably convey different forms of positive affect including peace/serenity and honor/valor (Hejmadhi, Davidson, & Rozin, 2000).

A major insight provided by the data on the neural substrates of positive and negative emotion is that the circuitry underlying these emotional dispositions are at least partially independent. The evidence in support of this claim will be described later, but for now, we wish to simply underscore the fact that these data are consistent with the bivalent conception of emotion championed by Cacioppo and colleagues (e.g., Cacioppo & Gardner, 1999) as well as others (e.g., Watson, Wiesse, Vaidya, & Tellegen, 1999). On this view, different modes of activation of positive and negative affective systems are possible, including reciprocal activation (e.g., positive goes up while negative goes down) and coactivation (e.g., both positive and negative go up simultaneously). There are important conceptual and methodological implications of this view that we will elaborate on in different sections that follow.

This chapter will present an overview of the major facts about the functional neuroanatomy of positive affect in humans. Compassion is a form of positive emotion, and it is important that we develop an understanding of some of the simpler forms of positive affect from which compassion may at least in part be constituted.

The first section of this chapter will sketch a model of differentiation between two types of positive affect that is based on a consideration of underlying neural circuitry. Data on the functional neuroanatomy of this circuitry will then be reviewed with an emphasis on evidence accrued from brain-imaging studies. The data provide a foundation for a consideration of individual differences in components of this circuitry. The third section of this chapter will focus on the nomological network of associations that define one form of positive affective style. The consequences of this style for a broad range of phenomena including immune function, neuroendocrine function, and cognitive processing will be considered. The fourth section will address the question of plasticity. To what extent do these circuits exhibit plasticity? Are there developmental changes in these systems? What is the impact of early experience? Are there interventions in adulthood that might change the activation levels in this circuitry? The final section will consider some of the implications of these data for a variety of interrelated issues including self-efficacy and mastery, physical health, resilience and illness, and invulnerability to psychopathology. Finally, we will conclude by explicitly considering what bearing these data might have on understanding the biological bases of compassion.

Distinctions among Forms of Positive Affect

Most of the evidence on differentiation among forms of positive affect in humans comes from studies that have utilized self-report methods. For example, models of emotion that assume two orthogonal factors of valence and arousal postulate different forms of positive affect in the two positive affect quadrants of this map of affective space. In the low arousal quadrant are positive affects such as contentment, while in the high arousal quadrant we have enthusiasm and ecstasy (e.g., Watson, Clark, & Tellegen, 1988). While this formulation and similar schemes have helped to call attention to potentially important variations among forms of positive affect, it is inherently limited because such data may provide more information about people's conceptions or lay theories of emotion than about the actual operations of emotion.

We have elected to parse the domain of positive affect on the basis of hypothesized underlying neural circuitry rather than on the basis of studies of the emotion lexicon. While it is likely that this strategy may be a fruitful one for a variety of different forms of positive affect, only one principal distinction is made here.

Based on numerous studies from my laboratory and from other laboratories, several territories within the prefrontal cortex (PFC) appear to be activated during the experimental elicitation of emotion. Moreover, there is an asymmetric pattern to this activation such that greater relative left-sided prefrontal activation is observed during the elicitation of certain positive emotions, while greater relative right-sided PFC activation is observed during the elicitation of certain negative emotions (see Davidson, 2000, for review). We have hypothesized that the role of left PFC activation during positive emotion is associated with the instantiation of positive or appetitive goals. There is a certain class of positive affect that is generated as an individual moves progressively closer toward a desired goal. The PFC is likely to maintain the representation of a goal state online in the absence of the physical cues of that goal. The online maintenance of the goal state facilitates the direction of behavior toward the acquisition of the goal. Thus, on this view, positive affect that is associated with left PFC activation has been described as "pre-goal attainment positive affect" (Davidson, 1994; Davidson & Irwin, 1999). This form of positive affect should be associated with motivational tendencies toward goal acquisition and should resemble the high arousal forms of positive affect described in the self-report literature (e.g., enthusiastic, energetic, etc).

Individuals differ reliably in baseline activation levels in the left and right PFC. Using both positron emission tomography and brain electrical activity measures, we have found differences among individuals in activation asymmetries in specific prefrontal territories, and these patterns of baseline activation are stable over time and predict important features of affective style (Davidson, 1998; Davidson, 2000). Individuals with tonically high levels of activation in regions of the left PFC or other components of the circuit underlying this form of emotion should have an affective style that exemplifies these characteristics—they should display high levels of pregoal attainment positive affect. It is likely that individuals with high levels of left prefrontal activation are also skilled at finding solutions that promote goal attainment and are able to effectively inhibit responding to both exogenous and endogenous stimuli that might detract or deter from pursuing the goal in question. Of particular importance here is the ability to inhibit negative affect that may have a deleterious effect on the promotion of anticipatory positive affect.

The contrasting form of positive affect is postgoal attainment positive affect. Emotion terms that have been used to describe this form of positive affect include contentment and satiation. Davidson has hypothesized that this form of positive affect arises following the acquisition of a desired goal and is associated with the PFC going "offline" (Davidson, 1994). There is little evidence for this conjecture at this time, though it is empirically tractable (e.g., Sutton, Shackman, & Davidson, 1998).

The distinction made here between pre- and post-goal attainment positive affect is similar to one made in the addiction literature between wanting and liking (Robinson & Berridge, 1993). The wanting system is conceptually similar to our conception of pre-goal attainment positive affect, while the liking system is comparable to our conception of postgoal attainment positive affect. However, the activation levels of these circuits in response to pharmacological challenge far exceed what is typical in response to naturally occurring incentives (see e.g., Breiter et al., 1997).

In the next section of this chapter, some of the highlights of recent research on the functional neuroanatomy of positive affect, particularly the pregoal attainment variety, will be described.

The Functional Neuroanatomy of Positive Affect

Although the emphasis in this section will be on studies of positive affect in normal individuals, it is instructive to begin with research that has examined the loss of positive affect in patients with selective brain lesions. In a series of studies of patients with unilateral brain damage mostly produced by stroke, Robinson and his colleagues have amassed a corpus of evidence that indicates that those with left-sided prefrontal and basal ganglia damage selectively display greater levels of depression and have increased frequency of depression compared with patients having damage elsewhere (see Robinson & Downhill, 1995, for review). In a very recent study (Morris, Robinson, Raphael, & Hopwood, 1996) by Robinson's group that included the largest number of patients examined in a single study of this kind, it was observed that it was particularly for patients with small lesions that the relationship between left prefrontal damage and depression was observed. Davidson and his colleagues (e.g., Davidson, 1995; Davidson & Irwin, 1999) have interpreted these data to indicate that territories within the left PFC play an important role in certain forms of positive affect, particularly the pregoal attainment variety, and that when damaged, a deficit in the capacity to experience such positive affect is observed. To extend this prediction to neurologically intact depressed patients, we measured regional brain electrical activity in a group of clinically depressed patients and controls (Henriques & Davidson, 1991) and found that the patients exhibited a pattern of left prefrontal hypoactivation. Moreover, in a sample of currently euthymic but previously depressed individuals, a similar pattern of left prefrontal hypoactivation was evident, suggesting that this pattern may represent a trait like vulnerability factor (Henriques & Davidson, 1990; see Reid, Duke, & Allen, 1998, and Davidson, 1998, for additional complexities).

The notion that the left prefrontal hypoactivation found in depressed patients or produced by lesion is associated with deficits in positive affect is consistent with other self-report (e.g., Watson, Clark, Weber, Assenheimer, Strauss, & McCormick, 1995) and behavioral (Henriques, Glowicki, & Davidson, 1994; Henriques & Davidson, 2000) data that indicate that at least a subgroup of depressed patients shows a selective deficit on measures that reflect the capacity to experience positive affect. For example, using signal detection methods in a memory task administered under monetary reward and punishment contingencies, we demonstrated that depressed individuals, unlike controls, failed to liberalize their response bias to rewarded trials but showed performance comparable to controls on punishment trials (Henriques, Glowacki, & Davidson, 1994; Henriques & Davidson, 2000). These data argue for a selective deficit in reward-related reactivity among depressed individuals and support the interpretation of the left PFC hypoactivation as reflecting a deficit in positive affect.

In a series of electrophysiological studies on normal individuals, we have demonstrated that activation of positive affect is associated with increased left prefrontal activation. This pattern has been obtained in response to a variety of different types of elicitors in human infants and adults, as well as in rhesus monkeys, and includes tastes differing in hedonic valence (Fox & Davidson, 1986), film clips (Davidson, Ekman, Saron, Senulis, & Friesen, 1990; Ekman, Davidson, & Friesen, 1990), sensory-motor tasks administered under different monetary incentive conditions (Sobotka, Davidson, & Senulis, 1992), voluntary smiling (Ekman & Davidson, 1993), and pharmacological challenges (Davidson, Kalin, & Shelton, 1992; Zinser, Fiore, Davidson, & Baker, 1999), among others (see Davidson, 1995, for review). These findings have been consistent in showing that when positive affect is elicited, there is an increase in left prefrontal activation compared with a neutral baseline or in comparison to negative emotion induction. While these findings have helped to establish the importance of changes in PFC activation asymmetry during emotion, they are not capable of providing fine-grained spatial resolution and thus cannot be used to make inferences about where in PFC such asymmetric effects might reside. Moreover, measures of brain electrical activity for the most part reflect neuronal activity in superficial layers of cortex and thus cannot reveal activation in subcortical structures, such as the basal ganglia, that are likely to be important parts of the circuit that generates pregoal attainment positive affect. In light of these limitations, we turn to studies in nonhuman primates where recordings from neurons in the orbital prefrontal cortex and ventral striatum reveal patterns of firing in anticipation of reward. Complementing these data at the animal level is functional neuroimaging in humans that provides corroborating evidence on where in the brain these positive affect–related activations may arise and examines the relationships between these patterns of activation and subjective and objective measures of emotion.

Using an extended picture presentation paradigm to induce consistent changes in positive or negative mood (Sutton, Davidson, Donzella, Irwin, & Dottl, 1997a), Davidson and his colleagues (Sutton, Ward, Larson, Holden, Perlman, & Davidson, 1997b) measured regional glucose metabolism using positron emission tomography while the presence of the intended emotional states was independently verified using emotion-modulated startle and facial electromyography. During the production of negative affect, right-sided increases in metabolic rate were found in both inferior and superior regions of the PFC, including the anterior orbital, inferior frontal, middle frontal gyrus, and superior frontal gyri. During the production of positive affect, a pattern of predominantly left-sided activation was observed with a somewhat more posterior distribution compared with negative affect. During positive affect, left-sided metabolic increases were observed in the region of the pre- and post-central gyri. In addition, increases were observed in the region that included the left nucleus accumbens.

Recent studies in animals on the role of dopamine signals from the ventral tegmental area (VTA) to the prefrontal cortex provide an important clue regarding the function of PFC activations associated with reward. From single-cell recordings in the VTA, Schultz and his colleagues (e.g, Schultz, Dayan, & Montague, 1997) have reported that the dopamine signal to PFC from the VTA codes for a deviation between the actual reward received and the reward that was predicted. If an unexpected or an unexpectedly large reward is received, VTA neurons emit a positive signal, whereas if the reward is exactly as expected or less than expected, either no signal or a negative signal (decreased spike production) occurs respectively. The PFC in turn implements the reward expectancy or prediction and is updated by input from the VTA. Pregoal attainment positive affect is associated with the implementation of reward expectancies with the VTA providing input to the PFC regarding the progressive decrease in the prediction reward signal as the individual moves closer to a desired goal.

Some studies have reported on decreased blood flow or metabolism during induced positive affect in brain regions hypothesized to play a role in negative affect. Such findings would be compatible with a model of reciprocal activation as described earlier in this chapter. George et al. (1995) reported that induced happiness was associated with a significant reduction in activation in the right superior PFC. In an fMRI study of the effects of cocaine in cocaine addicts, Breiter and colleagues (Breiter et al., 1997) reported significant deactivation of the amygdala during cocaine-induced "highs." Using another pharmacological challenge procedure with the anesthetic procaine, Ketter et al. (1996) compared those individuals who reported euphoric versus dysphoric responses to the challenge. Subjects with the euphoric affective response to the procaine had significantly less activation of the amygdala as detected by positron emission tomography (PET) compared with those showing a dysphoric response. Moreover, amygdala blood flow correlated positively with fear and negatively with euphoria on self-report measures of emotional intensity.

Corticosterone in rodents has been found to potentiate neural activity in the amygdala and also to accentuate behavioral responses that are amygdala-dependent such as fear-potentiated startle (e.g., Schulkin, Gold, & McEwen, 1998). In light of the evidence reviewed above indicating that the phasic activation of drug-induced positive affect transiently suppresses activation in the amygdala, we might expect that the elicitation of positive affect in humans would decrease cortisol. Lovallo and colleagues have recently reported that the presentation of a 30-minute medley of positive film clips led to a significant pre- to post-film reduction in levels of salivary cortisol, while a stressful challenge had the opposite effect (Buchanan, al'Absi, & Lovallo, 1999).

Breiter et al. (1997), in their study of the activations produced by cocaine, compared the effects of cocaine versus saline infusion on magnetic resonance signal change in cocaine addicts. They found activation in a distributed circuit that included cortical and subcortical regions. Of note is the strong activation observed in regions of the ventral striatum, which includes the caudate, putamen and the nucleus accumbens. Activation in this latter region is consistent with a large corpus of nonhuman data demonstrating the critical role played by the mesolimbic dopaminergic pathway in positive affect and addictive behaviors (Depue & Collins, 1999; Koob, 1992). Stein et al. (1998) in the first fMRI study of the effects of nicotine on regional brain activation in cigarette smokers also found activation of the nucleus accumbens during infusion of nicotine compared with saline. In the PET study from Davidson's group described earlier, which used pleasant and unpleasant pictures in an extended picture paradigm (Sutton & Davidson, 1997), activation was observed in a region including the nucleus accumbens during the picture-induced positive affect.

In addition to the ventral striatum and the prefrontal cortex, along with the role of dopamine in this circuit featured in the earlier discussion, other systems clearly play a critical role in different, but related forms of positive affect. Insel and his colleagues have amassed a large corpus of evidence on the role of oxytocin and vasopressin in social attachment (Insel, 1997). Oxytocin receptors are concentrated in the basal forebrain cholinergic nuclei among other regions, while vasopressin receptors are concentrated in the lateral septum and the amygdala. When oxytocin is administered in the brain to females of the monogamous species prairie voles, it has been found to facilitate partner preference in the absence of mating. For males of this species, it is apparently vasopressin that is critical in the formation of pair bonds.

In humans, pituitary oxytocin is secreted into circulation during parturition and nursing. Insel (1997) suggests that one important function of the central release of this peptide during labor and nursing is to facilitate the affiliative bond between the mother and her infant. In the developing neonate, it is of interest to note that there is a transient, but marked overproduction (relative to the adult) of both oxytocin and vasopressin receptors in various limbic regions in the first few postnatal weeks. These binding sites are particularly dense in the cingulate cortex, a region critically implicated in various aspects of emotion (see, e.g., Devinsky, Morrell, & Vogt, 1995), including separation distress. However, we do not know if these receptors are functional at this age, nor do we know why they disappear by the time of weaning.

Very few studies at the human level have examined the relationship between activity in these peptide systems and social emotions. In part, this is a function of the fact that peripheral measures of these peptides do not bear any simple relation to brain levels. However, there have been a few studies showing relationships between peripheral levels of oxytocin and personality traits such as interpersonal warmth and calm (Uvnäs-Moberg, 1997). Additional research examining the role of these peptides in positive social emotions is clearly required.

Individual Differences

That there is pronounced variability in humans' capacity to experience happiness was eloquently captured by the well-known clinical psychologist Paul Meehl. In a visionary article (1975), he explained that "not only are some persons born with more cerebral joy juice than others, but also that this variable is fraught with clinical consequences" (p. 299). In some of his early investigations of prefrontal brain electrical asymmetries associated with positive and negative affect, Davidson and colleagues (1979) noticed that stimulus-induced phasic shifts in asymmetric activation were superimposed on what appeared to be more stable tonic differences in asymmetric activation (see also Davidson & Tomarken, 1989). These tonic or baseline differences, which were present in both infants and adults, were related to various parameters of affective reactivity. In infants, Davidson and Fox (1989) reported that ten-month-old babies who exhibited resilience in response to maternal separation, showing no crying and exhibiting exploratory behavior, were more likely to have greater left- and less right-sided prefrontal activation during a preceding resting baseline compared with those infants who cried in response to this challenge.

During the initial explorations of this phenomenon, Davidson and colleagues needed to determine if baseline electrophysiological measures of prefrontal asymmetry were reliable and stable over time and thus could be used as a trait-like measure. Tomarken, Davidson, Wheeler, and Kinney (1992) recorded baseline brain electrical activity from 90 normal subjects on two separate occasions, approximately 3 weeks apart. At each testing session, brain activity was recorded during eight 1-minute trials, four eyes open and four eyes closed, presented in counterbalanced order. The major finding of import from this study was the demonstration that electrophysiological measures of activation asymmetry from prefrontal scalp electrodes showed both high internal consistency and reliability and acceptable test-retest reliability to be considered a trait-like index.

On the basis of our prior data and theory, we reasoned that extreme left and extreme right frontally activated subjects would show systematic differences in dispositional positive and negative affect. We administered the trait version of the Positive and Negative Affect Scales (PANAS; Watson, Clark, & Tellegen, 1988) to examine this question and found that the left-frontally activated subjects reported more positive and less negative affect than their right-frontally activated counterparts (Tomarken, Davidson, Wheeler, & Doss, 1992). The adjectives endorsed by those with high levels of left-prefrontal activation include enthusiastic, alert, and interested. More recently, Sutton and Davidson (1997) showed that scores on a self-report measure designed to operationalize

Gray's concepts of Behavioral Inhibition and Behavioral Activation (the BIS/BAS scales; Carver & White, 1994) were even more strongly predicted by electrophysiological measures of prefrontal asymmetry than were scores on the PANAS scales. Subjects with greater left-sided prefrontal activation reported more relative BAS to BIS activity compared with subjects exhibiting more right-sided prefrontal activation. Extreme left-frontally activated subjects endorsed items such as "When I'm doing well at something, I love to keep at it" and "When I see an opportunity for something I like, I get excited right away."

It was also hypothesized that measures of prefrontal asymmetry would predict reactivity to experimental elicitors of emotion. The model that has been developed over the past several years (see Davidson, 1992, 1994, 1995, for background) features individual differences in prefrontal activation asymmetry as a reflection of a diathesis that modulates reactivity to emotionally significant events. According to this model, individuals who differ in prefrontal asymmetry should respond differently to an elicitor of positive or negative emotion, even when baseline mood is partialed out. Davidson and colleagues performed several studies (e.g., Tomarken, Davidson, & Henriques, 1990; Wheeler, Davidson, & Tomarken, 1993) to examine this question. In one study, subjects were presented with short film clips designed to elicit positive or negative emotion. Brain electrical activity was recorded prior to the presentation of the film clips. Just after the clips were presented, subjects were asked to rate their emotional experience during the preceding film clip. In addition, subjects completed scales that were designed to reflect their mood at baseline. We found that individual differences in prefrontal asymmetry predicted the emotional response to the films even after measures of baseline mood were statistically removed. Those individuals with more left-sided prefrontal activation at baseline reported more positive affect to the positive film clips compared with their right frontally activated counterparts, while this latter group showed the reverse pattern. These findings support the idea that individual differences in electrophysiological measures of prefrontal activation asymmetry mark some aspect of vulnerability to positive and negative emotion elicitors. The fact that such relationships were obtained following the statistical removal of baseline mood indicates that any difference between left and right frontally activated subjects in baseline mood cannot account for the prediction of film-elicited emotion effects that were observed.

In a very recent study, we (Larson, Sutton, & Davidson, 1998) examined relations between individual differences in prefrontal activation asymmetry and the capacity to rapidly recover from a negative event. We used the emotion-modulated startle to probe the time course of emotional responding (see Davidson, 2000, for discussion). In this study, we presented pleasant and unpleasant pictures while acoustic startle probes were presented and the EMG-measured blink response from the orbicularis oculi muscle region was recorded (see Sutton, Davidson, Donzella, Irwin, & Dottl, 1997, for basic methods). Startle probes were presented both during the 6-second slide exposure as well as after the offset of the pictures, on separate trials. We interpreted startle magnitude during picture exposure as providing an index related to the peak of emotional response, while startle magnitude following the *offset* of the pictures was taken to reflect the recovery from emotional challenge. Used in this way, startle probe methods can potentially provide new information on the time course of emotional responding. We expected that individual differences following picture presentation would be particularly pronounced since we reasoned that subjects are more likely to differ in the time required for recovery than in their response during the negative picture itself. Similarly, we predicted that individual differences in prefrontal asymmetry would account for more variance in predicting magnitude of recovery (i.e., startle magnitude post-stimulus) than in predicting startle magnitude during the stimulus. Our findings were consistent with our predictions and indicated that subjects with greater left-sided prefrontal activation show a smaller blink magnitude following the offset of the negative stimuli, after the variance in blink magnitude *during* the negative stimulus was partialed out. Measures of prefrontal asymmetry did not reliably predict startle magnitude during picture presentation. The findings from this study are consistent with our hypothesis and indicate that individual differences in prefrontal asymmetry are associated with the time course of affective responding, particularly the recovery following emotional challenge. Individuals with greater left-sided prefrontal activation recover more quickly following a negative emotional stimulus than their right-activated counterparts. The findings also suggest that left-sided prefrontal activation may play a causal role in the shortening of the duration of negative affective responding.

In addition to the studies described earlier using self-report and psychophysiological measures of emotion, we have also examined relationships between individual differences in electrophysiological measures of prefrontal asymmetry and other biological indices that in turn have been related to differential reactivity to stressful events. Two recent examples from my laboratory include measures of immune function and cortisol.

In the case of the former, we examined differences between left and right prefrontally activated subjects in natural killer cell activity, since declines in NK activity have been reported in response to stressful, negative events (Kiecolt-Glaser & Glaser, 1991). We predicted that subjects with left prefrontal activation would exhibit higher baseline levels of NK activity compared with their right-activated counterparts because the former type of subject has been found to report more dispositional positive affect, to show higher relative BAS activity, and to respond less intensely to negative emotional stimuli and more intensely to positive emotional stimuli. We found that left frontally activated subjects indeed had higher levels of NK activity compared to their right frontally activated counterparts (Kang, Davidson, Coe, Wheeler, Tomarken, & Ershler, 1991). These findings have recently been replicated in a larger, independent sample and extended by showing that subjects with left-sided prefrontal activation also showed less decline in NK activity in response to an acute stress (Davidson, Coe, Dolski, & Donzella, 1999). These findings on associations between individual differences in anterior activation asymmetry and immune function begin to help us understand the mechanisms by which emotion may impact on physical health. Although a connection between emotional disposition and health has been assumed by many in the popular literature, little systematic scientific analysis of the mechanisms by which such interaction might occur has been performed. New findings on neural-immune interactions at both integrative and cellular levels will be crucial in understanding these important connections in the future.

Similar individual differences in scalp-recorded measures of prefrontal activation asymmetry have been identified in rhesus monkeys (Davidson, Kalin, & Shelton, 1992, 1993). Recently, we (Kalin, Larson, Shelton, & Davidson, 1998) acquired measures of brain electrical activity from a large sample of rhesus monkeys ($N = 50$). EEG measures were obtained during periods of manual restraint. A subsample of 15 of these monkeys were tested on two occasions, 4 months apart. We found that the test-retest correlation for measures of prefrontal asymmetry was .62, suggesting similar stability of this metric in monkey and man. In the group of 50 animals, we also obtained measures of plasma cortisol during the early morning. We hypothesized that if individual differences in prefrontal asymmetry were associated with dispositional affective style, such differences should be correlated with cortisol, since individual differences in baseline cortisol have been related to various aspects of trait-related stressful behavior and psychopathology (see e.g., Gold, Goodwin, & Chrousos, 1988). We found that animals with left-sided prefrontal activation had lower levels of baseline cortisol than their right frontally activated counterparts. When we included a group of animals that showed a symmetric pattern of prefrontal activation as a control group, it was found that only the left-sided animals differed from the other two groups. These findings indicate that left-sided prefrontal activation is associated with lower levels of cortisol rather than right-sided activation being associated with higher levels of cortisol. The symmetric and right-activated animals did not differ in their cortisol levels. Moreover, when blood samples were collected 2 years following our initial testing, animals classified as showing extreme left-sided prefrontal activation at age 1 year had significantly lower baseline cortisol levels when they were 3 years of age compared with animals who were classified at age 1 year as displaying extreme right-sided prefrontal activation. These findings indicate that individual differences in prefrontal asymmetry are present in nonhuman primates and that such differences are associated with a specific pattern of peripheral biology (high NK activity, low cortisol) that may be salubrious for health.

Affective Plasticity

As we noted in the discussion of the central circuitry of emotion, the amygdala is an important site of plasticity in the brain. It is involved in emotional learning, whether or not it is itself the site of storage of new stimulus-threat associations. Recent work by LeDoux and his colleagues is beginning to characterize the molecular changes in the amygdala that accompany newly acquired aversive learning (Schafe, Nadel, Sullivan, Harris, & LeDoux, 1999; Weisskopf & LeDoux, 1999). These findings underscore the fact that while there are stable individual differences in activation patterns in the central circuitry of emotion, there is also pronounced plasticity in this circuitry. One of the major challenges for human affective neuroscience in the next century is to better understand the environmental forces that shape the circuitry of emotion. Answers to this question will depend on the findings from longitudinal studies where sensitive measures of both brain function and structure can be obtained along with measures of environmental change and behavioral measures of emotional reactivity.

For now, most of the extant data directly relevant to this issue are at the animal level. In a series of studies, Meaney and his colleagues (Caldji,

Tannenbaum, Sharma, Francis, Plotsky, & Meaney, 1998; Liu, Diorio, Tannenbaum, Caldji, Francis, & Freedman, 1997; Meaney, Aitken, van Berkel, Bhatnagar, & Sapolsky, 1998; see Francis & Meaney, 1999 for recent review) have demonstrated that an early environmental manipulation in rats—frequency of maternal licking/grooming and arched-back nursing—produces a cascade of biological changes in the offspring that shape the central circuitry of emotion and, consequently, alter the animal's behavioral and biological responsivity to stress. This work provides an elegant model for plasticity in this central circuitry and provides important clues for the study of similar influences at the human level. These animal data present a variety of important implications for understanding the role of plastic changes in the circuitry of emotion in humans. These findings indicate that the PFC, amygdala, and hippocampus are all sites where plasticity is known to occur. One of the interesting puzzles in the human literature on prefrontal asymmetries associated with affective style is that while measures of baseline prefrontal asymmetries are stable in adults, they are not stable during early childhood (Davidson & Rickman, 1999). When brain electrical measures of baseline prefrontal activation asymmetry were examined over an 8-year period from 3 to 11 years of age in a cohort of approximately 65 children, little evidence of stability was found (Davidson & Rickman, 1999). This is a period during which pronounced plasticity is likely to occur in the central circuitry of emotion, particularly in the PFC, which is still undergoing important developmental change at least until puberty (Huttenlocher, 1990). An important challenge for future research is to obtain better measures of life course events, parental influence, and other important environmental factors and relate the occurrences of these to shifts in patterns of prefrontal activation.

Little is known about the impact of interventions designed to promote positive affect on plastic changes in the circuitry of emotion. Though there are some data on the impact of antidepressant medication on brain function (e.g., Bench, Frackowiak, & Dolan, 1995) and one study on the effects of cognitive therapy on regional glucose metabolism in patients with obsessive-compulsive disorder (Baxter et al., 1992), there are very few data on plastic changes in the brain as a consequence of practicing methods designed to increase positive affect, such as meditation. The Dalai Lama has called attention to this possibility in his recent bestseller *The Art of Happiness* (His Holiness the Dalai Lama & Cutler, 1998). In this book, he discusses the implications of research on neural plasticity for increasing levels of happiness and explains: "The systematic training of the mind—the cultivation of happiness, the genuine inner transformation by deliberately selecting and focusing on positive mental states and challenging negative mental states—is possible because of the very structure and function of the brain. . . . But the wiring in our brains is not static, not irrevocably fixed. Our brains are also adaptable" (pp. 44–45).

We have recently completed a study (Davidson, Kabat-Zinn, 2001) designed to examine the short-term consequences of meditation on brain and immune function. Brain electrical activity was recorded before and after an 8-week course in mindfulness meditation taught by Jon Kabat-Zinn (see Kabat-Zinn, 1994, for a description of the training). Individuals from a high-tech corporation volunteered for this study and were randomly assigned to either the meditation group or to a wait-list control group. Participants in each group were assessed on laboratory biological measures at the same points in time. At the end of the 8-week training, participants in both groups were administered an influenza vaccine and blood samples were then collected approximately 4- and 8 weeks after the vaccination. Subjects in the meditation group showed significantly greater increases in left-sided anterior activation compared with subjects in the wait-list control group. In addition, subjects in the meditation group evinced a significantly greater rise in antibody titers to the vaccine from the 4- to the 8-week blood draw. Moreover, the magnitude of change in left anterior cortical activation correlated positively with the magnitude of increase in antibody titers. These are among the first data to show reliable short-term changes in baseline brain activity produced by meditation. This study clearly raises many more questions than it answers. We do not know the extent to which the meditation-produced changes persist. Nor do we know whether longer-term training would be associated with more pronounced changes or which components of the intervention were most responsible for the changes that occurred. Of particular note in this regard are pilot data collected as part of the TTM project (see chapter 1) in one older monk who had been engaged in daily practices to cultivate compassion for more than 30 years. We measured brain electrical activity during the baseline state in this monk and found that he exhibited the most extreme left prefrontal activation compared with a normative sample of 175 Wisconsin students. Although no definitive conclusions can be drawn from this single case report, it was nonetheless intriguing and underscores the need for longitudinal research on the impact of these interventions on brain function and behavior. Collectively, the group study and the single case report both underscore the possibility of plasticity even in adulthood for functional activity in critical brain circuits that underlie individual differences in emotional reactivity.

Implications and Conclusions

Although we just recently ended the decade of the brain, it is at the dawning of the new millennium that we finally have both the theory and methods to begin addressing some of the most important questions about human brain function that have for so long eluded rigorous study. Understanding how feeling is instantiated in the brain and using the brain's architecture to meaningfully parse the domain of emotion are now possible using the modern methods of affective neuroscience. Research on plasticity has given us new information about and realistic hope for ways to shape the circuitry of emotion to promote increased well-being and positive affect. The downstream consequences of these patterns of neural activity for endocrine, autonomic, and immune function can be studied to provide clues to the mechanistic understanding of how emotion might affect physical health and disease.

Still to come is systematic research on other forms of positive affect, such as compassion, that have featured significantly in non-Western traditions. Based on the theory and data presented in this chapter, it is likely that individuals who show more frequent and prominent signs of compassion will likely be individuals who exhibit other traits of positive affect as well. Some of the same neural systems identified in pregoal attainment positive affect are likely to be implicated in compassion since, when compassion arises, it is often associated with the impulse to act so as to relieve suffering. This impulse to act, to approach, may be associated with a pattern of neuronal activation that includes left-sided prefrontal activation. This pattern of left-prefrontal activation may be combined with a state in which oxytocin is released since compassion arises out of social interconnectedness that oxytocin may facilitate. Surely other brain systems and additional complexities will be found once compassion becomes a serious focus of scientific scrutiny. It will also be important to examine the peripheral biological consequences of the generation of compassion. It may well be that there are robust immune and endocrine changes produced by the cultivation of compassion that have salubrious effects for physical health. This may provide a clue to the mechanism by which compassion may have some evolutionary advantage. Though such questions will prove to be both conceptually and methodologically challenging to study, it is imperative that we remain mindful of the extraordinary range of human emotional characteristics and not be too easily seduced into the illusion of understanding based on the limited lexicon for positive emotion in the traditional biobehavioral nomenclature. The field of affective neuroscience offers great promise for achieving significant new insights about these qualities of human experience that appear to be so essential for optimal functioning. It is essential that we not dismiss the centuries-old wisdom of the East prematurely, for it may provide important clues regarding practical methods for achieving plasticity in the central circuitry of emotion.

REFERENCES

Baxter, L. R., Schwartz, J. M., Bergman, K. S., Szuba, M. P., Guze, B. H., Mazziota, J. C., Alazraki, A., Selin, C. E. , Ferng, H. K., Munford, P., & et.al. (1992). Caudate glucose metabolic rate changes with both drug and behavior therapy for obsessive-compulsive disorder. *Archives of General Psychiatry, 49,* 681–699.

Bench, C. J., Frackowiak, R. S., & Dolan, R. J. (1995). Changes in regional cerebral blood flow on recovery from depression. *Psychological Medicine, 25,* 247–251.

Breiter, H. C., Gollub, R. L., Wwisskoff, R. M., Kennedy, D. N., Makris, N., Berde, J. D., Goodman, J. M., Kantor, H. L., Gastfriend, D. R., Riorden, J. P., Matthew, R. T., Rossen, B. R., & Hyman, S. E. (1997). Acute effects of cocaine on human brain activity and emotion. *Neuron, 19,* 591–611.

Buchanan, T. W., al'Absi, M., & Lovallo, W. R. (1999). Cortisol fluctuates with increases and decreases in negative affect. *Psychoneuroendocrinology, 24,* 227–241.

Cacioppo, J. T., & Gardner, W. L. (1999). Emotion. *Annual Review of Psychology, 50,* 191–214.

Caldji, C., Tannenbaum, B., Sharma, S., Francis, D., Plotsky, P. M., & Meaney, M. J. (1998). Maternal care during infancy regulates the development of neural systems mediating the expression of fearfulness in the rat. *Proceedings of the National Academy of Sciences, 95,* 5335–5340.

Carver, C. S., & White, T. L. (1994). Behavioral inhibition, behavioral activation and affective responses to impending reward and punishment: The BIS/BAS scales. *Journal of Personality and Social Psychology, 67,* 319–333.

Dalai Lama, & Cutler, H. C. (1998). *The Art of Happiness.* New York: Riverhead Books.

Davidson, R. J. (1992). Emotion and affective style: Hemispheric substrates. *Psychological Science, 3,* 39–43.

Davidson, R. J. (1994). Asymmetric brain function, affective style and psychopathology: The role of early experience and plasticity. *Development and Psychopathology, 6*, 741–758.

Davidson, R.J. (1995). Cerebral asymmetry, emotion and affective style. In R. J. Davidson & K. Hugdahl (Eds.), *Brain Asymmetry* (pp. 361–387). Cambridge, MA: MIT Press.

Davidson, R. J. (1998). Affective style and affective disorders: Perspectives from affective neuroscience. *Cognition and Emotion, 12*, 307–320.

Davidson, R. J. (2000). Affective style, psychopathology and resilience: Brain mechanisms and plasticity. *American Psychologist, 55*, 1193–1214.

Davidson, R. J., Coe, C. C., Dolski, I., & Donzella, B. (1999). Individual differences in prefrontal activation asymmetry predict natural killer cell activity at rest and in response to challenge. *Brain, Behavior, and Immunity, 13*, 93–108.

Davidson, R. J., Ekman, P., Saron, C., Senulis, J., & Friesen, W. V. (1990). Approach/withdrawal and cerebral asymmetry: Emotional expression and brain physiology, I. *Journal of Personality and Social Psychology, 58*, 330–341.

Davidson, R. J., & Fox, N. A. (1989). Frontal brain asymmetry predicts infants' response to maternal separation. *Journal of Abnormal Psychology, 98*, 127–131.

Davidson, R. J., & Irwin, W. (1999). The functional neuroanatomy of emotion and affective style. *Trends in Cognitive Sciences, 3*, 11–21.

Davidson, R. J., Kabat-Zinn, J., Schumacher, J., Rosenkranz, M., Muller, D., Santorelli, S. F., Urbanowski, F., & Harrington, A. (2001). Alterations in brain and immune function produced by mindfulness meditation. Submitted for publication.

Davidson, R. J., Kalin, N. H., & Shelton, S. E. (1992). Lateralized effects of diazepam on frontal brain electrical asymmetries in rhesus monkeys. *Biological Psychiatry, 32*, 438–451.

Davidson, R. J., Putnam, K. M., & Larson, C. L. (2000). Dysfunction in the Neural Circuitry of Emotion Regulation—A possible prelude to violence. *Science, 289*, 591–594.

Davidson, R. J., & Rickman, M. D. (1999). Behavioral inhibition and the emotional circuitry of the brain: Stability and plasticity during the early childhood years. In L. A. Schmidt & J. Schulkin (Eds.), *Extreme Fear, Shyness, and Social Phobia: Origins, Biological Mechanisms, and Clinical Outcomes* (pp. 67–87). New York: Oxford University Press.

Davidson, R. J., Schwartz, G. E., Saron, C., Bennett, J., & Goleman, D. J. (1979). Frontal versus parietal EEG asymmetry during positive and negative affect [Abstract]. *Psychophysiology, 16*, 202–203.

Davidson, R. J., & Tomarken, A. J. (1989). Laterality and emotion: An electrophysiological approach. In F. Boller & J. Grafman (Eds.), *Handbook of Neuropsychology, Vol. 3* (pp. 419–441). Amsterdam: Elsevier.

Depue, R. A., & Collins, P. F. (1999). Neurobiology of the structure of personality: Dopamine, facilitation of incentive motivation, and extraversion. *Behavioral and Brain Sciences, 22*(3), 491–569.

Devinsky, O., Morrell, M. J. & Vogt, B. A. (1995). Contributions of anterior cingulate cortex to behaviour. *Brain, 118,* 279–306.

Ekman, P. (1993). Facial expression and emotion. *American Psychologist, 48*(4), 384–392.

Ekman, P., Davidson, R. J., & Friesen, W. V. (1990). Duchenne's smile: Emotional expression and brain physiology, II. *Journal of Personality and Social Psychology, 58,* 342–353.

Ekman, P., & Davidson, R. J. (1993). Voluntary smiling changes regional brain activity. *Psychological Science, 4,* 342–345.

Fox, N. A., & Davidson, R. J. (1986). Taste-elicited changes in facial signs of emotion and the asymmetry of brain electrical activity in human newborns. *Neuropsychologia, 24,* 417–422.

Francis, D., & Meaney, M. J. (1999). Maternal care and development of stress responses. *Current Opinion in Neurobiology, 9,* 128–134.

George, M. S., Ketter, T. A., Parekh, P. I., Horwitz, B., Herscovitch, P., & Post, R.M. (1995). Brain activity during transient sadness and happiness in healthy women. *American Journal of Psychiatry, 152,* 341–351.

Gold, P. W., Goodwin, F. K., & Chrousos, G. P. (1988). Clinical and biochemical manifestations of depression: Relation to the neurobiology of stress. *New England Journal of Medicine, 314,* 348–353.

Hejmadi, A., Davidson, R. J., & Rozin, P. (2000). Exploring Hindu Indian Emotion Expressions: Evidence for accurate recognition by Americans and Indians. *Psychological Science, 2*(3), 183–187.

Henriques, J. B., & Davidson, R. J. (1990). EEG activation asymmetries discrimante between depressed and control subjects [Abstract]. *Psychophysiology, 27,* S38.

Henriques, J. B., & Davidson, R. J. (1991). Left frontal hypoactivation in depression. *Journal of Abnormal Psychology, 100,* 535–545.

Henriques, J. B., & Davidson, R. J. (2000). Decreased responsiveness to reward in depression. *Cognition and Emotion, 15*(5), 711–724.

Henriques, J. B., Glowacki, J. M., & Davidson, R.J. (1994). Reward fails to alter response bias in depression. *Journal of Abnormal Psychology, 103,* 460–466.

Huttenlocher, P. R. (1990). Morphometric study of human cerebral cortex development. *Neuropsychologia, 28,* 517–527.

Insel, T. R. (1997). A neurobiological basis of social attachment. *American Journal of Psychiatry, 154,* 726–735.

Kabat-Zinn, J. (1994). *Wherever You Go There You Are.* New York: Hyperion.

Kang, D. H., Davidson, R. J., Coe, C. L., Wheeler, R. W., Tomarken, A. J., & Ershler, W. B. (1991). Frontal brain asymmetry and immune function. *Behavioral Neuroscience, 105,* 860–869.

Ketter, T. A., Andreason, P. J., George, M. S., Lee, C., Gill, D. S., Parekh, P. I., Willis, M. W., Herscovitch, P., & Post, R. M. (1996). Anterior paralimbic mediation of procaine-induced emotional and psychosensory experiences. *Archives of General Psychiatry, 53*, 59–69.

Kiecolt-Glaser, J. K., & Glaser, R. (1981). Stress and immune function in humans. In R. Ader, D. L. Felten, & N. Cohen (Eds.), *Psychoneuroimmunology* (pp. 849–867). San Diego, CA: Academic Press.

Koob, G. F. (1992). Neurobiological mechanisms of cocaine and opiate dependence. In C. P. O'Brien & J. H. Faffe (Eds.), *Addictive States* (pp. 171–191). New York: Raven Press.

Larson, C. L., Sutton, S. K., & Davidson, R. J. (1998). Affective style, frontal EEG asymmetry and the time course of the emotion-modulated startle [Abstract]. *Psychophysiology, 35*, S52.

LeDoux, J. E. (1996). *The Emotional Brain: The Mysterious Underpinnings of Emotional Lift.* New York: Simon & Schuster.

Liu, D., Diorio, J., Tannenbaum, B., Caldji, C., Francis, D., & Freedman, A. (1997). Maternal care, hippocampal glucocorticoid receptors, and hypothalamic-pituitary-adrenal responses to stress. *Science, 277*, 1659–1662.

Meaney, M. J., Aitken, D. H., van Berkel, C., Bhatnagar, S., & Sapolsky, R. M. (1988). Effect of neonatal handling on age-related impairments associated with the hippocampus. *Science, 239*, 766–768.

Meehl, P. E. (1975). Hedonic capacity: Some conjectures. *Bulletin of the Menninger Clinic, 39*, 295–307.

Morris, P. L. P., Robinson, R. G., Raphael, B., & Hopwood, M. J. (1996). Lesion location and poststroke depression. *Journal of Neuropsychiatry and Clinical Neurosciences, 8*, 399–403.

Reid, S. A., Duke, L. M., & Allen, J. J. (1998). Resting frontal electroencephalographic asymmetry in depression: Inconsistencies suggest the need to identify mediating factors. *Psychophysiology, 35*(4), 389–404.

Robinson, R. G., & Downhill, J. E. (1995). Lateralization of psychopathology in response to focal brain injury. In R. J. Davidson & K. Hugdahl (Eds.), *Brain Asymmetry.* (pp. 693–711). Cambridge, MA: MIT Press.

Robinson, T. E., & Berridge, K. C. (1993). The neural basis of drug craving: An incentive-sensitization theory of addiction. *Brain Research Reviews, 18*, 247–291.

Ryff, C. D. & Singer, B. (1998). The contours of positive psychological health. *Psychological Inquiry, 9*, 1–28.

Schafe, G. E., Nadel, N. V., Sullivan, G. M., Harris, A., & LeDoux, J. E. (1999). Memory consolidation for contextual and auditory fear conditioning is dependent on protein synthesis, PKA, and MAP kinase. *Learning and Memory, 6*, 97–110.

Schulkin, J., Gold, P. W., & McEwen, B. S. (1998). Induction of corticotropin-releasing hormone gene expression by glucocorticoids: Implication for understanding the states of fear and anxiety and allostatic load. *Psychoneuroendocrinology, 23*(3), 219–243.

Schultz, W., Dayan, P., & Montague, P. R. (1997). A neural substrate for prediction and reward. *Science, 275*, 1593–1599.

Sobotka, S. S., Davidson, R. J., & Senulis, J. A. (1992). Anterior brain electrical asymmetries in response to reward and punishment. *Electroencephalography and Clinical Neurophysiology, 83*, 236–247.

Stein, E. A., Pankiewicz, J., Harsch, H. H., Cho, J. K., Fuller, S. A., Hoffmann, R. G., Hawkins, M., Rao, S. M., Bandettini, P. A., & Bloom, A. S. (1998). Nicotine-induced limbic cortical activation in the human brain: A functional MRI study. *American Journal of Psychiatry, 155*(8), 1009–1015.

Sutton, S. K., & Davidson, R. J. (1997). Prefrontal brain asymmetry: A biological substrate of the behavioral approach and inhibition systems. *Psychological Science, 8*, 204–210.

Sutton, S. K., Davidson, R. J., Donzella, B., Irwin, W., & Dottl, D. A. (1997a). Manipulating affective state using extended picture presentation. *Psychophysiology, 34*, 217–226.

Sutton, S. K., Shackman, A. J., & Davidson, R. J. (1998). Monetary incentive and working memory load modulate anterior brain activity [Abstract]. *Psychophysiology, 35*, S81.

Sutton, S. K., Ward, R. T., Larson, C. L., Holden, J. E., Perlman, S. B., & Davidson, R. J. (1997b). Asymmetry in prefrontal glucose metabolism during appetitive and aversive emotional states: An FDG-PET study. *Psychophysiology, 34*, S89.

Tomarken, A. J., Davidson, R. J., & Henriques, J. B. (1990). Resting frontal activation asymmetry predicts emotional reactivity to film clips. *Journal of Personality and Social Psychology, 59*, 791–801.

Tomarken, A. J., Davidson, R. J., Wheeler, R. E., & Doss, R. C. (1992). Individual differences in anterior brain asymmetry and fundamental dimensions of emotion. *Journal of Personality and Social Psychology, 62*, 676–687.

Tomarken, A. J., Davidson, R. J., Wheeler, R. E., & Kinney, L. (1992). Psychometric properties of resting anterior EEG asymmetry: Temporal stability and internal consistency. *Psychophysiology, 29*, 576–592.

Uvnäs-Moberg, K. (1997). Physiological and endocrine effects of social contact. *Annals of the New York Academy of Sciences, 807*, 146–163.

Watson, D., Clark, L. A., & Tellegen, A. (1988). Developmental and validation of brief measures of positive and negative affect: The PANAS scales. *Journal of Personality and Social Psychology, 54*, 1063–1070.

Watson, D., Clark, L. A., Weber, K., Assenheimer, J. S., Strauss, M. E., & McCormick, R. A. (1995). Testing a tripartite model: I. Evaluating the convergent and discriminant validity of anxiety and depression symptom scales. *Journal of Abnormal Psychology, 104*, 3–14.

Watson, D., Wiese, D., Vaidya, J., & Tellegen, A. (1999). The two general activation systems of affect: Structural findings, evolutionary considerations, and psychobiological evidence. *Journal of Personality and Social Psychology, 76*, 820–838.

Weisskopf, M. G., & LeDoux, J. E. (1999). Distinct populations of NMDA receptors at subcortical and cortical inputs to principal cells of the lateral amygdala. *Journal of Neurophysiology, 81*, 930–934.

Wheeler, R. E., Davidson, R. J., & Tomarken, A .J. (1993). Frontal brain asymmetry and emotional reactivity: A biological substrate of affective style. *Psychophysiology, 30*, 82–89.

Zinser, M. C., Fiore, M. C., Davidson, R. J., & Baker, T. B. (1999). Manipulating smoking motivation: Impact on an electrophysiological index of approach motivation. *Journal of Abnormal Psychology, 108*(2), 240–254.

7

Empathy-Related Emotional Responses, Altruism, and Their Socialization

NANCY EISENBERG

Since early adulthood, I have been interested in what motivates people to be concerned about the needs of others and issues of justice. As a college student at the University of Michigan in the late 1960s and early 1970s, I was exposed to, and somewhat involved in, anti-Vietnam war protests, a strike related to resources for African-American students, and efforts to educate high school children about the effects of racism. Because of the political climate of the time, it was not uncommon to be engaged in discussions of political and social issues pertaining to justice, human rights, and the welfare of individuals.

Given this background, it is not surprising that my initial area of research in psychology graduate school was the development of humanitarian political attitudes. I sought out Dr. Paul Mussen as my mentor; he was actively engaged in work on this topic. When I started to review the literature relevant to the development of humanitarian political attitudes, it was natural that I would quickly turn to the nascent literature on helping behavior and empathy. People with humanitarian political attitudes generally support policies that are helpful to the socially and economically deprived, and empathy or compassion seemed a likely candidate for the motivational bases of other-oriented attitudes and behavior. In addition, people's reasoning about moral issues appeared to contribute to the development of humanitarian attitudes.

Thus, since early in my career, I have studied other-oriented versus egoistic cognitions, behavior, and emotional reactions. Given this orientation, the Dalai Lama fascinated me, although I did not know a great deal about him. In my work, I have often cited studies of exemplars of altruism such as individuals involved in the civil rights movement at a personal cost and rescuers of Jews in Nazi Europe. When the Dalai Lama received the Noble Peace Prize, he was officially recognized for his humanitarian contributions. Moreover, in contrast to the level of corruption and self-interest associated with most governments and political leaders, the Dalai Lama appeared to be an interesting exception. It is my perception that in the United States and many other countries, people motivated by moral principles and an other-orientation seldom emerge as political leaders; when they do, they do not last long. Because the Dalai Lama embodies a nonviolent, humanitarian philosophy while also being the religious and political leader of millions of people, it seemed likely that the Buddhist culture and religion were different in fundamental ways from Western culture.

Indeed, I have always felt that Buddhism was a more benign religion than the Western religions I had been exposed to, although I really knew relatively little about the teachings or content of Buddhism. I did know that I was unimpressed (indeed, appalled) with the history of oppression, killing, and discrimination that is part of most Western religions. Too often religion has been used as a justification for inhumane attitudes and behavior. Although compassion and helping tend to be part of the ideology in most Western religions, they are not central to the religion, and often religious leaders and members have been compassionate only toward members of the ingroup. Thus, because compassion is a central construct in Buddhism, I was curious to learn more about its doctrine, as well as its influence on the everyday life of community members.

I knew very little about Buddhism when I went to Dharamsala, and unfortunately my knowledge is still quite limited. This is in part because the Dalai Lama was more interested in learning our perspective on compassion than in telling us his perspective. However, I did some reading on basic tenets of the religion and was exposed to the Dalai Lama as an exemplar of a Buddhist leader. Initially, I was very impressed that helping and compassion are deemed necessary in Buddhism for an individual to be reincarnated at a higher level in the next life. Even more interesting was the notion that Buddhists should be motivated to achieve the state of nothingness (*Nibbana*, the highest state) because in this state they are believed to be omnipotent and can therefore help more living beings than in lower states of being. So helping and compassion are both the means of achieving a desired endstate and the endstate itself (although it is believed that some very small percentage of people can achieve the highest level of being through meditation and related acts and rites).

Clearly, Buddhists have done a lot of thinking about compassion and altruism, much more than most of us in the West. In fact, many moral virtues are discussed in the *via positiva*, which outlines the virtues necessary to reach *Nibbana*. These include *dana* (giving), *metta* (kindness), *mudita* (sympathetic joy), *karuna* (compassion), and *upekkha* (equanimity). What is particularly interesting is the number of prosocial virtues discussed in the doctrine, as well as the orientation toward including all living beings in the domain of recipients of one's caring and altruism. For example, the virtue and state of *dana* implicitly connotes the development of a will to give benevolently and without reservation. Buddhism recognizes that it is better to give than receive and that the giver benefits at least as much as the recipient (Tachibana, 1975). In the Buddhist way of reckoning, a person who has fully cultivated *dana* will overcome what is bad by what is good (*The Milanda*, p. 117). Similarly, achieving the virtue of *metta* is said to occur when one can consider the joys, sorrows, and well-being of others, even those considered to be enemies. Closely connected with *metta* is the virtue of *mudita*, which is thought to liberate the heart from envy and jealousy. It reflects open-heartedness created by the joyful state of mind one finds in the success of others. In Buddhism, *karuna* represents love and compassion and is considered to be an effective antidote to greed and hatred (Saddhatissa, 1971). The practice of *karuna* helps a person to overcome indifference and provides an understanding of the suffering of others and a willingness to go out of one's way to help those in distress. The final virtue, *upekkha*, is Buddha's cure for anxiety, frustration, and agitation. This virtue allows one to meet difficult situations with an unperturbed mind. In this way, one will not be frustrated if his or her attempts at *karuna* or *metta* are met with hostility or rejection (Quintos, 1977). Thus, Buddhists have thought a lot about the importance of being other-oriented toward all individuals and of ways to counteract our tendencies to become prey to emotions such as envy, hostility, anxiety, and frustration that can undermine prosocial efforts. I return to this issue later in discussing the limitations of Western work on other-oriented emotions and behavior.

I found Buddhism's inclusivity to be reflected in the Dalai Lama's comments during our meetings. For example, he noted that he does not believe in missionary efforts; in his view, it does not matter what religion others may be as long as they act in moral and caring ways. He further stated that he believes that all people are born basically caring and good, and that it is society that corrupts their nature. Thus, all people—Buddhist or not—are initially good; this contrasts with the view common in some religions that one must become a member of a particular religious group to be a good person.

Given the centrality of compassion and helping in Buddhist doctrine and the salience and importance of religious ideas in the lives of many Buddhists, I have become more aware of the tremendous potential for a religious philosophy to influence socialization, particularly if the people's lives are immersed in and shaped by this religion. In such a case, the community may be as important a socializer of children as are parents. Yet in most of the research on the socialization of empathy and altruism stemming from Western psychology, the family is the unit of analysis. This is clearly a limitation of Western research on the topic, especially if one wishes to generalize the findings to Eastern cultures. At the conference in Dharamsala I discussed socialization primarily in the context of the family, although I came away with the certainty that such work must be supplemented more by an understanding of how the community and a prevailing philosophy shape children's other-oriented cognitions, behavior, and emotions. The pervasiveness of the Buddhist philosophy in the lives of many people clearly is greater than the influence of the Judaic-Christian doctrine in the lives of most Westerners, but Western social and behavioral scientists frequently have not fully recognized the implications of this reality.

In the next section of this chapter, I present the research ideas discussed at the conference in Dharamsala. Then I return to the issue of insights I gained, or questions raised, from my participation in this conference.

Empathy-Related Responding and Prosocial Actions

Everyday in the newspaper and on television there are reports of inhuman actions, including brutal murders, random shootings or bombings, and the abuse or neglect of children. One factor frequently cited by social scientists as contributing to behaviors ranging from child abuse to psychopathic murders is the inability to feel others' emotions and, consequently, to experience concern for them—that is, the absence of empathy and sympathy. These capacities to feel others' emotions and to experience concern for their welfare, as well as the prosocial behavior that is believed to result from other-oriented concern, are the focus of this chapter. In particular, the relation between empathy-related responding and prosocial behavior is discussed briefly, after which the socialization correlates of empathy/sympathy and prosocial behaviors are reviewed.

Over the last 40 years—indeed, over the last century—empathy has been defined in a variety of diverse ways. The definitions that my colleagues and I have used reflect current usage in the developmental and social psychological literatures. In our work, empathy is defined as an affective response that stems from the apprehension or comprehension of another's emotional state or condition, and that is similar to what the other person is feeling or would be expected to feel. Thus, if a person views another person crying and is sad as a consequence, he or she is experiencing empathy. Sympathy is an affective response that frequently stems from empathy, but does not consist merely of feeling the same emotion as the other is experiencing (or is expected to experience). Rather, sympathy consists of feelings of sorrow or concern for the distressed or needy other. When defined in this way, sympathy seems close to the Buddhist virtue of *metta*.

Personal distress is another emotional response that frequently stems from the apprehension of the others' state or condition; however, it is a self-focused, aversive emotional reaction to another's emotion or condition. It is experienced as discomfort, anxiety, or concern about one's own welfare (Batson, 1991). Thus, if a person views another person who is sad and, as a consequence, feels anxious and uncomfortable, this is personal distress.

My interest in empathy-related responding grew out of my prior work in prosocial behavior—that is, voluntary behavior intended to benefit others, including actions such as sharing, helping, and comforting. Most of my early efforts at understanding prosocial behavior were directed toward delineating developmental changes in children's moral reasoning about prosocial actions and the relation of such reasoning to behavior. However, I quickly realized that to gain a better understanding of prosocial behavior, I would have to move beyond the study of cognitive contributing factors such as moral judgment to a focus on the role of emotion in prosocial responding. This realization is consistent, I believe, with the Buddhist perspective in that feelings are an important part of several virtues (e.g., *metta, mudita*) that appear to be closely linked to *dana* (giving).

A shift to emotional factors contributing to prosocial behavior naturally leads to a focus on empathy. For centuries philosophers such as Hume (1777/1966), and for decades psychologists such as Hoffman (1975b) and Staub (1979), have argued that prosocial behavior is frequently motivated by empathy or sympathy. Indeed, for a time there seemed to be a fair degree of consensus on the issue. However, in 1982, Underwood and Moore published a meta-analysis in *Psychological Bulletin* in which they examined the relation between affective empathy and prosocial behavior in the empirical literature, and much to nearly everyone's surprise, they found essentially no correlation between the two.

As it turns out, there does appear to be a relation between empathy-related emotional responding and prosocial behavior, but whether or not such a relation is obtained depends on how empathy-related responding is conceptualized and how researchers measure empathy-related responding. Batson (1991) was the first to systematically differentiate between sympathy (which he calls empathy) and personal distress. He argued that sympathy and personal distress should be associated with different motivations and relate differently to prosocial behavior. Specifically, sympathy was hypothesized to be intimately linked with other-oriented motivations and, consequently, with other-oriented, altruistic helping behavior. In contrast, personal distress is viewed as involving the egoistic motivation of alleviating one's own distressed; consequently, it is linked with prosocial behavior only when the easiest way to reduce one's own distress is to eliminate distress in the needy or distressed other (e.g., when one cannot escape contact with the empathy-inducing person). Consistent with his theorizing, Batson and his colleagues, in their studies of adults in the laboratory, have found that sympathy is more likely to be associated with helping than is personal distress when it is easy for people to escape contact with the person needing assistance (see Batson, 1991).

However, Batson's work was solely with adults. There was still a question as to whether similar relations of sympathy and personal distress with prosocial behavior could be found for children. Unfortunately, the self-report methods and laboratory manipulations used in Batson's studies with adults did not seem particularly appropriate for use with children, in part because a prior review of the literature (Eisenberg & Miller, 1987) indicated that there was no relation between young children's self-reported empathy-related responding and their prosocial behavior.

Thus, in the mid-1980s, my colleague Richard Fabes, our students, and I started a program of research in which two of the primary goals were to differentiate between sympathetic and personal distress reactions using non-self-report indexes as well as self-report measures and to examine the relations of these indexes to prosocial behavior. In a series of studies, we demonstrated that we could use heart rate, skin conductance, facial reactions, and, to a limited degree, self-reported emotional reactions to differentiate between children's distress and sympathetic reactions. For example, children and adults viewed film clips selected to induce sympathy or emotion akin to distress, and their self-reported, facial, and physiological reactions were assessed. In general, people tended to report more distress, exhibited higher heart rate and skin conductance, and exhibited more facial distress in distress-inducing contexts. In contrast, they exhibited more concerned attention and sadness, reported more sympathy (particularly for older children and adults), and exhibited heart rate decelerations when exposed to a sympathy-inducing situation.

Next, in a second set of studies, we demonstrated that people who exhibited sympathy (as assessed with our physiological, facial, and self-report measures) were relatively likely to help others for who were the target of their sympathy, whereas children who appeared to experience personal distress in reaction to viewing needy or distressed people were relatively unlikely to assist (see Eisenberg & Fabes, 1990, 1991; Eisenberg et al., 1989; Fabes, Eisenberg, & Eisenbud, 1993). In these studies, children or adults typically viewed others in empathy-inducing situations while their facial and physiological responses were monitored. Soon afterward, they had an opportunity to report their emotional reactions and to help the people in need or distress (or others like them). In general, adults who reported sympathy, and children and adults who facially exhibited concern rather than distress and whose heart rates declined rather than accelerated at sympathy inducing moments, were those who were more likely to help (see Eisenberg & Fabes, 1990; Eisenberg, Fabes, Schaller et al., 1991).

Given that there does seem to be a link between empathy-related responding and prosocial behavior, it is useful to examine factors that might determine whether a given person tends to experience sympathy or personal distress when confronted with others who are in need. With this purpose in mind, I review some of the findings on the socialization of empathy-related emotion reactions in children. In addition, I summarize some of the larger body of literature about socialization of children's prosocial behavior (e.g., their helping, sharing, and comforting behaviors).

A Conceptualization of the Role of Regulation and Emotionality in Empathy-Related Responding

Prior to discussing the socialization of empathy-related responding, it is useful to consider in more detail the nature of sympathy and personal distress. The intensity of an individual's vicarious negative emotion when exposed to others in distress or need seems to be related to whether people experience sympathy or personal distress. Eisenberg et al. (1994) proposed that when people experience very high levels of negative emotional arousal in response to others' distress or need, they become over-aroused by the negative emotion, find it aversive, and, consequently, focus on their own needs rather than those of the distressed person (see also Hoffman, 1982). This self-focused, aversive reaction is personal distress. Consistent with this view, high levels of general negative emotional arousal have been found to result in a self-focus (Wood, Saltzberg, & Goldsamt, 1990), and empathically induced distress reactions are associated with higher skin conductance reactivity than is sympathy (Eisenberg, Fabes, Schaller, Carlo, & Miller, 1991; Eisenberg, Fabes, Schaller, Miller et al., 1991). In contrast, if people experience others' negative emotion but can maintain their vicarious emotional reaction to another's distress at a tolerable range, they are likely to experience how needy or distressed others feel, but are relatively unlikely to become self-focused and overwhelmed by their emotion.

Based on this line of reasoning, Eisenberg and Fabes (1992) proposed that *individual differences* in the tendency to experience sympathy versus personal distress vary as a function of dispositional or individual differences in both typical level of emotional intensity (Larsen & Diener, 1987) and individuals' ability to regulate their emotional reactions. People high in constructive modes of regulation such as behavioral and emotion regulation skills (e.g., who have control over their ability to focus and shift attention; Derryberry & Rothbart, 1988) were hypothesized to be relatively high in sympathy regardless of emotional intensity; those moderately high in emotional intensity were expected to be particularly sympathetic only if they also were well regulated. Well-regulated people would be expected to modulate their negative vicarious emotion and maintain an optimal level of emotional arousal—one that has emotional force and enhances attention but is not so aversive and physiologically arousing that it engenders a self-focus. In contrast, people low in the ability to regulate their emotions, especially if they are emotionally intense, were hypothesized to be low in dispositional sympathy and high in personal distress.

These ideas seem to be somewhat consistent with the Buddhist perspective. Practices such as meditation help the individual to regulate negative emotions and cultivate the virtues related to prosocial behavior and empathy. For example, the practice of *karuna* helps a person to overcome indifference and provide an understanding of the suffering of others and a willingness to go out of one's way to help those in distress. Thus, *karuna* seems to involve regulation of thought and behavior. *Upekkha* (equanimity) is the cure for anxiety, frustration, and agitation and helps a person to meet difficult situations with an unperturbed mind; thus, cultivating *upekkha* would be expected to involve the regulation of negative emotional states.

Some support has been obtained for our assumption that emotionality and regulation are linked to empathy-related responding (see Eisenberg, Wentzel, & Harris, 1999). Regulation has been linked to high sympathy and low personal distress (Eisenberg & Fabes, 1995; Eisenberg, Fabes, Murphy, Karbon et al., 1996; Eisenberg & Okun, 1996), whereas personal distress has been associated with low regulation among adults (Eisenberg, Fabes, Murphy, Karbon, Maszk et al., 1994; Eisenberg & Okun, 1996; compare with Eisenberg & Fabes, 1995) and infants (Ungerer et al., 1990). Furthermore, low and moderate levels of negative emotional intensity, but not high levels, have been associated with concern for another in a specific context (Eisenberg & Fabes, 1995), and children who experience more negative emotion than that of the empathy-eliciting stimulus person (i.e., become overaroused) are relatively low in empathy/sympathy (Strayer, 1993). In addition, there is limited evidence that unregulated children are low in sympathy regardless of their level of emotional intensity whereas, for moderately and highly regulated children, level of sympathy increases with level of emotional intensity (Eisenberg, Fabes, Murphy, Karbon et al., 1996; also see Eisenberg, Fabes, Karbon, Murphy, Wosinski et al., 1996; Lenrow, 1965).

The obvious next question is why do some people seem to be prone to empathic overarousal and personal distress whereas others seem to be prone to sympathy? It is likely that individual differences in this regard are due partially to genetic factors. Twin studies suggest that the tendency to experience empathy is partially inherited (Matthews, Batson, Horn, & Rosenman, 1981; Rushton, Fulker, Neale, Nias, & Eysenck,

1986; Zahn-Waxler, Robinson, & Emde, 1992). Moreover, aspects of temperament such as negative emotionality appear to have a genetic basis (Plomin & Stocker, 1989). Furthermore, parents' socialization practices may reflect to some degree parents' genetic makeup, a genetic makeup that is passed on to offspring and may affect children's capacity for empathy. However, observation of and interactions with socializers likely contribute to individual differences in empathy, sympathy, and personal distress above and beyond any contribution due to heredity. I now discuss some of the literature concerning the socialization of empathy-related responses.

Socialization of Empathy-Related Responding

Despite the importance of empathy to human social relationships, research on the socialization of empathy-related responding is sparse. Most of the existing work concerns the relations of children's empathy-related responding to (a) parents' empathy-related responding, (b) the quality of the parent-child relationship, (c) parental general disciplinary practices (often assessed in relation to perceived wrongdoing on the child's part), (d) parental emotion-related disciplinary practices, and (e) parental and family expressivity. Most of the relevant research has been conducted in Western cultures; thus, one cannot automatically assume that the same pattern of findings would be obtained in Asian cultures. Each of these topics is now discussed.

The Relation Between Parent and Child Empathy-Related Responding. Numerous investigators have examined the relation between measures of parents' and children's empathy, sympathy, or personal distress. Usually researchers have not differentiated between sympathy and personal distress but have used measures of global empathy. Findings in studies involving such global measures are inconsistent. In some studies, few significant relations have been found (Kalliopuska, 1984; Strayer & Roberts, 1989); in other studies, significant relations have been obtained (Trommsdorff, 1991) or the pattern of relations has been complex and difficult to explain (e.g., Barnett, King, Howard, & Dino, 1980).

In a few studies, the associations of parental sympathy and personal distress to children's sympathy and personal distress have been assessed (rather than merely focusing on global empathy). In these studies, girls' sympathy has been positively related to mothers' sympathy (or perspective taking combined with sympathy; Eisenberg et al., 1992; Eisenberg

& McNally, 1993; Fabes, Eisenberg, & Miller, 1990) or negatively related to daughters' personal distress (Eisenberg, Fabes, Schaller, Carlo, & Miller, 1991). In contrast, mothers' personal distress sometimes has been correlated with either daughters' low empathic responding or daughters' and sons' inappropriate positive affect in response to viewing distressed or needy others (Eisenberg et al., 1992; Fabes, Eisenberg, & Miller, 1990). Mothers' sympathy seldom has been related to sons' sympathy (although it was positively related in Eisenberg et al., 1992); however, there is some evidence that sympathetic fathers have sympathetic sons (Eisenberg, Fabes, Schaller, Carlo, & Miller, 1991). Thus, when sympathy and personal distress have been examined, parental responding has been linked with children's empathy-related reactions, but primarily for same-sex children.

The Relation between Quality of the Parent-Child Relationship and Children's Vicarious Responding. Given that children learn about the value of other people in their social interactions, it is not surprising that empathic and sympathetic children have high quality relationships with their mother early in life. Children who are securely attached to their mothers, in comparison to insecurely attached children, tend to be sympathetic with peers at 3 ½ years of age (Waters, Wippman, & Sroufe, 1979) and exhibit relatively high levels of empathic and prosocial behaviors in preschool (Kestenbaum, Farber, & Sroufe, 1989). Although Iannotti, Cummings, Pierrehumbert, Milano, and Zahn-Waxler (1992) did not find a relation between quality of attachment and a self-report measure of children's empathy, they found that quality of the attachment at age 2 predicted children's prosocial behavior toward peers at age 5. Furthermore, attachments with grandparents and other older people may foster empathy. In one study, the degree to which grandparents were emotionally important predicted girls' (but not boys') empathy. In addition, children who were more involved with their grandparents were higher in contemporaneous empathy (and, when assessed at age 7, empathy 3 years later). Furthermore, children who engaged in more intimate talks with people in the grandparents' generation were more empathic than other children (Bryant, 1987).

Consistent with the aforementioned findings on the quality of the parent-child relationship, abusive parents are low in empathy (Feshbach, 1987) and tend to have children low in empathy (Main & George, 1985; see Miller & Eisenberg, 1988). Moreover, there is empirical evidence of a link between children's empathy and warm, empathic parenting

(Trommsdorff, 1991; Zahn-Waxler, Radke-Yarrow, & King, 1979) and parental affection (Barnett, Howard, King, & Dino, 1980; Eisenberg-Berg & Mussen, 1978; Krevans & Gibbs, 1996), although not all studies have shown such relations (e.g., Barnett, King, Howard, & Dino, 1980; Eisenberg, Fabes, Schaller, Carlo, & Miller, 1991; Fabes et al., 1994; Janssens & Gerris, 1992; Iannotti et al., 1992). Conversely, Hastings, Zahn-Waxler, Robinson, Usher, and Bridges (2000) found that mothers who reported experiencing or expressing negative affect with their child (e.g., anger, disappointment, and conflict) when their children were age 5 had children who, at age 7, were relatively low in some (but not all) measures of empathy and concern for others. Although Bryant (1987) found no relationship between general parental support and empathy for 7- and 10-year-olds, maternal (but not paternal) report of expressions of support during times of stress predicted girls' concurrent empathy. In addition, mothers' expressive reactions to children's stressful experiences at age 10 predicted boys' and girls' empathy at age 14. Thus, parental support when children are under stress may foster empathy more than does a general level of support.

The relation of parental affection and support to children's empathy-related reactions likely varies as a function of other practices used by the parent. For example, Yarrow, Scott, and Waxler (1973) found that exposure to nurturant familiar adults who modeled prosocial behavior enhanced children's expressions of sympathy. Furthermore, authoritative parents, who are warm and directive, might be expected to have more empathic children than permissive parents (who are warm but nondirective; see Baumrind, 1971). In fact, in empirical studies, children viewed by teachers and peers as prosocial tended to have mothers who are authoritative in their parenting—that is, they were warm, used a democratic parenting style, expected and demanded mature and independent behavior from their children, and provided suggestions and information to their children. In contrast, children viewed by others as low in prosocial behavior had mothers and fathers who were authoritarian in their parenting (i.e, were low in warmth for fathers and were directive and negative for both parents; Dekovic & Janssens, 1992; see also Janssens & Dekovic, 1997). Authoritative parenting also has been linked to relatively high levels of reasoning about moral dilemmas (Janssens & Dekovic, 1997; Pratt et al., 1999). The blend of parenting behaviors that constitutes an authoritative parenting style also would be expected to promote sympathy. Although there is relatively little research testing this idea, authoritarian (versus authoritative) parenting has been related to low empathy and concern in U.S. 7-year-olds (Hastings et al., 2000). Moreover, Krevans and Gibbs (1996) found that characteristics of parenting associated with authoritative rather than authoritarian parenting (i.e., high nurturance, low power assertion, and high use of inductive discipline) were associated with children's empathy/sympathy. Thus, initial findings support the hypothesis that parental authoritative rather than authoritarian parenting is associated with offspring's empathy and sympathy.

The Relations of Parental Disciplinary Practices to Children's Empathy-Related Responding. Empirical work examining the relation of parental discipline to children's empathy-related responding is scant. However, Hoffman (1970, 1983) and others frequently have hypothesized regarding the relations of discipline to empathy and sympathy.

A type of discipline of great interest to psychologists studying moral development is parental use of reasoning or inductions, particularly those that point out the consequences of children's behavior for others. Hoffman (1983, 2000) reasoned that inductions are likely to promote moral development for a variety of reasons, including the following: (a) inductions direct and focus children's attention on others' affective states and the consequences of their behavior for others, thereby capitalizing on children's capacity to empathize and experience guilt; (b) inductions implicitly or explicitly communicate to the child that he or she is responsible and that morality is internal; (c) inductions induce an optimal level of arousal for learning—that is, they elicit the child's attention, but are unlikely to produce high levels that are disruptive to learning; (d) inductions are not likely to be viewed by the child as arbitrary and therefore are unlikely to induce resistance; and (e) parents who use inductions provide a rational, controlled model for imitation. Hoffman further argued that, over time, inductive messages are experienced as internalized (i.e., deriving from within the child) because the child plays an active role in processing the information embedded in the induction. This information is encoded and integrated with information contained in other inductions and becomes disassociated from the particular disciplinary event. Furthermore, the focus when socializers use inductions is on the child's action and its consequences rather than on the parent as the disciplinary agent. Consequently, over time children are likely to remember the causal link between their actions and consequences for others rather than the external pressure or the specific disciplinary context.

Empirical findings regarding links between parental general disciplinary practices and children's empathy are somewhat inconsistent, perhaps in part because investigators seldom have differentiated between sympathy and personal distress in this research. In studies of global empathy, some investigators have found that parental practices are unrelated to children's empathy (Barnett, King, Howard, & Dino, 1980). However, others have obtained evidence suggesting that inductive practices (e.g., parental use of reasoning) are positively related to children's empathy or sympathy (e.g., Janssens & Gerris, 1992; Krevans & Gibbs, 1996; Miller, Eisenberg, Fabes, Shell, & Gular, 1989; Zahn-Waxler et al., 1979). Power-assertive discipline is defined as involving physical punishment, deprivation of privileges, or the threat of these punishments. Parental power assertion was negatively related to empathy in one study (Janssens & Gerris, 1992), albeit not in others (Bryant, 1987; Feshbach, 1978). However, in a study of sympathy and personal distress rather than global empathy, mothers' use of negative control (i.e., nonphysical power assertion or negative appraisals of the child), albeit not physical control (physical punishment or physically guiding the child's actions), was linked to low levels of sympathy in preschool children (Miller et al., 1989). Thus, although one would expect negative relations between harsh parental practices and empathy/sympathy, the findings are scant and unclear. Critical variables are probably the degree to which parental practices are overly harsh and the overall configuration of parenting behavior.

The relations of parental demandingness versus permissiveness vary with the measure of empathy. In one study parental permissiveness and a low level of parental overcontrol were positively related to 6- to 8-year-old girls' (but not boys') empathy (Feshbach, 1978). However, serious questions have been raised about the method used to assess empathy in this study (Eisenberg & Lennon, 1983). In contrast, in other research, mothers' and fathers' demandingness (i.e., expectations of mature behavior) was associated with 9- to 12-year-old children's empathy (Janssens & Gerris, 1992). In contrast, paternal (but not maternal) indulgence has been associated with low levels of empathy for boys (findings were mixed for girls; Bryant, 1987). In the same study, paternal limit-setting was positively related to empathy at ages 7 and 10 for boys and girls (Bryant, 1987). In combination, these findings suggest that parents who are overindulgent and do not expect their children to live up to certain standards are likely to be low in sympathy or empathy.

Parental Emotion-Related Disciplinary Practices. In some studies of the socialization of empathy-related responding, investigators have focused on parental reactions to and discussions of children's emotional displays and emotion-related behavior rather than on general disciplinary practices. In this research, measures of empathy-related responding often included facial and/or physiological responses, as well as self-report measures of sympathy and distress rather than global empathy.

Parents may influence children's emotion-related behavior in a variety of ways (Eisenberg, Cumberland, & Spinrad, 1998). First, socialization experiences may influence whether children tend to focus on others' needs or on their own needs or desires in situations involving empathy-related emotion. For example, parents' verbal messages, if other-oriented, may help children to focus on others' emotional states and needs. In addition, adults who are empathic in their parenting behavior may model an other-orientation to their children.

Second, how socializers react to the expression of emotion in general may affect the likelihood of children acknowledging, accepting, and showing negative emotions, including vicarious negative emotions such as sympathy (Eisenberg, Schaller et al., 1988), and whether emotional situations become intrinsically distressing for the child. Buck (1984) suggested that sanctions for emotional expressiveness in the home are associated with physiological but not external markers of emotional responding in adults. This is because children who receive negative reactions to their displays of emotion are expected to gradually learn to hide their emotions but would be expected to feel anxious when in emotionally evocative situations (due to prior associations between punishment and emotional expressivity). Similarly, Tomkins (1963) suggested that children learn to express distress without shame and to respond sympathetically to others if their parents respond openly with sympathy and nurturance to children's feelings of distress and helplessness.

In addition, socializers' reactions to children's emotions may teach children specific methods for dealing with and regulating their emotions. For example, whereas some parents teach their children to hide or control their emotions, others emphasize techniques such as seeking social support or dealing instrumentally with problems and stressors (e.g., Hardy, Power, & Jaedicke, 1994; Roberts & Strayer, 1987).

Finally, socializers' willingness to discuss emotions with their children would be expected to relate to children's awareness of others' emotional states (Dunn, Bretherton, & Munn, 1987). Emotion-related language in the culture and in the family is viewed as sharpening the child's awareness of emotional states and as promoting the development of emotional memory and an abstract emotion-related conceptual system. Emotional concepts are viewed as playing a crucial role in structuring emotional experience and in the development of subtler feelings that are part of sympathy (Malatesta & Haviland, 1985). Of course, discussion of emotion often is part of a larger pattern of socialization practices.

In general, parental practices that help children to cope with their own negative emotion appear to foster sympathy rather than personal distress. This presumably is because children who cannot adequately cope with their emotions tend to become overaroused and, consequently, experience a self-focused aversive response (i.e., personal distress) when confronted with another's distress (Eisenberg et al., 1994).

For example, Eisenberg, Fabes, Schaller, Carlo, and Miller (1991) found that parents who reported being restrictive with regard to children's expression of their own negative emotion tended to have sons prone to experience personal distress rather than sympathy when exposed to distressed or needy others. Specifically, mothers' emphasis on controlling emotions that were unlikely to injure another person (e.g., children's own sadness and anxiety) was associated with boys' facial and physiological (skin conductance and heart rate) markers of distress when viewing an empathy-inducing film, accompanied by self-reports of low distress in reaction to the film. Thus, these boys seemed prone to experience distress when confronted with others' distress, but did not want others to know what they were feeling. Boys whose parents stress control of emotions such as anxiety may have difficulty dealing with these emotions in social settings.

In contrast, parents who are restrictive with regard to emotional displays that could be *hurtful to others* (e.g., gaping at a disfigured person) tend to have same-sex elementary school children who are high in self-reported dispositional and situational sympathy (Eisenberg, Fabes, Schaller, Carlo, & Miller, 1991). Parents who discourage their children from expressing hurtful emotions may be educating their children about the effects of children's emotional displays on others. However, maternal restrictiveness with regard to the display of hurtful emotions also has been linked to personal distress in kindergarten girls. It appeared that mothers who were restrictive in this regard with their young daughters were less supportive in general; thus, for younger children, such maternal restrictiveness may have reflected age-inappropriate restrictiveness or low levels of support (Eisenberg et al., 1992).

As noted previously, it seems likely that parents who talk about emotions with their children in a constructive manner have children who are relatively mature in their abilities to understand and regulate emotion (Gottman, Katz, & Hooven, 1996). In fact, Barnett, Howard, King, and Dino (1980) found that empathic undergraduates, in comparison to less empathic undergraduates, reported that their parents were more likely to discuss feelings with them. However, Barnett, King, Howard, and Dino (1980) found that fathers' reports of discussing emotions in nondisciplinary settings were negatively related to girls' empathy (mothers' reports were unrelated to children's empathy). In another study, mothers' references to their own sympathy and sadness were associated with boys' reports of sympathy and sadness (Eisenberg et al., 1992). Thus, empirical findings in regard to this issue are inconsistent, although it is possible that discussion of emotion that is not overly arousing is associated with the capacity for sympathy.

Maternal techniques that direct that child's attention to another's situation or help the child to feel the other's distress seem to foster sympathy. For example, mothers who were warm but also directed their children's attention to an empathy-inducing story tended to have elementary school children who were sympathetic and helpful. This did not hold for kindergartners, perhaps because mothers of younger children seemed to be attempting to modulate their children's negative affect with their own displays of positive emotion when telling the stories (Fabes et al., 1994). In another study in which mothers viewed an empathy-inducing film with their child, mothers' verbal linking of the events in the film with children's own experiences was associated with children's heightened vicarious emotional responding of all kinds (sadness, distress, and sympathy); furthermore, mothers' statements about perspective taking or referring to the film protagonist's feelings or situation were associated with boys' reports of sympathy and sadness (Eisenberg et al., 1992).

One method of coping with emotional stress is through directly acting on the problem—that is, trying to change factors in the environment that have caused the distress (Lazarus & Folkman, 1984). Initial findings indicate that boys whose parents encourage them to deal instrumentally with situations that have caused their own sadness or anxiety are likely to experience sympathy rather than personal distress in empathy-inducing contexts (Eisenberg, Fabes, Schaller, Carlo, & Miller, 1991). Moreover, parents who model instrumental coping have children who are relatively high in social competence (Roberts & Strayer, 1987). Parents who teach sons to instrumentally deal with negative emotions and stressful situations may be less likely to become overaroused when experiencing vicariously induced negative emotion and may be more likely to experience sympathy. It is unclear why this same relation was not obtained for girls; perhaps, due to gender roles, instrumental coping often is less effective for girls.

Findings such as these support the view that children's tendencies to respond with sympathy versus personal distress are in part learned, although the relevant socialization processes are likely to be complex and may involve genetic factors. Indeed, it is important to note that the socialization process is not a one-way street. For example, in one study, mothers' perceptions of how distressed their children become when exposed to others' distress were greater for younger (kindergarten) than older (second grade) children. Mothers of these younger children were warmer and displayed more positive and less negative emotion when telling stories about people in distress to younger children than were mothers of older children. It appeared that mothers were trying to buffer younger children's reactions to the stories. Indeed, if mothers perceived their kindergartners as emotionally vulnerable, they were more likely to display positive rather than negative emotion while telling the stories (Fabes et al., 1994).

Furthermore, children with difficult temperaments often may elicit negative reactions from their parents when they display negative emotions. In a study of 4- to 6-year-olds, mothers who described their children as prone to express negative emotions and as low in the ability to regulate their attention reported minimizing or punishing their children's expressions of negative emotions. Mothers who viewed their children as not only prone to negative emotions but also as experiencing intense negative emotions reported reacting with distress and avoidance when their children exhibited negative affect. In contrast, mothers' perceptions of their children's temperament generally were unrelated to mothers' reports of comforting, encouraging the expression of emotion, or attempts to get their children to instrumentally deal with a problem when their children express negative emotion (Eisenberg & Fabes, 1994). Thus, some types of parental emotion socialization-related behaviors (particularly negative parental reactions) often may vary based on children's characteristics, whereas others (probably supportive reactions) may vary more as a function of parental beliefs and parenting goals.

The Relations of Family and Parental Expressiveness to Children's Empathy-Related Responding. The degree to which socializers express their emotions may influence whether children feel that it is appropriate to experience and display their emotions. For example, the amount of emotional expressivity in the family has been correlated with offspring's own emotional reactivity (Cassidy, Parke, Butkovsky, & Braungart, 1992; Halberstadt, 1986; Halberstadt, Crisp, & Eaton, 1999). Socializers who display their own negative emotions not only model expressivity but also may communicate that it is acceptable to experience negative emotions. However, as is discussed briefly, socializers' expressions of different emotions may relate differently to empathy-related responding.

Initial research is consistent with the view that the ways in which families deal with the expression of emotion are associated with children's tendencies to experience vicariously induced emotion, but primarily for girls and women. Young adult women (but not men) who reported a relatively high degree of expression of positive emotions and gentle negative emotions (e.g., apologizing, expressing a sense of loss) in their homes of origin reported relatively high levels of vicarious emotions (e.g., sadness, sympathy, and distress) in reaction to viewing sympathy-inducing and distressing films (Eisenberg, Fabes, Schaller, Carlo, Poulin et al., 1991). Among children, the expression of gentle negative emotions in the home has been associated with girls' (especially younger girls') sympathy. In contrast, boys and girls from homes in which hostile negative emotions frequently are expressed seem to be prone to personal distress or low sympathy (Eisenberg et al., 1992; Eisenberg et al., 2001). In Indonesia, parental expression of both hostile and more gentle negative emotions has been linked to low levels of sympathy among third graders (Eisenberg, Liew, & Pidada, 2001). It is likely that degree and valence of family expressiveness not only reflect the quality of family interactions, but also implicitly teach children what emotions, and how much emotion, they are expected to display or experience (see Halberstadt, 1986). Moreover, in homes in which a lot of hostile negative emotion is expressed, negative emotion may be viewed as particularly threatening and as something to be avoided if possible.

Summary

In summary, although empirical research on the socialization of empathy-related responding is relatively sparse, it appears that certain parental practices and behaviors, particularly those related to the socialization of emotion, are associated with Western children's empathy-related reactions. Much more research is needed, including work with different ethnic and cultural groups. It is interesting to speculate whether the same pattern of findings would be obtained in Tibetan Buddhist families as in Western families. Perhaps the messages embedded in Buddhism regarding compassion are so pervasive in the culture that parental practices such as induction are less important in teaching compassion. However, even if children are exposed to an ideology that encourages compassion and helpfulness, it is likely that children must learn to regulate their own emotions and emotion-related behavior if they are to enact behaviors that reflect compassion. Thus, it is reasonable to hypothesize that familial practices related to the socialization of emotion-related regulation would be linked to sympathy in Asian Buddhist families as well as in Western families, although only time and research on the topic will tell.

The Socialization of Sympathy versus the Socialization of Prosocial Behavior

There is considerably more information on the socialization of prosocial behavior and, in general, the pattern of findings regarding the socialization correlates of prosocial behavior is somewhat similar to that for the socialization of sympathy/empathy (see Eisenberg, 1992; Moore & Eisenberg, 1984; Radke-Yarrow, Zahn-Waxler, & Chapman, 1983). However, it is important to note that although sympathy is positively related to prosocial behavior, the socialization correlates of the two may differ somewhat. For example, children who are sympathetic may not enact prosocial behaviors because they are shy (Stanhope, Bell, & Parker-Cohen, 1987), do not know how to assist (Oliner & Oliner, 1988; Peterson, 1983), or are not sufficiently assertive (Barrett & Yarrow, 1977). Thus, socialization techniques that enhance children's assertiveness and feelings of efficacy may be particularly important for some types of prosocial behavior but not for the development of sympathy. In addition, many prosocial behaviors are not motivated by sympathy; they may be based on internalized moral values or they may not be altruistic or moral in motive. Indeed, many everyday instances of prosocial actions simply may reflect socially appropriate behaviors that are enacted habitually. It is likely that the socialization correlates of prosocial behaviors that do not stem from sympathy differ somewhat from the socialization correlates of sympathy and empathy.

It appears that a variety of socialization variables may be associated with the development of prosocial behavior, particularly in combination. A few of the more consistent findings are now summarized briefly.

Discipline

In general, parental discipline that involves reasoning (i.e., induction) rather than power assertion is associated with prosocial behavior, particularly for middle-class Western children. Inductions that are victim- or peer-oriented—for example, that point out the consequences of the child's behavior to others—most often have been linked with children's prosocial behavior. However, inductions appear to be most effective for children who have a history of exposure to inductive discipline and when combined with a democratic parenting style, including support and demands for mature behavior rather than power assertion (see Eisenberg & Fabes, 1998; Hoffman, 1983; Janssens & Gerris, 1992).

In contrast to inductive discipline, in general, power assertion has been either negatively related or unrelated to children's prosocial behavior (Eisenberg & Fabes, 1998; Krevens & Gibbs, 1996). Moreover, as noted previously, physical abuse of children has been linked to low levels of children's empathy and prosocial behavior, as well as lack of understanding of others' emotions and inappropriate behavior (George & Main, 1979; Howes & Eldredge, 1985; Main & George, 1985; see Eisenberg & Fabes, 1998; Miller & Eisenberg, 1988). As argued by Hoffman (1983), children often attribute prosocial behavior induced by power-assertive techniques to external motives such as fear of detection or punishment (Dix & Grusec, 1983; Smith, Gelfand, Hartmann, & Partlow, 1979). Furthermore, power assertion would be expected to focus the child's attention on punishment rather than on the consequences of their behavior for others and likely induces a level of arousal inimicable to learning (Hoffman, 1983, 2000).

Nonetheless, there is a difference between the occasional use of power-assertive techniques in the context of a positive parent-child relationship and the use of punishment as the preferred, predominant mode of discipline. When power-assertive techniques are used in a measured and rational manner by parents who generally are supportive and use nonpower-assertive disciplinary techniques, there may be no negative effects on children's social behavior. For example, rescuers of Jews in Nazi Europe reported that the punishment they received from their parents was not a routine response and was linked to specific behaviors rather than unprovoked (Oliner & Oliner, 1988).

Of course, punishment can induce immediate compliance with socializers' demands for prosocial behavior if the socializer monitors the child's behavior. However, there is little evidence that physical punishment, particularly when used as a primary mode of discipline, fosters the development of internalized prosocial behavior. Indeed, it likely undermines the development of self-initiated, internalized prosocial behavior.

Parental Warmth

The role of parental warmth and support in children's prosocial behavior is complex. Parental warmth by itself is not consistently related to prosocial behavior (Eisenberg & Fabes, 1998; Radke-Yarrow et al., 1983). However, quality of the parent-child relationship has been linked to prosocial behavior, as well as empathy and sympathy (e.g., Kestenbaum et al., 1989; see Eisenberg & Fabes, 1998).

It is likely that parental warmth and support provide a context in which other positive parental practices are optimally effective. For example, Dekovic and Janssens (1992) found that democratic parenting, involving both parental warmth and support, combined with inductions, demandingness, and the provision of suggestions, information, and positive comments, was associated with Dutch children's prosocial behavior as reported by teachers and peers. If children have a warm and secure relationship with their parents, they are more likely to try to live up to parental expectations. In contrast, parental warmth combined with a highly permissive parenting style may result in low levels of prosocial behavior.

Modeling

One of the most consistent findings in the prosocial literature is that children model prosocial and selfish behavior that they observe, be it depicted by unknown adults or parents (see Eisenberg & Fabes, 1998). This finding has been obtained numerous times in laboratory studies in which exposure to models was manipulated, as well as in correlational studies of families. Although powerful and competent models are imitated more than other models, children sometimes imitate prosocial actions of their peers (Eisenberg & Fabes, 1998). Furthermore, nurturant models who have ongoing relationships with children may be particularly effective models. For example, preschoolers who viewed lifelike prosocial behaviors enacted by adults with whom they had had nurturant interactions over a period of time in the classroom were likely to exhibit prosocial behavior at a later time (Yarrow, Scott, & Waxler, 1973).

Nondisciplinary Verbalizations

In general, children are more likely to share or donate with others if they hear an adult say that he or she is going to help. In addition, children tend to engage in more prosocial behavior if exposed to preachings from adults that are other-oriented in content (e.g., that point out the effects of assisting for another) and focus on the positive effects of prosocial action on others' emotional states (e.g., "They would be so happy and excited if they could buy food and toys. . ."). In general, preachings that are normative in content—that is, indicate that it is good or right to give—are less effective than preachings that emphasize the effects of prosocial behavior on others (Eisenberg & Fabes, 1998). Preachings also may be most effective if children feel that they have a choice of whether to assist. For example, McGrath, Wilson, and Frassetto (1995) found that adults' appeals enhanced donating if they referred to the peer-beneficiary in the appeal and if children did not feel forced to give. In addition, children were more generous if exposed to a message stating that the focus of the appeal (adult or child) would be happy if they donated rather than sad if they did not.

Reinforcement for Prosocial Behavior

Children often engage in prosocial behavior in the immediate situation if they receive material rewards or social reinforcements (e.g., praise) for doing so. However, concrete rewards do not seem to enhance prosocial tendencies outside of the rewarded context (Fabes et al., 1989). Furthermore, the effects of praise seem to vary with type of praise and age of the recipient (Eisenberg & Fabes, 1998; also see Eisenberg et al., 1993). Praise that attributes the child's positive behavior in his or her dispositional kindness or internal motives (e.g., "I guess you're the kind of person who likes to help others whenever you can. Yes, you are a very nice and helpful person") seems to be more effective than praise that simply labels the act as positive or good, particularly for children aged 8 and older who have a firm understanding of the consistency of personality (e.g., Grusec & Redler, 1980). In addition, social reinforcement for prosocial actions (without an internal attribution) increases elementary school children's prosocial behavior in the immediate context and, for older elementary school children, is associated with more prosocial behavior in a new situation. Grusec and Redler (1980) hypothesized that older children may interpret reinforcement for a specific action (e.g., "It was good that you gave some of your marbles to the poor children. Yes, that was a nice and helpful thing to do") as having implications for a variety of situations, whereas younger children do not view praise for a given act as having broader relevance.

Learning by Doing

Children who are induced to engage in prosocial behavior without feeling forced to do so seem to be relatively prosocial in other contexts (e.g., Eisenberg, Cialdini, McCreath, & Shell, 1987). In addition, the assignment of chores that have positive consequences for others has been linked to prosocial proclivities in children. Thus, practice in assisting others seems to foster prosocial tendencies, at least in some circumstances (Eisenberg & Fabes, 1998). It is possible that children who behave prosocially come to think of themselves as helpful people, although evidence for this explanation is mixed (Eisenberg et al., 1987; Eisenberg & Fabes, 1998). In addition, by engaging in prosocial actions children may learn new helping behaviors, may develop feelings of efficacy in regard to assisting others, and may discover that there are empathic rewards when one improves the state of another.

Parental Emphasis on Prosocial Values

As would be expected, parents who hold and try to teach prosocial values to their children tend to have children who are relatively kind and helpful (e.g., Hoffman, 1975a; Eisenberg & Fabes, 1998). One of the more dramatic pieces of evidence for this assertion comes from studies of people who have exhibited unusual tendencies toward altruism. For example, rescuers in Nazi Europe often recalled learning values of caring from parents or from another very influential person in their lives. Rescuers also reported that their parents felt that ethical values were universal—that is, were to be extended to all human beings. Interestingly, rescuers did not differ from nonrescuers in reported exposure to nonprosocial values such as honesty or equity, only in prosocial-relevant values (Oliner & Oliner, 1988).

Conflict in the Home

Conflict in the family seems to play a role in children's prosocial behavior, albeit in a complex manner. Conflict has been correlated with prosocial behavior toward family members, such as parents and siblings, particularly if conflict is frequent and physical in nature (Cummings, Zahn-Waxler, & Radke-Yarrow, 1981, 1984). However, conflict is also associated with problem behaviors and emotional dysregulation in children (Davies & Cummings, 1994). Moreover, in general, reports and displays of maternal anger and externalizing emotion have been associated with low levels of peer-directed prosocial behavior, low sympathy, and high levels of personal distress (see Eisenberg & Fabes, 1998). Eisenberg and Fabes (1998) noted that this apparently discrepant pattern of findings can be interpreted in a meaningful way if exposure to adult conflict is viewed as undermining children's emotional security, inducing distress, and evoking coping responses from the child calculated to minimize the stress in the child's social environment (see Davies & Cummings, 1994). Children frequently cannot readily escape from conflict in the home; thus, they often may attempt to alleviate their distress by intervening and comforting family members. However, children exposed to high intensity or ongoing anger may tend to become overaroused when exposed to others' negative emotions and experience self-focused personal distress as a consequence. If this is true, children would be expected to try to escape from dealing with others' distress if possible. In brief, it appears that exposure to high levels of anger and conflict may elicit attempts by children to minimize self-related negative emotional and physical consequences of conflict but undermines the capacity for sympathy or other-oriented (rather than self-oriented) prosocial behavior.

Summary

The constellation of socializers' practices, beliefs, and characteristics, as well as the emotional atmosphere of the home, seems to be related to children's prosocial development. Parents who are supportive; use inductive discipline; provide opportunities for prosocial activity; model, value, and preach other-oriented behavior; uphold high standards for their children; and encourage the development of sympathy and perspective taking are most likely to rear prosocial children. Moreover, practices that help children manage their own negative emotion and parental provision of an emotionally positive home environment seem to be related to the development of prosocial and sympathetic responding. However, most researchers studying socialization correlates of prosocial responding have not adequately considered the role of the child's characteristics (e.g., compliance, temperament) in the socialization process. It is likely that children's personality and temperament interact with parental characteristics and beliefs in determining the quality of the parent-child relationship and parental socialization efforts.

An important question for future research on prosocial tendencies is one raised by His Holiness during the discussion at the conference. As noted previously, he argued that children are born loving and caring; he cited the fact that infants so easily become attached to their caregivers as evidence of the tendency toward caring. His Holiness further argued that it is the child's experience within the family and community that sometimes undermines this basic tendency toward caring. Some of the speakers at the conference, including me, argued that infants are born with the capacity for both caring and aggression and that it is not solely the environment that is responsible for the development of uncaring, aggressive, or hurtful behavior. Although the issue of whether humans are basically good or bad has been debated for centuries, it is possible for researchers to obtain data that address this issue. Initial research has shown that children aged 1 to 2 years sometimes exhibit prosocial behaviors and signs of empathy (e.g., Zahn-Waxler, Radke-Yarrow, Wagner, & Chapman, 1992); moreover, there is some evidence that genetic factors may play a role in young children's sympathy and prosocial behavior (Zahn-Waxler, Robinson, & Emde, 1992). Thus, an important goal for behavioral scientists is to determine the degree to which young children's positive tendencies co-occur with negative tendencies and how the social environment enhances or undermines the development of prosocial and antisocial tendencies.

In addition, relatively little is known about the ways in which parental socialization effects are modified or enhanced by socialization experiences with siblings, teachers, peers, and adults in community institutions. In a community of Buddhists, especially Tibetan Buddhists, it seems likely that community and family leaders, as well as the extended family, play an important role in socialization, especially teaching support for the prosocial virtues that are the core of Buddhism. The study of the transmission of values related to compassion and prosocial behavior in Buddhist communities perhaps could shed light on the layers of socialization that contribute to children's development, especially in traditional communities united by tradition and religion.

Of particular interest is research on how children learn to sympathize with, assist, and care about justice for groups of people outside of their own group. The tendency not to differentiate between ingroup members and those dissimilar to the self as targets of concern and caring behavior was an important difference between rescuers of Jews in Nazi Europe and their peers who were bystanders (Oliner & Oliner, 1988). Although children in traditional cultures appear to be relatively prosocial toward ingroup members, it is not at all clear that they are especially prosocial to people outside of their own group (see Eisenberg & Fabes, 1998). One wonders if the philosophical stance of Buddhism toward considering all living things as equally worthy of care and help (indeed, Buddhists are instructed to think that all people may have been their mother in a past life) actually influences the behavior and vicarious emotional responding of children toward people that are not part of the community and are not known. If it does, this would be very important information for socializers concerned with teaching children to care about the larger community of humankind.

As noted previously, most of the research reviewed in this chapter has involved middle-class children and mothers from Western societies, so the generalizability of the work to other populations and to socializers besides mothers is not known. One important outcome for me of my brief exposure to the Tibetan community in India and the ideas of the Dalai Lama was to stimulate thinking on how the development of compassion and altruism may vary in different cultures and subcultures. Socialization obviously is a complex and multifaceted process, and too little attention has been paid to cultural values and their implications for prosocial development. One hopes that a positive outcome of the shrinking world (in terms of travel and communication) is that there will be more communication and collaboration among social and behavioral scientists in various parts of the world. I have recently begun work on children's conflicts and their social and emotional development in Indonesia (with Dr. Sri Pidada), a culture with a much stronger emphasis on the group, collectivist values, and the avoidance of interpersonal conflict than in the mainstream culture of the United States. I hope that collaborations of this sort will serve to broaden our understanding of the role of culture in positive development.

ACKNOWLEDGEMENTS   Work on this chapter was supported by grants from the National Science Foundation (DBS-9208375) and the National Institute of Mental Health (1 R01 HH55052) and Research Scientist Development and

Research Scientist Awards from the National Institute of Mental Health (K02 MH00903 and K05 M801321). I would like to acknowledge the input of Richard A. Fabes, who collaborated with me on a number of studies discussed in this chapter.

REFERENCES

Barnett, M. A., Howard, J. A., King, L. M., & Dino, G. A. (1980). Antecedents of empathy: Retrospective accounts of early socialization. *Personality and Social Psychology Bulletin, 6*, 361–365.

Barnett, M. A., King, L. M., Howard, J. A., & Dino, G. A. (1980). Empathy in young children: Relation to parents' empathy, affection, and emphasis on the feelings of others. *Developmental Psychology, 16*, 243–244.

Barrett, D. E., & Yarrow, M. R. (1977). Prosocial behavior, social inferential ability, and assertiveness in young children. *Child Development, 48*, 475–481.

Batson, C. D. (1991). *The altruism question: Toward a social-psychological answer.* Hillsdale, NJ: Erlbaum.

Baumrind, D. (1971). Current patterns of parental authority. *Developmental Psychology Monographs, 4*, 1–103.

Bryant, B. K. (1987). Mental health, temperament, family, and friends: Perspectives on children's empathy and social perspective taking. In N. Eisenberg & J. Strayer (Eds.), *Empathy and its development* (pp. 245–270). Cambridge, UK: Cambridge University Press.

Buck, R. (1984). *The communication of emotion.* New York: Guilford Press.

Cassidy, J., Parke, R. D., Butkovsky, L., & Braungart, J. M. (1992). Family-peer connections: The roles of emotional expressiveness within the family and children's understanding of emotion. *Child Development, 63*, 603–618.

Cummings, E. M., Zahn-Waxler, C., & Radke-Yarrow, M. (1981). Young children's responses to expressions of anger and affection by others in the family. *Child Development, 52*, 1274–1282.

Cummings, E. M., Zahn-Waxler, C., & Radke-Yarrow, M. (1984). Developmental changes in children's reactions to anger in the home. *Journal of Child Psychology and Psychiatry, 25*, 63–74.

Davies, P. T., & Cummings, E. M. (1994). Marital conflict and child adjustment: An emotional security hypothesis. *Psychological Bulletin, 116*, 387–411.

Derryberry, D., & Rothbart, M. K. (1988). Arousal, affect, and attention as components of temperament. *Journal of Personality and Social Psychology, 55*, 958–966.

Dekovic, M., & Janssens, J. M. A. M. (1992). Parents' child-rearing style and children's sociometric status. *Developmental Psychology, 28*, 925–932.

Dix, T., & Grusec, J. E. (1983). Parental influence techniques: An attributional analysis. *Child Development, 54*, 645–652.

Dunn, J., Bretherton, I., & Munn, P. (1987). Conversations about feeling states between mothers and their young children. *Developmental Psychology, 23,* 132–139.

Eisenberg, N. (1992). *The caring child.* Harvard University Press.

Eisenberg, N., Cialdini, R., McCreath, H., & Shell, R. (1987). Consistency-based compliance: When and why do children become vulnerable? *Journal of Personality and Social Psychology, 52,* 1174–1181.

Eisenberg, N., Cumberland, A., & Spinrad, T. L. (1998). Parental socialization of emotion. *Pyschological Inquiry, 9,* 241–273.

Eisenberg, N., & Fabes, R. A. (1990). Empathy: Conceptualization, assessment, and relation to prosocial behavior. *Motivation and Emotion, 14,* 131–149.

Eisenberg, N., & Fabes, R. A. (1991). Prosocial behavior and empathy: A multi-method, developmental perspective. In P. Clark (Ed.), *Review of personality and social psychology* (Vol. 12, pp. 34–61). Newbury Park, CA: Sage.

Eisenberg, N., & Fabes, R. A. (1992). Emotion, regulation, the development of and social competence. In M. S. Clark (Ed.), *Review of personality and social psychology, Vol. 14. Emotion and social behavior* (pp. 119–150). Newbury Park, CA: Sage.

Eisenberg, N., & Fabes, R. A. (1994). Mothers' reactions to children's negative emotions: Relations to children's temperament and anger behavior. *Merrill-Palmer Quarterly, 40,* 138–156.

Eisenberg, N., & Fabes, R. A. (1995). The relation of young children's vicarious emotional responding to social competence, regulation, and emotionality. *Cognition and Emotion, 9,* 203–228.

Eisenberg, N., & Fabes, R. A. (1998). Prosocial development. In W. Damon (Series Ed.) & N. Eisenberg (Vol. Ed), *Handbook of child psychology: Vol. 3. Social, emotional, and personality development* (pp. 701–778); 5th ed., pp. 701–778). New York: Wiley.

Eisenberg, N., Fabes, R. A., Carlo, G., Speer, A. L., Switzer, G., Karbon, M., & Troyer, D. (1993). The relations of empathy-related emotions and maternal practices to children's comforting behavior. *Journal of Experimental Child Psychology, 55,* 131–150.

Eisenberg, N., Fabes, R. A., Carlo, G., Troyer, D., Speer, A. L., Karbon, M., & Switzer, G. (1992). The relations of maternal practices and characteristics to children's vicarious emotional responsiveness. *Child Development, 63,* 583–602.

Eisenberg, N., Fabes, R. A., Karbon, M., Murphy, B. C., Wosinski, M., Polazzi, L., Carlo, G., & Juhnke, C. (1996). The relations of children's dispositional prosocial behavior to emotionality, regulation, and social functioning. *Child Development, 67,* 974–992.

Eisenberg, N., Fabes, R. A., Miller, P. A., Fultz, J., Mathy, R. M., Shell, R., & Reno, R. R. (1989). The relations of sympathy and personal distress to prosocial behavior: A multimethod study. *Journal of Personality and Social Psychology, 57,* 55–66.

Eisenberg, N., Fabes, R. A., Murphy, B., Karbon, M., Maszk, P., Smith, M., O'Boyle, C., & Suh, K. (1994). The relations of emotionality and regulation to dispositional and situational empathy-related responding. *Journal of Personality and Social Psychology, 66,* 776–797.

Eisenberg, N., Fabes, R. A., Murphy, B., Karbon, M., Smith, M., & Maszk, P. (1996). The relations of children's dispositional empathy-related responding to their emotionality, regulation, and social functioning. *Developmental Psychology, 32,* 195–209.

Eisenberg, N., Fabes, R. A., Schaller, M., Miller, P. A., Carlo, G., Poulin, R., Shea, C., & Shell, R. (1991). Personality and socialization correlates of vicarious emotional responding. *Journal of Personality and Social Psychology, 61,* 459–471.

Eisenberg, N., Fabes, R. A., Schaller, M., Carlo, G., & Miller, P. A. (1991). The relations of parental characteristics and practices to children's vicarious emotional responding. *Child Development, 62,* 1393–1408.

Eisenberg, N., Gershoff, E. T., Fabes, R. A., Shepard, S. A., Cumberland, A. J., Losoya, S. H., Guthrie, I. K., & Murphy, B. C. (2001). Mothers' emotional expressivity and children's behavior problems and social competence: Mediation through children's regulation. *Developmental Psychology, 37,* 475–490.

Eisenberg, N., & Lennon, R. (1983). Gender differences in empathy and related capacities. *Psychological Bulletin, 94,* 100–131.

Eisenberg, N., Liew, J., & Pidada, S. (in press). The relations of parental emotional expressivity with the quality of Indonesian children's social functioning. *Emotion.*

Eisenberg, N., & McNally, S. (1993). Socialization and mothers' and adolescents' empathy-related characteristics. *Journal of Research on Adolescence, 3,* 171–191.

Eisenberg, N., & Miller, P. (1987). The relation of empathy to prosocial and related behaviors. *Psychological Bulletin, 101,* 91–119.

Eisenberg, N., & Okun, M. A. (1996). The relations of dispositional regulation and emotionality to elders' empathy-related responding and affect while volunteering. *Journal of Personality, 64,* 157–183.

Eisenberg, N., Schaller, M., Fabes, R. A., Bustamante, D., Mathy, R., Shell, R., & Rhodes, K. (1988). The differentiation of personal distress and sympathy in children and adults. *Developmental Psychology, 24,* 766–775.

Eisenberg, N., Wentzel, M., & Harris, J. D. (1998). The role of emotionality and regulation in empathy-related responding. *School Psychology Review, 27,* 506–521 (invited article).

Eisenberg-Berg, N., & Mussen P. (1978). Empathy and moral development in adolescence. *Developmental Psychology, 14,* 185–186.

Fabes, R. A., Eisenberg, N., & Eisenbud, L. (1993). Behavioral and physiological correlates of children's reactions to others' distress. *Developmental Psychology, 29,* 655–663.

Fabes, R. A., Eisenberg, N., Karbon, M., Bernzweig, J., Speer, A. L., & Carlo, G. (1994) Socialization of children's vicarious emotional responding and prosocial behavior: Relations with mothers' perceptions of children's emotional reactivity. *Developmental Psychology, 30*, 44–55.

Fabes, R. A., Eisenberg, N., & Miller, P. (1990). Maternal correlates of children's vicarious emotional responsiveness. *Developmental Psychology, 26*, 639–648.

Fabes, R. A., Fultz, J., Eisenberg, N., May-Plumlee, T., & Christopher, F., S. (1989). The effects of reward on children's prosocial motivation: A socialization study. *Developmental Psychology, 25*, 509–515.

Feshbach, N. D. (1978). Studies of empathic behavior in children. In B. A. Maher (Ed.), *Progress in experimental personality research* (Vol. 8, pp. 1–47). New York: Academic Press.

Feshbach, N. D. (1987). Parental empathy and child adjustment/maladjustment. In N. Eisenberg & J. Strayer (Eds.), *Empathy and its development* (pp. 271–291). New York: Cambridge University Press.

George, C., & Main, M. (1979). Social interactions of young abused children: Approach, avoidance, and aggression. *Child Development, 50*, 306–318.

Gottman, J. M., Katz, L. F., & Hooven, C. (1996). Parental meta-emotion philosophy and the emotional life of families: Theoretical models and preliminary data. *Journal of Family Psychology, 10*, 243–268.

Grusec, J. E., & Redler, E. (1980). Attribution, reinforcement, and altruism: A developmental analysis. *Developmental Psychology, 16*, 525–534.

Halberstadt, A. G. (1986). Family socialization of emotional expression and nonverbal communication styles and skills. *Journal of Personality and Social Psychology, 51*, 827–836.

Halberstadt, A. G., Crisp, V. W., & Eaton, K. L. (1999). Family expressiveness: A retrospective and new directions for research. In P. Philippot, R. S. Feldman, & E. Coats (Eds.), *The social context of nonverbal behavior* (pp. 109–155) New York: Cambridge University Press.

Hardy, D. F., Power, T. G., & Jaedicke, S. (1993). Examining the relation of parenting to children's coping with everyday stress. *Child Development, 64*, 1829–1841.

Hastings, P. D., Zahn-Waxler, C., Robinson, J., Usher, B., and Bridges, D. (2000). The development of concern for others in children with behavior problems. *Developmental Psychology, 36*, 531–546.

Hoffman, M. L. (1970). Moral development. In P. H. Mussen (Ed.), *Carmichael's manual of child development* (Vol. 2, pp. 261–359). New York: Wiley.

Hoffman, M. L. (1975a). Altruistic behavior and the parent-child relationship. *Journal of Personality and Social Psychology, 31*, 937–943.

Hoffman, M. L. (1975b). Developmental synthesis of affect and cognition and its implications for altruistic motivation. *Developmental Psychology, 11*, 607–622.

Hoffman, M. L. (1982). Development of prosocial motivation: Empathy and guilt. In N. Eisenberg (Ed.), *The development of prosocial behavior* (pp. 281–313). New York: Academic Press.

Hoffman, M. L. (1983). Affective and cognitive processes in moral internalization. In E. T. Higgins, D. N. Ruble, & W. W. Hartup (Eds.), *Social cognition and social development: A sociocultural perspective* (pp. 236–274). Cambridge, MA: Cambridge University Press.

Hoffman, M. L. (2000). *Empathy and moral development: Implications for caring and justice*. Cambridge: Cambridge University Press.

Howes, C., & Eldredge, R. (1985). Responses of abused, neglected, and nonmaltreated children to the behaviors of their peers. *Journal of Applied Developmental Psychology, 6*, 261–270.

Hume, D. (1966). *Enquiries concerning the human understanding and concerning the principles of morals* (2nd ed). Oxford, England: Clarendon Press. (Originally published, 1777.)

Iannotti, R. J., Cummings, E. M., Pierrehumbert, B., Milano, M. J., & Zahn-Waxler, C. (1992). Parental influences on prosocial behavior and empathy in early childhood. In J. M. A. M. Janssens & J. R. M. Gerris (Eds.), *Child rearing: Influence on prosocial and moral development* (pp. 77–100). Amsterdam: Swets & Zeitlinger.

Janssens, J. M. A. M., & Dekovic, M. (1997). Child rearing, prosocial moral reasoning, and prosocial behavior. *International Journal of Behavioral Development, 20*, 509–527.

Janssens, J. M. A. M., & Gerris, J. R. M. (1992). Child rearing, empathy and prosocial development. In J. M. A. M. Janssens & J. R. M. Gerris (Eds.), *Child rearing: Influence on prosocial and moral development* (pp. 57–75). Amsterdam: Swets & Zeitlinger.

Kalliopuska, M. (1984). Relation between children's and parents' empathy. *Psychological Reports, 54*, 295–299.

Kestenbaum, R., Farber, E. A., & Sroufe, L. A. (1989). Individual differences in empathy among preschoolers: Relation to attachment history. *New Directions in Child Development, 44*, 51–64.

Krevans, J., & Gibbs, J. C. (1996). Parents' use of inductive discipline: Relations to children's empathy and prosocial behavior. *Child Development, 67*, 3263–3277.

Larsen, R. J., & Diener, E. (1987). Affect intensity as an individual difference characteristic: A review. *Journal of Research in Personality, 21*, 1–39.

Lazarus, R. S., & Folkman, S. (1984). *Stress, appraisal, and coping* (pp. 282–325). New York: Springer.

Lenrow, R. B. (1965). Studies of sympathy. In S. S. Tompkins & Izard, C. E. (Eds.), *Affect, cognition, and personality* (pp. 264–294). New York: Springer.

Main, M., & George, C. (1985). Responses of abused and disadvantaged toddlers to distress in agemates: A study in the day care setting. *Developmental Psychology, 21*, 407–412.

Malatesta, C. Z., & Haviland, J. M. (1985). Signals, symbols, and socialization: The modification of emotional expression in human development. In M. Lewis & C. Saarni (Eds.), *The socialization of emotions* (pp. 89–116). New York: Plenum.

Matthews, K. A., Batson, C. D., Horn, J., & Rosenman, R. H. (1981). Principles in his nature which interest him in the fortune of others: The heritability of empathic concern for others. *Journal of Personality, 49,* 237–247.

McGrath, M. P., Wilson, S. R., & Frassetto, S. J. (1995). Why some forms of induction are better than others at encouraging prosocial behavior. *Merrill-Palmer Quarterly, 41,* 347–360.

Miller, P., & Eisenberg, N. (1988). The relation of empathy to aggression and externalizing/antisocial behavior. *Psychological Bulletin, 103,* 324–344.

Miller, P. A., Eisenberg, N., Fabes, R. A., Shell, R., & Gular, S. (1989). Socialization of empathic and sympathetic responding. In N. Eisenberg (Ed.), The development of empathy and related vicarious responses. *New Directions in Child Development* (pp. 65–83). San Francisco: Jossey-Bass.

Moore, B., & Eisenberg, N. (1984). The development of altruism. In G. Whitehurst (Ed.), *Annuals in child development*, Vol. 1 (pp. 107–174). New York: JSI Press.

Oliner, S. P. & Oliner, P. M. (1988). *The altruistic personality: Rescuers of Jews in Nazi Europe.* New York: Free Press.

Peterson, L. (1983). Influence of age, task competence, and responsibility focus on children's altruism. *Developmental Psychology, 19,* 141–148.

Plomin, R., & Stocker, C. (1989). Behavioral genetics and emotionality. In J. S. Reznick (Ed.), *Perspectives on behavioral inhibition* (pp. 219–240). Chicago: Chicago University Press.

Pratt, M. W., Arnold, M. L., Pratt, A. T., & Diessner, R. (1999). Predicting adolescent moral reasoning from family climate: A longitudinal study. *Journal of Early Adolescence, 10,* 148–175.

Quintos, L. (1977). *The moral system of Buddhism.* Manila: Cardinal Bea Institute.

Radke-Yarrow, M., Zahn-Waxler, C., & Chapman, M. (1983). Prosocial dispositions and behavior. In P. Mussen (Series Ed.), *Manual of child psychology: Vol. 4. Socialization, personality, and social development* (pp. 469–545); E. M. Hetherington, Volume Ed.). New York: Wiley.

Roberts, W., & Strayer, J. (1987). Parents' responses to the emotional distress of their children: Relations with children's competence. *Developmental Psychology, 23,* 415–432.

Rushton, J. P., Fulker, D. W., Neal, M. C., Nias, D. K. B., & Eysenck, H. J. (1986). Altruism and aggression: The heritability of individual differences. *Journal of Personality and Social Psychology, 50,* 1192–1198.

Saddhatissa, H. (1971). *Buddhist ethics.* New York: Braziller.

Smith, C. L., Gelfand, D. M., Hartmann, D. P., & Partlow, M. E. Y. (1979). Children's causal attributions regarding help giving. *Child Development, 50,* 203–210.

Stanhope, L., Bell, R. Q., & Parker-Cohen, N. Y. (1987). Temperament and helping behavior in preschool children. *Developmental Psychology, 23,* 347–353.

Staub, E. (1979). *Positive social behavior and morality: Vol 2: Socialization and development.* New York: Academic Press.

Strayer, J. (1993). Children's concordant emotions and cognitions in response to observed emotions. *Child Development, 64,* 188–201.

Strayer, J., & Roberts, W. (1989). Children's empathy and role taking: Child and parental factors, and relations to prosocial behavior. *Journal of Applied Developmental Psychology, 10,* 227–239.

Tachibana, S. (1975).*The ethics of Buddhism.* London: Oxford University Press.

Tomkins, S. S. (1963). *Affect, imagery, consciousness. Vol. 2 Negative affects.* New York: Springer.

Trommsdorff, G. (1991). Child-rearing and children's empathy.*Perceptual Motor Skills, 72,* 387–390.

Underwood, B., & Moore, B. S. (1982). Perspective-taking and altruism. *Psychological Bulletin, 91,* 143–173.

Ungerer, J. A., Dolby, R., Waters, B., Barnett, B., Kelk, N., & Lewin, V. (1990). The early development of empathy: Self-regulation and individual differences in the first year. *Motivation and Emotion, 14,* 93–106.

Waters, E., Wippman, J., & Sroufe, L. A. (1979). Attachment, positive affect, and competence in the peer group: Two studies in construct validation. *Child Development, 50,* 821–829.

Wood, J. V., Saltzberg, J. A., & Goldsamt, L. A. (1990). Does affect induce self-focused attention? *Journal of Personality and Social Psychology, 58,* 899–908.

Yarrow, M. R., Scott, P. M., & Waxler, C. Z. (1973). Learning concern for others. *Developmental Psychology, 8,* 240–260.

Zahn-Waxler, C., Radke-Yarrow, M., & King, R. A. (1979). Child rearing and children's prosocial initiations toward victims of distress. *Child Development, 50,* 319–330.

Zahn-Waxler, C., Robinson, J., & Emde, R. N. (1992). The development of empathy in twins. *Developmental Psychology, 28,* 1038–1047.

Zahn-Waxler, Radke-Yarrow, Wagner, E., & Chapman, M. (1992). Development of concern for others. *Developmental Psychology, 28,* 126–136.

8

Emergency Helping, Genocidal Violence, and the
Evolution of Responsibility and Altruism in Children

ERVIN STAUB

In this chapter I will describe three interconnected areas of theory and research. The first part of the chapter examines what leads people to help
others rather than remain passive when somebody is suddenly in pain or
danger. The second part looks at what leads groups to turn against other
groups in genocidal violence. What are the cultural, societal, and psychological origins of such extreme violence? The third part considers
ways of raising caring and nonviolent children, who are more likely to
help others in emergencies and less likely to participate in, or remain passive bystanders to, genocidal violence.

Helping and Passivity in Emergencies

The first domain of work has been referred to as research on bystanders
in emergencies. The social psychologists who initiated this research (Latane & Darley, 1970) responded to the highly publicized murder of Kitty
Genovese. Kitty Genovese was on her way home from work in the middle of the night in Queens, New York, when she was attacked by a man.

In response to her cries for help people in adjoining buildings turned on lights—someone even shouted out the window "leave that woman alone"—but 38 witnesses in adjoining buildings did nothing more. The attacker fled, returned again, fled one more time, and then finally killed Kitty Genovese. Only one person called the police after it was all over, first calling his attorney to make sure that he was not legally liable.

As I define the term, bystanders are simply people who witness events. They can remain passive or respond and take action. The passivity of bystanders in situations like the murder of Kitty Genovese was first interpreted as the result of the callousness of life in a big city. However, the line of research initiated by Latane and Darley and continued by other researchers showed that many influences effect whether people help someone in such an emergency or remain passive (Myers, 1999).

Some of these influences are situational. Latane and Darley (1970) found that the greater the number of witnesses who are present, or who are believed by those present to be able to hear or see another's distress, the less likely it is that any one person will help. Other reseachers found that the clearer the need is, the less ambiguous the situation, the more likely that people will help. For example, when someone who is in distress calls out for help, helping increases (for reviews see Staub, 1978; Piliavin, Dividio, Goertner, & Clark, 1981). The competencies and roles of other witnesses also affect helping. For example, when people believe that one of the witnesses is a doctor, they are less likely to initiate action to help a person in physical distress (See Staub, 1978).

Latane and Darley proposed two primary explanations for bystander passivity in emergencies. Their concept of pluralistic ignorance suggested that people in public places tend to hide their emotions. As a result, they show little visible reaction to the sights and sounds of someone else's need or distress. As each bystander looks around and sees that others show no concern, each assumes that there is no serious need and no reason to act. In a rare study that found greater helping by pairs of bystanders than by an alone bystander, when pairs of kindergarten and first-grade children heard a crash and sounds of distress from another room, they reacted. They talked to each other, and influenced each other to act (Staub, 1970b). By fourth grade, children in pairs helped less than children who heard the distress sounds alone.

Latane and Darley's second primary explanation was diffusion of responsibility. When other people are present, each person feels less responsible to help and also less concerned about being blamed for not helping. A third presumed inhibitor of helping is fear of disapproval. In public situations, in the presence of others, people are concerned about acting inappropriately, about the negative reactions that may follow from other people.

Another way to describe what tends to happen in such situations is that the circumstances and the behavior of other people define the meaning of events as well as appropriate action. For example, in one of my studies (Staub, 1974), two people heard sounds of distress from another room. One of them was a participant in the experiment, another a confederate. In one experimental condition when there was a crash and sounds of distress coming from another room, the confederate said, "that sounds bad, maybe we should do something," but remained seated. In another condition, she said, "I don't know what that is but it probably has nothing to do with us. Maybe it's part of another experiment." In a third situation, she said, "That sounds bad, maybe we should do something," and then got up and said "You go in, I'll go and find the experimenter." How this person defined the meaning of the situation and the appropriate action greatly affected the other person's behavior. In the last situation, every person attempted to help by going into the other room. When she defined the distress sounds as irrelevant, only a third of the participants went into the another room. When she said help was needed but did nothing, two thirds of the participants attempted to help.

The responsibility can be diffused or it can be focused on a person. Being alone itself focuses responsibility. In one of our studies with young children, an adult verbally focused responsibility on some children, but not on others (Staub, 1970a). Each child was alone working on a drawing. Before the adult left the room, she told the child that there was another child in the adjoining room. When responsibility was focused on the child, the adult told the child that he or she is "in charge," in case anything happened. Each child later heard a crash and sounds of distress from the adjoining room. Kindergarteners did not help more when responsibility was focused on them, but a number of them plugged their ears with their fingers, which did not happen when responsibility was not focused on them. Apparently, feeling responsible but not ready to help, the distress sounds were more unpleasant, more distressful to them. In first grade, the children who were left in charge helped more.

In some of the research, we also found that overlearned social rules that guide everyday behavior can inhibit helping. In one study, we explored changes in helping with age (Staub, 1970b). Children heard distress sounds from an adjoining room either alone or in pairs. Helping increased from kindergarten to first and second grade, remained stable in fourth grade, and sharply declined by sixth grade to about the same level it was in kindergarten. This was surprising. As we engaged the older children in conversation, they expressed worry about the adult's reactions. It seemed that the sixth-grade children in our study have learned that stopping work on a task and going into a strange room in a strange environment were inappropriate behaviors. This inhibited them from helping.

To explore this further, in another study (Staub, 1971) children were either told that they can go into the other room if they needed more drawing pencils, that they were prohibited from going into the other room, or they received no information. The children who received permission to go into the other room helped substantially more than the children in the other two groups, who helped little. One of the girls who received permission listened to the distress sounds for a while, then broke the point of both of her drawing pencils and rushed into the other room.

So far I have focused on the influence of circumstances, age, and standards of behavior on helping. But the characteristics of people—who they are—greatly matters. Circumstances and personal characteristics jointly give rise to the thoughts, feelings, and psychological experiences that determine helping.

The theorizing and research about the influence of situations have suggested that the experience of responsibility may be crucial to helping or not helping. Research on personal characteristics supports this. In an early study, people who denied their responsibility for others' welfare were less likely to help in an emergency (Schwartz & Clausen, 1970). My associates and I found in a series of studies that a personal characteristic I came to call *prosocial value orientation* is strongly related to helping others, under a variety of conditions. Prosocial value orientation has three components: a positive evaluation of human beings, concern about others' welfare, and a feeling of personal responsibility for others' well-being.

Persons with a strong prosocial value orientation are more likely to help someone in either physical or psychological distress. In one study (Staub, 1974; Erkut, Jaquette & Staub, 1981), a participant in the study was alone in a room, working on a task, when there were sounds of distress coming from another room. If the participant did not enter the other room in response to the distress sounds, our confederate, who was in that room, came into the room where the participant was working. He lay down on the sofa, still in pain. The stronger the participants' prosocial value orientation, the more likely they were to initiate help by entering the other room. They were also more likely to agree to go to Harvard Square to fill a prescription, rather than call the distressed person's roommate, which would have resulted in much longer delay before the person in pain has received the necessary medication. In two other studies (Feinberg, 1978; Grodman, 1979; see Staub, 1978), persons with stronger prosocial orientations responded more helpfully to someone in psychological distress, (someone upset about something that has happened in his or her life).

Self-interest can also motivate people to help others; people may want approval or material gain through reciprocation, since reciprocity is a very strong and apparently universal norm of behavior (Staub, 1978). People can also help others for *moral reasons*, guided by their belief in norms and principles like justice or social responsibility, which prescribe helping people in need. When such moral principles lead to helping, the relationship is primarily between the actor and the principle, rather than the actor and a person in need or a person whose welfare would increase as a result of helping.

Empathy or sympathy, feeling others' pain and distress, also motivates people to help. As the chapter by Eisenberg (Chapter 7) in this book shows, when people respond with personal distress to someone else's distress, rather than with "other-oriented" empathy or sympathy, they will only help when escape from the presence of another person's need is difficult. However, feelings of empathy that are other-oriented, or sympathy with a person who suffers, include concern about the welfare of another that leads to a desire to help.

One of my studies suggests, however, that a feeling of responsibility added to empathy or caring further enhances helping. In a survey study, 7,000 people returned a questionnaire published in the magazine *Psychology Today* (Staub, 1991a). The questionnaire assessed empathy, "rule orientation," prosocial orientation, and a variety of forms of helping. The strongest association was between prosocial value orientation and helping (Staub, 1991b). I see prosocial value orientation as based on empathy, but added to empathy is the feeling of personal responsibility, which would lead people not only to feel with and care about others, but to act on that feeling. This is further supported by research on rescuers of Jews in Nazi Europe, people who endangered their lives to save the lives of Jews destined to be murdered. Some rescuers were primarily characterized by empathy, others by moral principles, but the largest percentage had characteristics that can best be identified as prosocial value orientation (Oliner & Oliner, 1988).

Other research also shows the importance of responsibility. Kohlberg and Candee (1984) described responsibility as an aspect of moral reasoning that can be present not only at the highest levels of reasoning that Kohlberg (1969) identified, Kohlberg's stages five and six, but also at lower levels, at stages three and four. Kohlberg had shown that persons with high levels of moral reasoning are less likely to fully obey the instructions given in Milgram's obedience research, in which the person in charge, the experimenter, tells subjects to administer increasingly intense electric shocks to another person. Subjects were told that this is ostensibly a part of an instructional procedure, the shock levels to be increased by the "teacher" when the "learner" makes a mistake. The reexamination of the research finding shows that resistance or disobedience occurs not as a function of the level of moral reasoning, but as a function of a feeling of responsibility. People who feel more personally responsible obey less.

Feelings of responsibility make it more likely that people help others who need help. Relinquishing resposibility for others' welfare is one of the psychological processes that enables people to harm others.

Genocide: Harming, Responsibility, and Evolution

In genocidal violence responsibility for members of the victims group is relinquished by perpetrators, and very frequently by bystanders as well. How does the motivation to harm and even to kill whole groups of other people arise? How do inhibitions that normally keep people from killing, including the feeling of responsibility, decline and disappear? The conception that I describe here has been supported by the analysis of a number of instances of genocides and mass killings, including the Holocaust, the genocide of the Armenians in Turkey, the autogenocide in Cambodia, and the disappearances in Argentina (Staub, 1989a). It is also applicable to other instances, such as the mass killings in Bosnia (Staub, 1996b), and the genocide in Rwanda (Staub, 1999).

Genocidal violence very frequently begins with extremely difficult life conditions in a society. There may be persistent economic problems, or intense and persistent political conflict, or rapid and very great social change. Most often there is a combination of these. Difficult life conditions activate basic needs that all human beings possess (Staub, 1989b, 1996b). One of these is the need for security, for believing that one's body will be safe from harm and that one will be able to find food and shelter for oneself and one's family. Another need is to have a positive identity. A further need is for effectiveness and control. All these needs are deeply frustrated by the difficulties of life and the social disorganization inherent in them.

Still another need is for comprehension of reality. In the chaos and disorganization that can take place in the midst of severe economic and political problems, people's world views become ineffective in understanding reality. They will turn to anything that offers them comprehension of the world and their own place in it. Connections between people, another basic need, are also weakened, as people focus on themselves and their own needs at a time when support and connection are especially important.

People could satisfy these needs by creating a vision of how to solve problems, with different subgroups of society working together. However, the chaos, disorganization, and lack of understanding of why things are the way they are make this unlikely. Under difficult life conditions the tendency is to satisfy basic psychological needs in ways that lead groups of people to turn against other groups.

Members of the dominant group, often guided by their leaders, elevate their group by devaluing others. They identify some subgroup of society as responsible for their life problems. Such scapegoating satisfies several basic needs, although in destructive ways. It provides an "understanding" of why life problems exist, shifts responsibility for them away from the self and the group, and thereby helps protect the identity of group members, creates connection as members of the group join in turning against the scapegoated group, and offers a solution to the life problems by "dealing" with the scapegoat.

Almost invariably people turn to ideologies that offer an image of a better future. Ideologies also help fulfill basic needs. They offer a comprehensible reality as they provide a vision of how to live life. They offer a sense of significance to people as they work for the ideology's fulfillment. And the ideological movement creates intense connection among followers. Unfortunately, such ideologies almost invariably identify an enemy who has to be destroyed to fulfill the ideology. The ideologies that groups adopt or create in difficult times can be nationalistic, focusing on the better future of the group. Or they can focus on the better future of all humanity, what I call "better world" ideology. Communism is an example of a better world ideology; Serbian nationalism was a nationalistic ideology. But many such ideologies have both nationalistic and betterworld components.

Scapegoating and destructive ideologies are more likely to arise when the group's culture has certain characteristics. One of these is a history of devaluation of a subgroup of the society. Such devaluation is present in many groups, and it "preselects" the scapegoat or ideological enemy. Another important cultural characteristic is a strong respect for authority within the group. This makes it more difficult for people to stand on their own in difficult times, makes it more likely that they turn to new authorities, and makes it less likely that they resist these authorities when they lead them to harm others. Certain cultural self-concepts, a monolithic rather than pluralistic society, and a history of violence in dealing with conflicts between groups are other characteristics that make turning against others as a way of dealing with life problems more likely.

As a dominant group or a government turns against an identified victim, an evolution begins. As they harm other people, individuals and progressively the whole society change. Human beings have a tendency to believe that the world is a just place (Lerner, 1980), and guided by that tendency, they assume that people who suffer have somehow deserved their suffering, due to their bad actions or bad character. As a result, they tend to devalue people who suffer. Ironically, perpetrators devalue their own victims as they engage in such "just world" thinking.

These and other psychological processes can lead perpetrators to so profoundly devalue victims that they exclude them from the moral and human realm (Opotaw, 1990; Staub, 1998b). This makes extreme violence against them possible. This process includes relinquishing all responsibility for the welfare of the victims, and even a reversal of morality. The "higher" ideals of the ideology lead perpetrators to believe that their actions are morally right, that by their actions they serve their group, or even all of humanity. Many of them become fanatically committed to the destruction of their victims.

In the course of this evolution, the norm, standards and institutions of the society change. Frequently, the boundaries of the victim group expand. New victims are included. For example, in Nazi Germany, near the end of the war, the Nazis contemplated the killing of physically unattractive German prison inmates (Lifton, 1986). Additional motives can also enter the picture. Perpetrators begin to harm victims not only in fulfillment of the ideology, but also to fulfill personal motives of wealth, sexual gratification, or competition (des Forges, 1999).

Genocidal violence does not always start with difficult life conditions. Another important starting point is group conflict. Differences between subgroups of society develop over time in status and power. The experience of injustice and conflicts over power, privilege, and rights can be the starting point of an evolution toward genocidal violence. Conflict over territory or other tangible resources also may be a starting point. At times the way a group defines its self-interest can lead it to turn against others, for example, in order to develop land on which an indigenous group lives. And frequently past histories of conflict, antagonism, and violence make the flareup or renewed violence between ethnic or other groups probable. However, even in these instances most of the influences and conditions I described are present, such as histories of devaluation, ideological visions, and progressive evolution. In the case of protracted conflict, it may be mutual harmdoing that creates the evolution and leads to cycles of violence.

As the perpetrators become increasingly committed to their destructive course, only bystanders, witnesses who are not themselves members of the perpetrator group, can inhibit the escalation of violence. Unfortunately, both internal bystanders, members of the population, and external bystanders—outside groups and nations—frequently remain passive. Internal bystanders, who are themselves affected by the difficult life conditions, tend to focus on their own needs. They are also affected by cultural characteristics, like the devaluation of the victim group, which makes it more difficult and less likely that they will separate themselves from their group in order to oppose harming the victims.

The passivity of the bystanders affirms the actions of the perpetrators. They interpret bystander passivity as support. It also changes the bystanders themselves. It is very difficult to see others suffer, do nothing, and remain caring and empathic. In order to reduce their own empathic distress and feelings of guilt, bystanders who remain passive will progressively distance themselves from victims. Over time some of them even become perpetrators (Staub, 1989a).

Nonetheless some bystanders, a small minority, attempted to help Jews in Nazi Europe. As I noted, they had some of the same characteristics that I described as important for helping others in emergencies. In addition to beliefs in principles of morality, possessing empathy, or a prosocial value orientation, they also tended to make less differentiation between members of their ingroup and people outside the group, including Jews (Oliner & Oliner, 1988).

Many rescuers first acted in response to a request for help. Having agreed to help, perhaps in a limited way, in the course of helping they changed. In their case an evolution took place toward more caring and helping (Staub, 1989b; 1993). Limited helping made them more concerned about the welfare of others. Having agreed to hide some people for a day or two, they continued to hide them. Many rescuers, if they succeeded moving people they hid to a safer area, continued to look for opportunities to help persecuted Jews.

As I noted, external bystanders, groups and nations also tend to be passive. Unfortunately, historically nations have not regarded themselves as moral agents; they have not seen themselves as responsible for the welfare of people outside their own borders. They have defined their national interest in terms of power, wealth, and influence. There have been some changes in this in terms of new international conventions, but only limited change in action, as demonstrated, for example, in the incredible passivity of the international community in the face of the genocide in Rwanda (des Forges, 1999; Staub 1999).

In order to prevent genocidal violence (Staub, 1995a, 1999, 2000), the community of nations has to respond to the beginnings of human rights violations, wherever it occurs. This requires certain institutions, as well as the will to act. Early warning that systematic human rights violations are taking place is necessary. Such early warning must lead to response. What kinds of response? Strong communication that violence against a minority is unacceptable and will not be tolerated can make a significant difference. What might have happened in the case of Bosnia if, at the very beginning, the foreign ministers of the main powers as well as the nations surrounding the former Yugoslavia had come to the Serb leaders, communicating that such aggression will not be tolerated. Sanctions and boycotts can be important. The earlier the response, the earlier the sanctions take place, the more likely they will be effective. The further the escalation of violence has gone, the greater the commitment that usually develops among perpetrators to an ideology or a course of violent action, and the less likely that continued violence can be inhibited without force.

In addition to responding to human rights violations, the community of nations needs to create institutions and procedures to help groups with histories of antagonism heal their hostility. In many regions of the world, deep-seated hostility exists between groups of people. Without active attempts to heal such antagonism, periods of peace will be followed by periods of violence, as has happened in the former Yugoslavia, in Rwanda, in Burundi, among other places. The community of nations must also help groups of victims heal from their victimization. Understandably, survivors of past victimization tend to feel vulnerable, see the world as dangerous, and when threatened are more likely to become violent (Staub, 1998, 1999, 2000). To inhibit a continued cycle of violence, it is necessary to attend to the wounds they carry as a result of their past history of victimization.

To heal such wounds requires that people engage with what has happened to them, under supportive conditions. It requires that they reconnect with and regain trust in people (Staub, 1998, 2000; Staub & Pearlman, 2001). To heal histories of antagonism also requires, among other things, deep engagement and positive connection between groups of people (Staub, 1989b, 1995, 1999). To prevent genocide, as well as to create a caring world in which human welfare is enhanced, it is also necessary to raise children who are caring, nonviolent, and able to resist influences within their group that leads to violence against other groups.

Raising Caring and Nonviolent Children

How can we create inclusive caring, caring that goes beyond the boundaries of the group? How can we create caring that includes "critical loyalty" to the group, the ability and willingness to oppose policies and practices in one's group that are contrary to basic human values, or to the long-term interests of the group itself?

To raise caring children requires the satisfaction of the basic human needs I have briefly described. Love and affection, the nurture and care of children, and their experience of benevolence—all are cornerstones supporting the development of a caring disposition that is reflected in how children behave toward others. Such experiences make children feel valued. They contribute to a positive sense of self. They also lead children to trust and value other people. These are basic requirements for caring about others and their welfare.

In one interesting study (Yarrow & Scott, 1972), small groups of children were supervised on several occasions by either a warm and affectionate person, or the same person who was trained to act in an indifferent manner—not hostile, or negative, just indifferent. Later when these children observed scenes acted out for them with small "diorama" figures, they remembered the same amount of what they saw, but they remembered different contents. The children who were exposed to the warm and affectionate caretaker remembered more of the positive events and actions in the scenes acted out for them, but the children who were cared for by the indifferent person remembered more of the negative events and behaviors.

Affection is not enough. Children also need structure and guidance. External structure and guidance can become internal structure and self-guidance. One form of guidance is provided through rules, which define what is right and what is wrong, acceptable or not. However, as the research I described earlier showed, rules can become overly prohibitive, inhibiting helping. Socializers must communicate the values that underlie rules and the relative importance of different values. While orderliness may be a reasonable value, it seems less important than valuing the well-being of people.

Guidance can be provided by reasoning with children, explaining to them the rationale for rules, and specifically the consequences of their behavior for others (Hoffman, 1970). Considering how other people feel when one's actions have been harmful to them, or when one has acted in prosocial, helpful ways toward them, has a variety of consequences. It helps the child understand the inner world of the other, his or her feelings and thoughts. It helps children understand their own power in influencing others' welfare. It can thus contribute to both empathy and feelings of responsibility (Staub, 1979).

Structure and guidance also require discipline, which at times is necessary to lead children to act on the rules and values communicated to them. However, disciplinary practices ought not be hostile and punitive, but moderate enough to be consistent with love and affection. Hostility, the frequent use of physical punishment by parents, as well as permissiveness or lack of guidance contribute to aggressive behavior tendencies in children and youth (Dodge, 1993; Eron, Gentry, & Schlegel, 1994; Huesmann & Eron, 1984; Staub, 1996a, 1996b).

Learning by doing, by participation, is an essential avenue for becoming caring and helpful. In a number of experiments I had children participate in various forms of helping others. Children made toys for hospitalized children, or older children taught younger children. On the whole, children who participated in helping others were later more helpful in other contexts (Staub, 1979). Research indicates that meaningful participation in the life of the family, children having responsibilities that actually matter (Whiting & Whiting, 1975), also contribute to increased helping behavior. Not responding to others' needs represents a closing off of the self. Opening up to others, taking their perspective, considering their needs and responding to them all lead to a continued evolution and growth not only of helping, but also of the self.

At times to take positive action requires separating oneself from the current actions, practices, or policies of one's group, whether the group is a peer group or one's society. This is extremely difficult for people, since staying apart and opposing one's group or its other members can lead to ostracism. Such opposition, especially constructive opposition, represents moral courage. A continued loyalty to one's group must be guided by basic human values as well as commitment to the group's ultimate welfare. In recent research, we differentiated between blind and constructive patriotism (Staub, 1997) and developed measures that have enabled us to identify blind and constructive patriots (Schatz & Staub, 1996). Constructive patriots express the belief that the love of their group requires them to question and if necessary to criticize and oppose practices within their group.

Involving children in decision making—having them participate in making rules in schools and at home—is one important way to develop a critical consciousness. Ideally, making one's own evaluation of the meaning of events will lead to the practice of critical loyalty and constructive patriotism. As children consider the right or desirable rules for their classroom, they have to think about their own needs, the needs of others, including the teacher, and the requirements for learning in the classroom (Staub, 1995b). In the process of such participation, in the school or at home, they can learn to stand up for their beliefs.

The evolution of inclusive caring requires the experience of genuine engagement with members of other groups. It is not sufficient for groups of people to be part of the same life space. Engagement, connection, joint activities, and shared goals are required (Staub 1996a). One form of such interaction can be cooperative learning in the schools. In the course of such cooperative learning children can teach each other and learn from each other (Aronson, Stephan, Sikes, Blaney, & Snapp, 1978), in a framework of equality (Allport, 1954).

Education about others' culture, especially understanding how cultures develop in response to the life conditions a group has faced, can be valuable. As children come to understand why other groups may have developed in certain ways, they can come to the realization that their own group has also developed in response to the life circumstances it has faced. This can help them see that the practices and values of their own group are not the standard by which all other groups are to be judged. This kind of education can help them learn to accept differences between groups, as well as appreciate underlying basic commonalities among human beings.

As I have noted, children who have experienced hostility and abuse rather than love and affection, or little structure or guidance, are likely to become hostile and aggressive. Aggressive children frequently are also ineffective (Pepler & Slaby, 1994). They do not function well in school; neither are they connected to other social systems. Their orientation to self, to others, and to society are all affected.

Given harmful, damaging, abusive experiences in childhood, is transformation possible? What kind of tranformational experiences counteract a negative orientation to others and to oneself, and feelings of hostility? The research findings indicate that a loving and affectionate connection to even one person can limit or counteract much of the damage done by negative environments (Garmezy & Rutter, 1983). While "redemptive" experiences in childhood can be profoundly important, how can people who have become traumatized and hostile to others undergo transformation later in life? How can they learn to trust others?

I believe that human beings seek the constructive fulfillment of their basic needs. When need fulfillment has become destructive, special experiences are required to open them to the possibilities of positive connection, affirmation of the self, and a positive view of the world. As a person gets older, the positive transformation may require more intensive experiences of care and support, of connection and community. The creation of these experiences is a profound challenge in a world where too many children and adolescents are treated harshly by people and by the circumstances of their lives.

REFERENCES

Allport, G. W. (1954). *The Nature of Prejudice*. Reading, MA: Addison-Wesley.
Aronson, E., Stephan, C., Sikes, J., Blaney, N., & Snapp, M. (1978). *The Jigsaw Classroom*. Beverly Hills, CA: Sage Publications, Inc.
Des Forges, A. (1999). *Leave none to tell the story: Genocide in Rwanda*. New York: Human Rights Watch.
Dodge, K. A. (1993). Social cognitive mechanisms in the development of conduct disorder and depression. *Annual Review of Psychology*, 44, 559–584.
Erkut, S., Jaquette, D., & Staub, E. (1981). Moral judgment-situation interaction as a basis for predicting social behavior. *Journal of Personality*, 49, 1–44.
Eron, L. D., Gentry, J. H., & Schlegel, P. (Eds.) (1994). *Reason to hope: A psychosocial perspective on violence and youth*. Washington, DC: American Psychological Association.
Feinberg, J. K. (1978). *Anatomy of a helping situation: Some personality and situational determinants of helping in a conflict situation involving another's psychological distress*. Unpublished doctoral dissertation, University of Massachusetts, Amherst.

Garmezy, N., & Rutter, M. (1983). *Stress, Coping, and Development in Children*. New York: McGraw-Hill.

Grodman, S. M. (1979). *The role of personality and situational variables in responding to and helping an individual in psychological distress*. Unpublished doctoral dissertation, University of Massachusetts, Amherst.

Hoffman, M. L. (1970). Moral Development. In P. H. Mussen (Ed.), *Carmichael's Manual of Child Development*. New York: Wiley.

Heusmann, L. R. & Eron, L. D. (1984). Cognitive processes and the persistence of aggressive behavior. *Aggressive behavior, 10,* 243–251.

Huesmann, L. R., Eron, L. D., Lefkowitz, M. M., & Walder, L. O. (1984). Stability of aggression over time and generations. *Developmental Psychology, 20, 6,* 1120–1134.

Johnson, D. W., Maruyama, G., Johnson, R., Nelson, D., & Skon, L. (1981). The effects of cooperative, competitive and individualistic goal structures on achievement: A meta analysis. *Psychological Bulletin, 89,* 47–62.

Kohlberg, L. (1969). Stage and sequence: The cognitive-developmental approach to socialization. In D.Goslin (Ed.), *Handbook of Socialization Theory and Research*. Chicago: Rand McNally.

Kohlberg, L., & Candee, L. (1984). The relationship of moral judgment to moral action. In W. M. Kurtines, & J. L. Gewirtz (Eds.), *Morality, Moral Behavior, and Moral Development,* 52–73.

Latane, B., & Darley, J. (1970). *The Unresponsive Bystander: Why Doesn't He Help?* New York: Appleton-Crofts.

Lerner, M. (1980). *The Belief in a Just World: A Fundamental Delusion*. New York: Plenum Press.

Lifton, R. J. (1986). *The Nazi Doctors: Medical Killing and the Psychology of Genocide*. New York: Basic Books.

Myers, D. (1999). *Social Psychology*. New York: McGraw Hill.

Oliner, S. B., & Oliner, P. (1988). *The Altruistic Personality: Rescuers of Jews in Nazi Europe*. New York: Free Press.

Opotaw, S. (Ed.) (1990). Moral exclusion and injustice. *Journal of Social Issues, 46,* (1).

Pepler, D. J., & Slaby, R. G. (1994). Theoretical and developmental perspectives on youth and violence. In Eron, L. D., Gentry, J. H., & Schlegel, P. (Eds.) *Reason to Hope: A Psychosocial Perspective on Youth & Violence* (pp. 27–58). Washington, DC: American Psychological Association.

Piliavin, J. A., & Piliavin, I. M. (1972). Effect of blood on reactions to a victim. *Journal of Personality & Social Psychology, 23,* 353–362.

Piliavin, J. A., Dividio, J. F., Goertner, S .L., & Clark, R. D.(1981). *Emergency Intervention*. New York: Academic Press.

Schatz, R. T., & Staub, E. (1997). Manifestations of blind and constructive patriotism: Personality correlates and individual-group relations. In Bar-Tal, D., & Staub, E. (Eds.). *Patriotism in the Life of Individuals and Nations*. Chicago: Nelson Hall Publishers.

Schwartz, S. H., & Clausen, G. T. (1970). Responsibility norms and helping in an emergency. *Journal of Personality and Social Psychology, 16,* 299–310.

Staub, E. (1970a). A child in distress: The effects of focusing responsibility on children on their attempts to help. *Developmental Psychology, 2,* 152–154.

Staub, E. (1970b). A child in distress: The influence of age and number of witnesses on children's attempts to help. *Journal of Personality and Social Psychology, 14,* 130–140.

Staub, E. (1971). Helping a person in distress: The influence of implicit and explicit "rules" of conduct on children and adults. *Journal of Personality and social Psychology, 17,* 137–145.

Staub, E. (1974). Helping a distressed person: Social, personality and stimulus determinants. In L. Berkowitz (Ed.), *Advances in Experimental Social Psychology* (Vol. 7). New York: Academic Press.

Staub, E. (1978). *Positive Social Behavior and Morality: Social and Personal Influences* (Vol. 1). New York: Academic Press.

Staub, E. (1979). *Positive Social Behavior and Morality: Socialization and Development* (Vol. 1). New York: Academic Press.

Staub, E. (1989a). Steps along the continuum of destruction: The evolution of bystanders: German psychoanalysts and lessons for today. *Political Psychology, 10,* 39–53.

Staub, E. (1989b). *The Roots of Evil: The Origins of Genocide and Other Group Violence.* New York: Cambridge University Press.

Staub, E. (1991a, May). The power to help others. *Psychology Today.*

Staub, E. (1991b). Values and helping, Unpublished manuscript, University of Msssachusetts, Amherst, MA.

Staub, E. (1993). The psychology of bystanders, perpetrators and heroic helpers. *International Journal of Intercultural Relations, 17,* 315–341.

Staub, E. (1995a). Preventing genocide: Activating bystanders, helping victims and the creation of caring. In *The Problems of Genocide.* Boston: The Zoryan Institute.

Staub, E. (1995b). The caring schools project: A program to develop caring, helping, positive self-esteem and nonviolence. Unpublished manuscript, University of Massachusetts, Amherst.

Staub, E. (1997). Blind versus constructive patriotism: Moving from embeddedness in the group to critical loyalty and action. In Bar-Tal, D., & Staub, E. (eds.). *Patriotism in the Lives of Individuals and Nations.* Nelson Hall Publishers.

Staub, E. (1996a). Altruism and aggression in children and youth: Origins and cures. In Feldman, R. *The psychology of adversity.* Amherst: University of Massachusetts Press.

Staub, E. (1996b). The cultural-societal roots of violence: The examples of genocidal violence and contemporary youth violence in the United States. *American Psychologist, 51,* 117–132.

Staub, E. (1998). Breaking the cycle of genocidal violence: Healing and reconciliation. In J. Harvey (ed.). *Perspectives on loss: A sourcebook*, Philadelphia: Taylor and Francis.

Staub, E. (1999). The origins and prevention of genocide, mass killing, and other collective violence. *Peace and Conflict: Journal of Peace Psychology, 5* (4), 303–336.

Staub, E. (2000). Genocide and mass killing: Origins, prevention, healing, and reconciliation. *Political Psychology, 21* (2), 367–382.

Staub, E., & Pearlman, L. A. (2001). Healing, reconciliation and forgiving after genocide and other collective violence. *Forgiveness and Reconciliation*, Radnor, PA: Templeton Foundation Press.

Whiting, B. B., & Edwards, C. P. (1988). *Children of Different Worlds: The Formation of Social Behavior*. Cambridge: Massachusetts Press.

Whiting, B. B., & Whiting, J. W. M. (1975). *Children of Six Cultures: A Psychocultural Analysis*. Cambridge, MA: Harvard University Press.

Yarrow, M. R., & Scott, P. M. (1972). Limitations of nurturant and nonnurturant models. *Journal of Personality and Social Psychology, 8*, 240–261.

Yarrow, M. R., & Waxler, C. Z. (1976). Dimensions and correlates of prosocial behavior in young children. *Child Development, 47*, 118–125.

9

Altruism in Competitive Environments

ROBERT H. FRANK

In his autobiography, Russell Baker tells of his mother's relatives sitting around the kitchen table late at night during the Depression talking about the long-lost family fortune. Its existence had been discovered many years earlier by his grandfather—"Papa"—when he journeyed to England to investigate the family history. There, he learned they were descended from a "fabulously rich old Bishop of London back in the time of Marlborough and Queen Anne."

The bishop, it seems, had willed his fortune to his Virginia kin—that is, to Baker's forebears—but the inheritance somehow never made it across the Atlantic. Papa was told it had all "reverted to the Crown" and was now the property of the Empire. The family felt sure, however, that their rightful fortune had been embezzled by "British connivers."

By their account, the loss was substantial. "Probably a million dollars in today's money," as Russell's Uncle Allen put it. "More like fifty or sixty million," according to his Uncle Hal.

Young Russell, age eleven, was intoxicated by the erstwhile family riches. But his sister Doris, two years younger, was more tough-minded. As Baker tells it:

My excitement about the great lost fortune was dampened by Doris when, grousing one evening about having to sell magazines, I said, "If Mama's father had got the family fortune, I wouldn't have to work."

"You don't believe any of that baloney, do you?" she replied.

I quit believing it then and there. No nine-year-old girl was going to beat me at skepticism.

Like young Baker, most Western behavioral scientists deeply fear being considered naive by their peers. They feel uneasy, for example, when called on to explain why a dentist serves without pay on the board of directors of a local charity. Perhaps he volunteers out of pure generosity of spirit, but worldly scholars are often reluctant to speak of such motives. They feel on much firmer ground when they imagine that the dentist hopes to win favorable attention, thereby to lure, in time, more teeth to extract. And sure enough, when we examine membership lists of Rotary Clubs and other "service" organizations, we find a surfeit of dentists, lawyers, insurance agents, and others with something to sell, but not many postal employees or airline pilots.

The self-interest model has served Western behavioral scientists well. It helps explain, for example, why divorce rates are higher in states that offer liberal welfare benefits; why manual transmissions now have four or five forward speeds instead of only three; why paper towels are replacing electric hand driers in public restrooms; and so on.

And yet the plain fact is that many people do not fit the me-first caricature. They give anonymously to public television stations and private charities. They donate bone marrow to strangers with leukemia. They endure great trouble and expense to see justice done, even when it will not undo the original injury. At great risk to themselves, they pull people from burning buildings and jump into icy rivers to rescue people who are about to drown. Soldiers throw their bodies atop live grenades to save their comrades. Seen through the lens of modern self-interest theory, such behavior is the human equivalent of planets traveling in square orbits.

Economists, philosophers, biologists, and others have invested much effort trying to account for such behavior. I will try to illustrate the thinking that has developed from these efforts in the context of a simple example—the custom of leaving a tip after restaurant meals.

What is the purpose of this custom? Why not simply add an equivalent amount to the waiter's paycheck and ask that he provide good service in return for his fair compensation? Perhaps the difficulty is that if the waiter knew the tip would *automatically* be included in his paycheck, his selfish tendencies might get the better of him. Thus, if the owner of the restaurant were off the premises, the waiter might provide slow, inattentive service—since that is presumably easier than providing fast, attentive service. If so, the diner wouldn't get the satisfying package he was willing to pay for and would be more likely to dine at home.

A tip seems like a natural solution to this incentive problem. In effect, it says to the diner, "we're going to reduce the price of your meal by a little bit and, at the end of the meal, if you're happy with the service you received, then you should give the waiter a small tip—let's say 15 percent, which happens to be the standard figure in the United States. So, the tipping custom is announced and customers find that it does indeed result in better service. Under competitive pressure, other restaurants begin to copy this practice because it seems to work so well.

Now we confront the first difficult question. If the tip comes at the end of the meal, as it usually does, why doesn't the diner renege? Having *already* received good service, why not just pay his bill and leave? This is the response that Darwin's theory of evolution by natural selection appears to predict. According to Darwin, motives and behavior are shaped by the organism's need to acquire the resources needed for survival and reproduction. Given the intensity of competition for these resources, the theory predicts that if an opportunity arises to acquire additional resources without penalty, organisms will seize it. Failure to tip seems to constitute just such an opportunity.

A recent theoretical development—Robert Axelrod's and William Hamilton's tit-for-tat theory of the evolution of cooperation—suggests a possible answer. Tit-for-tat theory is a theory of how cooperation develops when people interact together repeatedly. Many meals are eaten in restaurants in which patronage occurs on a regular, ongoing basis. In such cases, the incentives that confront waiters and diners are much like those in the repeated prisoner's dilemma. The diner might be tempted to go away without leaving a tip, but he knows if he does so he may not get good service in the future. This threat gives him an incentive to uphold his part of the bargain. The tit-for-tat theory thus appears to provide a rigorous account of why the tipping institution holds together and works to the benefit of all involved. In restaurants whose clientele consists largely of regular patrons, nobody really has any incentive to cheat.

But tit-for-tat cannot be the whole story, for tipping occurs not just in restaurants that people visit on a regular basis, but also in steak houses along interstate highways, most of whose patrons never expect to return. Why don't the patrons of these restaurants simply refrain from tipping? After all, the waiter is clearly not in any position to retaliate.

This is precisely the prediction made by the self-interest model favored by Western economists. In fact, however, researchers have found that tipping rates are only marginally lower in restaurants that have a lot of transient trade than in restaurants that depend mostly on local patrons. The prediction of the self-interest model is thus flatly rejected. Tipping at out-of-town restaurants remains very much a phenomenon to explain.

A second biological theory of altruism, William Hamilton's kin selection model, is of little help. Hamilton argued that the genetic goal of any biological organism is often equally well served—indeed, sometimes even better served—not by self-serving actions but by actions that benefit genetic relatives. For example, since full siblings contain half their genes in common, on average, it would be in a person's interest to sacrifice his life to save the lives of at least three siblings. The three would be likely to pass on more copies of their altruistic brother's genes than he himself could have done.

Of course, not all altruistic acts entail giving up one's own life. As the cost of the altruistic action falls, the degree of relatedness required to make altruism pay genetically also declines. But even though a 15 percent tip on a restaurant meal is a small sacrifice, the odds that a waiter will be genetically related to a random diner from out of town are essentially nil. The kin-selection model helps us understand why parents make big sacrifices on behalf of their children, but it cannot explain why people leave tips when they are dining on the road.

Another influential biological theory of cooperation is Robert Trivers's theory of reciprocal altruism. Consider a good swimmer who happens to be sitting on a dock when she notices that a swimmer below is in trouble. The risk involved in a rescue may be small, and there is a good chance the good deed will lead to some advantage in the future. The victim may reciprocate directly, for instance; but even if not, the rescue may enhance the rescuer's reputation, causing others to favor her in future interactions.

The desire to build a good reputation does indeed appear to motivate altruistic behavior in many cases. But this calculus does not seem to apply to diners on the road, for whom the odds are vanishingly small that failure to tip will entail any loss of reputation. The diner will either get nice treatment from strangers in the future, or he won't, irrespective of whether he leaves a tip. Or at least, so it seems.

Some will suggest people's tipping habits are forged for the most part in local restaurants, where tipping does pay. According to this view, it is simply not worthwhile to calculate whether tipping makes sense in each particular instance. Although this explanation has obvious force, it suggests that people would modify their behavior if someone pointed out to them that they could get away with not tipping on the road. And yet most people, when they are told of the self-interest model's argument about tipping on the road, seem disinclined to change their behavior. They seldom say, "Oh, I never thought of that. I'm going to start leaving no tip from now on." Rather, most people respond with a remark like, "Well, that's not why I leave a tip. I leave a tip because that's the responsible thing to do under the circumstances. The waiter's provided good service. He's lived up to his part of the agreement; I'd feel bad if I didn't live up to my part of the agreement."

So the puzzle remains: Why do people live up to their implicit obligation to tip when they're dining on the road? And why do they make anonymous donations to charity, engage in hazardous rescues, and make various other sacrifices on behalf of others? Many such actions, purposely taken with full knowledge of their consequences, are altruistic, if by this we mean actions that benefit others at net costs to the actor.[1] If people did not perform these actions, they would be better off—in the sense of having more resources for themselves and their families—and they know it.

As I will presently suggest, however, these same actions are often part of a larger pattern that is beneficial to the actor, or at least not harmful. The apparent contradiction arises not because of any hidden gains from the actions themselves, but because we face important problems that simply cannot be solved by purely selfish action. Not all of these problems involve altruism per se. But they all entail a choice between purely selfish behavior and behavior that is contrary to self-interest. Their common feature is that they can be solved only if we can make commitments to behave in ways that may later prove contrary to our interests.

The Commitment Problem

Thomas Schelling[2] provides a vivid illustration of this class of problems. He describes a kidnapper who suddenly gets cold feet. He wants to set his victim free, but is afraid the victim will go to the police. In return for his freedom, the victim gladly promises not to do so. The problem, however, is that both realize it will no longer be in the victim's interest to keep this promise once he is free. And so the kidnapper reluctantly concludes he must kill him.

Schelling suggests the following way out of the dilemma: "If the victim has committed an act whose disclosure could lead to blackmail, he may confess it; if not, he might commit one in the presence of his captor, to create a bond that will ensure his silence."[3] (Perhaps the victim could allow the kidnapper to photograph him in the process of some unspeakably degrading act.) The blackmailable act serves here as a commitment device, something that provides the victim with an incentive to keep his promise. Keeping it will still be unpleasant for him once he is freed; but clearly less so than not being able to make a credible promise in the first place.

In everyday economic and social interaction, we repeatedly encounter commitment problems like the one confronting Schelling's kidnapper and victim. Below I discuss four examples of commitment problems and in each case suggest how specific emotions can act as the commitment devices needed to solve them.

The Trust Problem

Suppose a business owner has identified an opportunity to open a franchise in another state that will be highly profitable if operated by an honest manager, but otherwise only marginally profitable. The owner would be willing to pay extra for someone who could commit himself to manage honestly. And a purely self-interested person would like to be able to make such a commitment in order to receive the higher rate of pay. The problem is that both know that this current intention by itself is insufficient, for, once hired, the manager can earn even more by being dishonest. If the owner is unable to identify an honest manager, he is likely to forego the venture altogether. But if the owner could somehow identify an honest manager, their commitment problem would be solved. The owner would reap the higher profits because of the manager's intrinsic motivation not to cheat, and the manager would command a premium salary for his honesty.

The Deterrence Problem

When I give lectures out of town, I usually bring along an expensive briefcase given to me by my wife several Christmases ago. If a stranger in the audience took a liking to my briefcase, and thought me to be a purely self-interested, rational person, he would be free to steal my briefcase with impunity. He would correctly calculate that the costs of my retaliating would be prohibitive. I would have to call the police and miss my flight home. Months later, I would have to return to testify at the trial. I would have to endure hostile cross-examination by the thief's attorney, who would try to make it seem somehow *my* fault that his client had taken my briefcase. Since these costs clearly exceed the value of the briefcase, a self-interestedly rational person would simply write the briefcase off.

But suppose potential thieves were somehow able to discern that I was not a self-interestedly rational person—that I would be likely to react angrily to the theft and be willing to endure high costs rather than see the crime go unpunished. In that case, my briefcase would be a much less inviting target. The irony is that being known as someone predisposed not to pursue material self-interest would again confer an important material advantage.

The Bargaining Problem

Another commitment problem arises when people negotiate the terms on which to divide the surplus from an economic or social exchange. Suppose you and a colleague have been offered $10,000 by an editor to write an article that only the two of you can write. Neither of you has sufficient knowledge to write the article alone, and it will take each of you one month to complete your respective parts. Imagine that there would be sufficient nonmonetary benefits from having the article in print under your names that each of you would have been willing to participate in the project for free. If your colleague supposes you to be a perfectly self-interested, rational person, and if he is such a person himself, he may then be tempted to have his lawyer draw up a contract that would insure that he would end up with the lion's share of the $10,000 fee. Suppose, for example, that he pledges to give $11,000 to the John Birch Society (or to some other cause he does not favor) in the event that you receive more than $100 as your share of the $10,000 fee. By signing such a contract, he can present you with an ultimatum: either accept $100 as your share or else the deal is off. You know he means it because if he agrees to give you any more than $100, he is committed under his contract to give up $11,000. If you are a self-interested, rational person, your best bet at that point is to accept the $100. After all, $100 is better than nothing, and you would have been willing to do the job for free.

But suppose your colleague had thought you were someone who might have reacted not rationally but emotionally to his offer. He might then have had grounds for worrying that your indignation would lead you to reject it outright. And this concern would have militated against making such an outrageous offer in the first place. Here again, the irony is that being known to be other than a purely self-interested, rational person confers material advantage. Someone who cares not only about the size of her payoff in absolute terms, but also about relative payoffs—how her payoff compares to her trading partner's—is much more likely to be an effective negotiator.

The Marriage Problem

Rational choice theories of assortative mating tell a story something like this: Each person, seeking a mate with desired characteristics, engages in dating rituals whose function is akin to the search for a job or a place to live. Because search is costly, it doesn't pay to examine each and every potential mate. Rather, a limited sample of potential partners is examined sequentially, and the search terminated when a suitably attractive partner is found. The logic of this process is captured in the heuristic, "marry the best person who will have you, but don't waste your whole life searching."

Once two people agree on a marriage, it serves their collective interests to terminate further search and get on with the task of raising a family. But where each *individual's* material incentives are concerned, it is not necessarily optimal to terminate further search. Suppose, for example, that several years into the marriage one partner discovered a mutual interest in someone much more attractive than her current mate. At that point it might pay, in strictly material terms, to terminate her current relationship and move on to the new one.

Needless to say, just such scenarios unfold from time to time. But if this were expected to happen whenever a spouse encountered someone more attractive than his or her current mate, then the heavy investment that marriage normally entails could scarcely be considered an attractive proposition. Perhaps this is why nature saw to it that couples who marry become bonded by emotional attachments strong enough to outweigh most countervailing material advantages. Only with the depth of commitment provided by a strong bond of love does it become worth undertaking the investment required to raise a family. Note once again the irony that the advantage that derives from such an emotional commitment is unavailable to the purely self-interested, rational actor.

Clues to Behavioral Predispositions

To recapitulate briefly, my claim is that common elements from the human emotional repertoire help solve trust, deterrence, bargaining, marriage, and other commitment problems. Sympathy for one's trading partner can make one trustworthy even when material incentives favor cheating. A sense of justice can lead people to incur the costs of retaliation, even when incurring those costs will not undo the original injury. Caring about relative payoffs can lead people to reject one-sided offers, even when their wealth would be increased by accepting them. And strong emotional bonds of love provide a measure of security that facilitates long-term investment in relationships that might otherwise seem too risky.

Note, however, that although emotions can clearly help shape behavior in these ways, alone they are insufficient to solve commitment problems. The solution requires not only that the relevant emotions be present, but also that one's potential partners have some way of discerning them. Unless the owner of a business can identify the employee whose emotions motivate trustworthy behavior, that employee cannot be offered the job whose high pay is predicated on trust. Unless the predator can identify the potential victim as someone whose emotions will motivate retaliation, the potential victim is likely to become an actual victim. Unless our trading partners can detect that we are emotionally predisposed to reject wealth-augmenting, but one-sided, offers, we are unable to deter such offers. And unless potential mates can discern in us the capacity to develop strong emotional bonds of love, we are unlikely to be regarded as suitable mates.

But how do people know that a person's feelings commit him to behave in non-self-interested ways? As the following episode made clear to me, there are at least *some* instances in which such behavior can be predicted very well indeed.

One fall day, some 35 years ago, black activist Ron Dellums was the speaker at a large rally on the University of California campus in Berkeley. Polls suggested he would soon become the Berkeley–North Oakland district's first radical congressman. Crowds were easily galvanized in those days, and this one was in especially high spirits. But at least one young man was not moved by Dellums's speech. He sat still as a stone on the steps of Sproul Plaza, lost to some drug, his face and eyes empty of expression.

Presently a large Irish Setter appeared, sniffing his way through the crowd. He moved directly to the young man sitting on the steps and circled him once. He paused, lifted his leg, and, with no apparent malice, soaked the young man's back. He then set off again into the crowd. The boy barely stirred.

Now, the Irish Setter is not a particularly intelligent breed. Yet this one had no difficulty locating the one person in that crowd who would not retaliate for being sprayed. Facial expressions and other aspects of demeanor apparently provide clues to behavior that even dogs can interpret. And although none of us had ever witnessed such a scene before, no one was really surprised when the boy did nothing. Before anything even happened, it was somehow *obvious* that he was just going to go right on sitting there.

Without doubt, however, the boy's behavior was unusual. Most of us would have responded angrily, some even violently. Yet we already know that no real advantage inheres in this "normal" response. After all, once the boy's shirt was soaked, it was already too late to undo the damage. And since he was unlikely ever to encounter that particular dog again, there was little point in trying to teach the dog a lesson. On the contrary, any attempt to do so would have courted the risk of being bitten.

Our young man's problem was not that he failed to respond angrily, but that he failed to communicate to the dog that he was *predisposed* to do so. The vacant expression on his face was somehow all the dog needed to know he was a safe target. Merely by wearing "normal" expressions, the rest of us were spared.

Since the publication of Charles Darwin's 1872 book, *The Expression of Emotions in Man and Animals*, much has been written about the observable manifestations of affective states. Ekman and Friesen and others, for example, have confirmed Darwin's claim that certain facial expressions are characteristic of specific emotions.[4] These expressions, which are the result of complex combinations of facial muscle movements, are extremely difficult to produce on demand, yet appear spontaneously when the corresponding emotion is experienced.

Consider, for instance, the schematic expression shown in Figure 9.1. The distinct configuration of the eyebrows—elevated in the center of the brow, sloping downward toward the sides—is produced by a specific combination of the pyramidal muscles (located near the bridge of the

FIGURE 9.1   The expression of grief, sadness, or concern.

nose) and the corrugator muscles (located near the center of the brow). Ekman reports that fewer than 15 percent of the subjects tested were able to produce this expression on demand.[5] By contrast, virtually all subjects exhibit it spontaneously when they experience grief, sadness, or concern.

Ekman and various coauthors have also found that posture and other elements of body language—the pitch and timbre of the voice, the rate of respiration, and even the cadence of speech—are systematically linked to underlying affective states.[6] Because the relevant linkages are beyond conscious control in most people, it is difficult to conceal from others the experience of certain emotions and equally difficult to feign the characteristic expressions of these emotions on occasions when they are not actually experienced. For this reason, we are able to employ such clues to form estimates of the emotional makeup of others, which in turn help us form judgments about their character.[7]

Assume, for the moment, that there exist reliable clues on which to base inferences about the presence of non-self-interested behavioral predispositions in others. What does this assumption imply about the ability of people with such predispositions to compete effectively in the material realm with purely self-interested rivals of the sort contemplated by traditional behavioral scientists?

To answer this question, let us focus on a single specific predisposition, say, trustworthiness. Imagine a population, some of whose members are trustworthy, others not. And suppose that the way people earn a living in this population is by interacting with others in joint ventures whose payoffs constitute a prisoner's dilemma. The trustworthy types always cooperate in these interactions, while the untrustworthy types always defect. If, contrary to our working assumption, the two types were perfectly indistinguishable, interactions would occur on a random basis and the average payoffs would be larger for the untrustworthy types (owing to the dominance of the defect strategy in all prisoner's dilemmas). Given the ecological rule that population types reproduce in proportion to their relative payoffs, the eventual result would be extinction for the trustworthy types. In highly simplified form, this is the Darwinian story that inclines many behavioral scientists to think that self-interest is inevitably the only important human motive.

But now suppose that the trustworthy types were distinguishable at a glance from the untrustworthy types. Then interaction would no longer take place on a random basis. Rather, the trustworthy types would pair off systematically with one another to reap the benefits of mutual cooperation. The untrustworthy types would be left to interact with one another and would receive the lower payoff associated with mutual defection. The eventual result this time is that the untrustworthy types would be driven to extinction.

Neither of these two polar cases seems descriptive of actual populations, which typically contain a mix of trustworthy and untrustworthy individuals. That is precisely the result we get if we make one small modification to the original story. Again suppose that trustworthy types are observably different from the untrustworthy types, but that some effort is required to make the distinction. If the population initially consisted almost entirely of trustworthy persons, it simply would not pay to expend this effort because one would be overwhelmingly likely to achieve the benefit of mutual cooperation merely by interacting at random with another person. In such an environment, the trustworthy types would cease to be vigilant in their choice of trading partners. Untrustworthy individuals would then find a ready pool of victims, and their resulting higher payoffs would cause their share of the total population to grow.

But as the untrustworthy types became more numerous, it would begin to pay the trustworthy types to exercise greater vigilance in their choice of partners. With sufficiently many untrustworthy types present in the population, the trustworthy types would be vigilant in the extreme, and we would again see exclusive pairing among trustworthy types. And that in turn would cause the prevalence of trustworthy types to grow. At some point, a stable balance would be struck in which the trustworthy types were just vigilant enough to prevent further encroachment by the untrustworthy types. The average payoff to the two types would be the same, and their population shares would remain constant. There would be, in other words, a stable niche for each type.

Similar ecological accounts can be constructed in support of the survival compatibility of love, envy, anger, sympathy, guilt, and a variety of other emotions that play no role in the traditional self-interest model. As we shall see, taking these emotions into account gives rise to predictions very different from those of the self-interest model.

The Problem of Mimicry

If there are genuine advantages in being vengeful or altruistic and being perceived as such, there are even greater advantages in appearing to have, but not actually having, these qualities. A liar who appears altruistic will have better opportunities than one who glances about furtively, sweats profusely, speaks in a quavering voice, and has difficulty making eye contact.

Adolf Hitler was apparently someone who could lie convincingly. In a September 1938 meeting, Hitler promised British Prime Minister Neville Chamberlain that he would not go to war if the borders of Czechoslovakia were redrawn to meet his demands. Following that meeting, Chamberlain wrote in a letter to his sister: "in spite of the hardness and ruthlessness I thought I saw in his face, I got the impression that here was a man who could be relied upon when he gave his word."[8]

Clues to behavioral predispositions are obviously not perfect. Even with the aid of all of their sophisticated machinery, experienced professional polygraph experts cannot be sure when someone is lying. Some emotions are more difficult to simulate than others. Someone who feigns outrage, for example, is apparently easier to catch than someone who pretends to feel joyful. But no matter what the emotion, we can almost never be certain.

Indeed, the forces at work are such that it will always be possible for at least *some* people to succeed at deception. In a world in which no one cheated, no one would be on the lookout. A climate thus lacking in vigilance would obviously create profitable opportunities for cheaters. So there will inevitably be a niche for at least some of them.

Useful lessons about the nature of this problem are contained in the similar instances of mimicry that abound in nature. There are butterflies, such as the Monarch, whose foul taste defends them against predators. This taste would be useless unless predators had some way of telling which butterflies to avoid. Predators have learned to interpret the Monarch's distinctive wing markings for this purpose.

The Monarch has created a profitable opportunity for other butter-flies, such as the Viceroy, who bear similar wing markings but lack the bad taste. Merely by looking like the unpalatable Monarchs, Viceroys have escaped predation without having had to expend the bodily re-sources needed to produce the objectionable taste itself.

In such instances, it is clear that if mimics could *perfectly* simulate the wing marking with neither cost nor delay, the entire edifice would crum-ble: The comparatively efficient mimics would eventually overwhelm the others, and the predators' original reason for avoiding that particular marking would thereby vanish. So in cases where mimics coexist along-side the genuine article for extended periods, we may infer that perfect mimicry either takes time or entails substantial costs. The fact that the bearer of the genuine trait has the first move in this game will often prove a decisive advantage.

Similar considerations apply in the case of those who mimic emo-tional traits. If the signals we use for detecting these traits had no value, we would have long since ceased to rely on them. And yet, by their very nature, they cannot be perfect. Symptoms of character, after all, cannot be scrutinized without effort. If no one ever cheated, it would never pay to expend this effort. The irony, of course, is that this would create fail-safe opportunities to cheat.

The inevitable result is an uneasy balance between people who really possess these traits and others who merely seem to. Those who are adept at reading the relevant signals will be more successful than others. There is also a payoff to those who are able to send effective signals about their own behavioral predispositions. And, sad to say, there will also be a niche for those who are skillful at pretending to have feelings they really lack.

Indeed, at first glance it might appear that the largest payoff of all goes to the shameless liar. In specific instances, this may well be true, but we must also bear in mind the special contempt we reserve for such persons. Most of us will go to great trouble to inform others when we stumble upon someone who lies with apparent sincerity. Even if such persons are caught only very rarely, it is on this account far from clear that they com-mand any special advantage.

The ecological balance between more and less opportunistic strategies is at once in harmony with the Western behavioral scientist's view that self-interest underlies all action and with the Buddhist tradition's view that people can and do transcend their selfish tendencies. The key to re-solving the tension between these views is to understand that the ruthless pursuit of self-interest is self-defeating. As the Buddhist tradition has recognized clearly from the beginning, the best outcome is sometimes possible only when people pursue their goals indirectly. The enlightened pursuit of self-interest often requires commitments to behave in ways that will, if triggered, prove deeply contrary to our interests.

Much of the time, the practical means for accomplishing these commitments will be emotions that have observable symptoms. Persuasive evidence suggests that at least some of these emotions are inborn. But even if they were transmitted only by cultural indoctrination, they would serve equally well. What is necessary in either case is that people who have them be observably different, on the average, from those who do not.

For convenience, I will use the term *commitment model* as shorthand for the notion that seemingly unselfish behavior is sometimes explained by emotional predispositions that help solve commitment problems. I will call the competing view that people always act efficiently in the pursuit of self-interest the *self-interest model*.

The commitment model's point of departure is that a person who is believed always to pursue self-interest will be excluded from many valuable opportunities. For example, no one would willingly hire such a person for a managerial position that involved failsafe opportunities to embezzle cash from the company. By contrast, a person who is believed to have a strong conscience is a much more attractive candidate for this position. The strict calculus of self-interest would still dictate that he steal the money; but a sufficiently strong emotional commitment to honesty can overcome this calculus.

On purely theoretical grounds, the commitment model thus suggests that the moving force behind moral behavior lies not in rational analysis but in the emotions. This view is consistent with an extensive body of empirical evidence reviewed by developmental psychologist Jerome Kagan. As he summarizes his interpretation of that evidence:

> Construction of a persuasive rational basis for behaving morally
> has been the problem on which most moral philosophers have
> stubbed their toes. I believe they will continue to do so until they
> recognize what Chinese philosophers have known for a long time:
> namely, feeling, not logic, sustains the superego.

The emotions may indeed sustain the superego. But the commitment model tells us that it may well be the logic of self-interest that ultimately sustains these emotions.

A Simple Thought Experiment

The critical assumption behind the commitment model, again, is that people can make reasonable inferences about character traits in others. Because it is so central, it may be useful to attempt a preliminary assessment of it before going further.

First, a simple point of clarification: "reasonable inference" does not mean that it is necessary to be able to predict other people's emotional predispositions with certainty. Just as a weather forecast of 20 percent chance of rain can be invaluable to someone who must plan outdoor activities, so can probabilistic assessments of character traits be of use to people who must choose someone to trust. It would obviously be nice to be accurate in every instance. But it will often suffice to be right only a fraction of the time.

Is it reasonable to assume we can infer emotional predispositions in others? I have found the following simple thought experiment helpful in coaxing out my own beliefs on this issue. Imagine you have just gotten home from a crowded concert and discover you have lost $1000 in cash. The cash had been in your coat pocket in a plain envelope with your name written on it. Do you know anyone, not related to you by blood or marriage, who you feel certain would return it to you if he or she found it?

For the sake of discussion, I will assume that you are not in the unenviable position of having to answer no. Think for a moment about the person you are sure would return your cash; call her "Virtue." Try to explain *why* you feel so confident about her. Note that the situation was one where, if she had kept the cash, you could not have known it. On the basis of your other experiences with her, the most you could possibly know is that she did not cheat you in *every* such instance in the past. Even if, for example, she returned some lost money of yours in the past, that would not prove she didn't cheat you on some other occasion. (After all, if she *had* cheated you in a similar situation, you wouldn't know it.) In any event, you almost certainly have no logical basis in experience for inferring that Virtue would not cheat you now. If you are like most participants in this thought experiment, you simply believe you can fathom her inner motives: You are sure she would return your cash because you are sure she would feel terrible if she did not.

The thought experiment also calls attention to the fact that such emotional predispositions may depend on circumstance. Think, for example, about your relationship with Virtue. Typically, she is a close friend.

This is a natural outcome for at least two reasons. First, you have had much more opportunity to observe the behavior of close friends, and if situations that shed light on a person's character occur only rarely, it is much more likely you will have witnessed one. But second, and perhaps more important, you are much more inclined to trust a friend because you believe she feels a special loyalty to you. Indeed, your belief that Virtue will return your cash does not necessarily imply a belief that she would have returned an envelope bearing the name of a perfect stranger. Her predisposition to return your money may be contingent on her relationship to you.

Your intuitions may also tell you that the amount of cash in the envelope could matter. Most people feel they know many more people who would return $100 than $1000. By the same token, a person who would unhesitatingly return $1000 might instead hang on to an envelope with $50,000.

People's feelings of right and wrong are clearly not the only forces that govern their behavior. As social psychologists have long emphasized, behavior of almost every sort is strongly influenced by the details and nuances of context. But despite the obvious importance of situational factors, they do not tell the whole story. On the contrary, most participants in this thought experiment respond that they know someone they feel sure would return the cash of a perfect stranger, or indeed even that of someone deeply disliked, no matter how large the amount. We need not deny the obvious importance of context when we speak of traits of character that differ between persons. It would be a mistake to pretend that character traits account for all important differences in behavior. But it is perhaps a more serious error to suppose that behavior is guided *only* by context.

Of course, the fact that you may feel sure that a particular person would return a stranger's cash does not necessarily make it so. Plenty of apparently trustworthy people have let even close friends down in situations like the one contemplated by the thought experiment. What the experiment does establish (on the assumption that you responded affirmatively) is that you accept the crucial premise of the commitment model.

Do Views about Human Nature Matter?

Views about human nature have important practical consequences. In the public policy arena, they affect the conduct of foreign affairs, the design and scope of economic regulation, and the structure of taxation. In the world of commerce, they dictate corporate strategies for preventing workers from shirking, for bargaining with unions, and for setting prices. In our personal lives, they affect how we choose mates and jobs, even how we spend our incomes.

More important, our beliefs about human nature help shape human nature itself. Our ideas about the limits of human potential mold what we aspire to become. They also shape what we teach our children, both at home and in the schools.

The commitment and self-interest models paint strikingly different pictures not only of human nature, but also of its consequences for material welfare. The traditional self-interest model says that people who love, who feel guilty when they cheat, vengeful when they are wronged, or resentful when they get less than their fair share will often behave in ways that reduce their material payoffs. But the commitment model tells us that precisely because of this, they may also enjoy opportunities that would not be available to a purely opportunistic person. In many cases, a person or society armed with this knowledge will make better choices than one exposed only to the self-interest tradition. Here are some illustrations.

Shirking on the Job

In the workplace, as in other areas of life, there are frequent opportunities to cheat and shirk. In recent decades, economists have written at length about this issue under the rubric of the so-called "principal-agent" problem. In the standard treatment, the firm, or principal, has some task it wants the worker—its agent—to perform. The problem is that it is costly to monitor the worker's performance.

Economists have focused on the design of contracts that provide material incentives not to shirk. One ingenious proposal makes use of the observation that firms can often rank the performance of different workers even when they cannot measure exactly how much each produces. Under these circumstances, firms can elicit better performance by making part of each worker's pay depend on his or her rank in the productivity ordering.

But even the most sophisticated of these contracts is limited by the fact that behavior is often virtually impossible to monitor. Workers often confront golden opportunities to shirk, ones that are altogether beyond the reach of material incentive contracts. In the modern industrial firm, people tend to work in teams rather than as individuals. The classical monitoring problem is that while the firm can easily discover how much a team produces, it has little way of knowing how much each individual contributes to this total. The self-interest model emphasizes that each worker thus has an incentive to free-ride on the efforts of his coworkers.

The commitment model suggests that one way of solving this problem is to hire workers who feel bad when they shirk. How can firms do this? The commitment model suggests a simple strategy, one based on the premise that most people have at least some capacity to experience the emotions that support cooperation. The extent to which they actually experience them depends strongly on environmental factors. The practical problem confronting the firm is thus to design a working environment that will encourage these emotions. A useful starting point is the observation that feelings of moral responsibility are much more focused on people with whom we have close personal ties. This suggests that shirking might be attacked by creating a work environment that fosters closer personal ties between coworkers.

Exactly this strategy has been followed by many successful firms in Japan. In the typical Japanese corporation, the worker "is a member of the company in a way resembling that in which persons are members of families, fraternal organizations, and other intimate and personal organizations in the United States."[10] Many Japanese companies provide housing, athletic, and medical facilities for their workers and educate their children in company schools. Coworkers vacation together in mountain or shore retreats maintained by the company. In contrast to the typical American worker, who works for many different firms during his lifetime, the Japanese ideal is lifetime tenure with a single employer.

This pattern enables the Japanese firm to solve monitoring problems in a way that the typical American firm cannot. Because of the close ties that exist between Japanese coworkers, their employers can link pay to the *group's* performance and rely on feelings of coworker solidarity to overcome the inherent free-rider problem. By contrast, the pay schemes suggested by the self-interest model, which focus on *individual* performance, not only do not encourage cooperation, they actively militate against it.

This is not to say that the particular solutions adopted by Japanese firms will always be appropriate in the United States, where we place such a high premium on individuality and mobility. On the contrary, firms that blindly imitate the behavior of Japanese firms, as many American companies have begun to do, are not likely to prosper. If the commitment model is useful here, it is because it suggests the specific purpose the Japanese practices serve, namely, to encourage the emotions that support cooperation. The successful firms will be those that find ways of solving this problem in the American context. The self-interest model, with its exclusive focus on material incentives, steers management's attention in entirely different directions.

Wage and Price Setting

Views on human nature affect not only a firm's policies for dealing with shirking, but also those toward wage and price setting. In highly profitable firms, for example, it is not uncommon for union members to threaten to abandon their jobs permanently in the event management does not accede to their demands. In these situations, management must decide whether to take the threat seriously.

Now, to abandon one's livelihood is an extraordinarily costly step—much more costly, most of the time, than the loss employees would suffer by moderating their demands. Threats of this sort would be utterly without credibility if union members behaved as predicted by the self-interest model. But if their concerns about fairness play a prominent role, it is easy to see why such threats are so often effective. A labor relations policy based on traditional rational bargaining models would serve a firm very poorly indeed.

Workers are not the only ones who care about how the economic pie is divided. Consumers, too, make frequent sacrifices in the name of fairness. In particular, they will often accept losses in order to avoid patronizing firms whose prices they perceive to be unfair. It is clear that firms take consumer attitudes about fairness very much to heart, often going to great lengths to frame their offerings in ways that make prices seem more in line with costs.

Richard Thaler cites the example of hotel room packages during Super Bowl weekend.[11] The Super Bowl is played each year on a Sunday late in January. In the host city, it is all but impossible to find a hotel room for the Saturday night before the game. And yet hotel chains are reluctant to charge a market-clearing price. They fear that customers would perceive $1000 per night as unfair and refuse to patronize their hotels in other cities or at other times.

The solution some hotels have adopted is to sell a Super Bowl package: a room from Thursday through Sunday for $1200 total. Since they have vacant rooms on the other nights anyway, including them in the package does not cost much. Making them part of the deal causes the buyer to see a price of $300 per night, which seems "fair." He is happy to pay it, even though he really didn't need a room for the other three nights.

Foreign Relations

Military and strategic planning has become increasingly dominated by game theory of the sort first employed for these purposes by the Rand Corporation in the 1950s. But the behaviors predicted by traditional game theory often bear little resemblance to the actual behavior of countries in conflict. For example, both the German bombardment of England during World War II and the American bombing of Vietnam 25 years later were undertaken in the belief that a military adversary could be bombed into submission. In both instances, however, the bombing served only to increase the adversary's determination to resist. From the perspective of the self-interest model, this outcome is puzzling. But the commitment model's portrayal of human nature makes it seem much more intelligible.

The self-interest and commitment models make conflicting observations about a variety of other strategic issues as well. One is the defense doctrine of Mutually Assured Destruction (MAD). The idea behind MAD is simple. It is to maintain sufficient armaments to be able to deliver a devastating counterstrike to any nation that might consider launching a nuclear first strike against us.

Rationalists have argued that this form of deterrence makes no sense. Once we know we are the victim of a first strike, they reason, it is obviously too late to deter anything. At that point, our interests clearly dictate that we *not* retaliate, for to do so would only increase the likelihood of total world destruction. The problem with the MAD strategy, they conclude, is that the potential launcher of a first strike knows perfectly well what our incentives will be once its attack is launched. And this knowledge completely undercuts the capacity of MAD to deter.

Taken at face value, the critics' case is correct. If a nation makes policy decisions by strict reliance on the self-interest model, MAD *is* an irrational strategy. In order for MAD to be rational, our adversaries must know we have either (1) a doomsday machine (a tamper-proof device that *automatically* retaliates); or (2) policy makers who do not react rationally. The commitment model makes clear that because human beings are in charge of such decisions, they may indeed react irrationally. With the stakes so high, no prudent nation would be willing to gamble on a perfectly rational response to its first strike.

The Importance of Stable Environments

The commitment model suggests why environments that encourage repeated interactions might be advantageous. After all, stable environments provide opportunities to discern traits of character and to foster personal ties and loyalty. These, in turn, can sustain cooperation even in situations where dishonesty is impossible to detect (and hence impossible to retaliate against). The model thus suggests a reason for the increased attractiveness of living in small towns, or of forming cohesive neighborhood groups in large cities.

The idea that geographic mobility is a good thing is firmly enshrined in American conventional wisdom. In defense of it, economists have stressed that incomes will be highest when resources are free to move to their most highly valued uses. Stated in this way, their claim seems true by definition. But it does not consider the possible effects that increased mobility may have on our ability to solve commitment problems. A stable population will naturally be much better able than a transient one to form effective bonds of trust. Being firmly rooted has economic costs, just as the self-interest model says. But it also has important economic benefits. People who turn down high-paying jobs in impersonal environments are not necessarily unmindful of their material welfare.

Behavior toward Institutions

The commitment model says that emotional predispositions are the driving force behind moral behavior. The role of emotion makes it easy to see why there are many people who would never dream of cheating a friend, yet think nothing of stealing company property or paying too little income tax. The sympathy that motivates proper conduct toward individuals tends to be much less strongly summoned by large institutions.

At an earlier point in human history, it did not much matter whether people were predisposed not to cheat large organizations, for there were none. But today, of course, they are a large and growing fixture of life, and it is clearly disadvantageous to live in a society where people feel free to cheat them.

The modern strategy for dealing with this problem has been to rely on detection and punishment—industrial stool pigeons, lie detectors, and drug tests for catching miscreants, and fines, lost jobs, or imprisonment for punishing them. The commitment model suggests that an effective alternative, or complement, to this strategy might be to *personalize* people's attitudes toward institutions. Institutions do, after all, act on behalf of real people. We establish governments to take actions for us that we find it impractical to undertake individually. Large corporations, similarly, exist because they enable us to produce more than we could on our own. When we cheat the government, we cheat our neighbors. When we steal from our employers or take drugs on the job, we steal from our coworkers. The difficulty is that we do not experience these connections directly. Because moral behavior is driven largely by emotion, and because emotion is more naturally summoned by persons than by institutions, it would surely help to stress these linkages when we teach our children moral values.

Motives for Honesty

When an opportunistic person is exhorted to behave morally, his immediate, if unspoken, question is "what's in it for me?" The traditional rationale for the maxim, "honesty is the best policy," responds that penalties for cheating are often severe, and you can never be sure you will not be caught. The rationale further asserts that living up to your promises on one occasion creates the impression you will do so in the future. This, in turn, makes people more inclined to trust you, which is often a decisive advantage.

In some cases it is easy to see why honesty might indeed be the best policy for the reasons traditionally given. Consider again the practice of tipping in restaurants. It is one clearly built on trust: Because tips are customarily left at the end of the meal, the waiter or waitress must rely on the diner's implicit promise to reward prompt and courteous service.[12] Having already received good service, the diner is in a position to stiff the waiter. But while this occasionally does happen, it would not be a sensible strategy for most people who eat repeatedly in the same restaurants. A person who leaves a generous tip each time he visits his favorite restaurant may thus be viewed as making a rational investment in obtaining good service in the future. Living up to his implicit promise is clearly consistent with—indeed, required by—the vigorous pursuit of self-interest.

The difficulty is that the tipper's behavior here does not really capture what we understand by the term "honesty." It is perhaps more fittingly described as "prudence." He has lived up to his implicit promise, to be sure; but since failure to do so would have led to bad service on future occasions, we cannot conclude that fidelity to the implicit promise was an important motivating factor.

Whether people honor their agreements when they expect to interact repeatedly with us is obviously important. But in much of life, we are concerned instead with how they behave either in fleeting encounters or in ones where their behavior simply cannot be observed. These cases, after all, are the ones that seriously test a person's character. In them, an honest action will be one that, by definition, requires personal sacrifice. Earlier we saw a clear example in the case of the tip left in a restaurant in a distant city. When a traveler breaks the implicit promise to tip, he will save some money and his disgruntled waiter will have no opportunity to retaliate.

With situations like these in mind, sophisticated people generally react cynically to the notion that honesty is the best policy. They realize that guaranteed success is *not* a prerequisite for cheating to be profitable. Of course, there is always *some* possibility that an angry waiter will make a scene that will be witnessed by someone you know. But celebrities apart, this risk is negligible, or at any rate far too small to be seriously considered a self-interested reason for tipping. The difficulty with traditional self-interested appeals to morality is that they suggest no reason not to cheat in situations where detection is all but impossible.

The commitment model suggests an altogether different rationale for honesty, one that is both self-interested and at the same time relevant for situations where cheating cannot be detected: If character traits like honesty are observable in a person, an honest person will benefit by being able to solve important commitment problems. He will be trustworthy in situations where the purely self-interested person would not and will therefore be much sought-after as a partner in situations that require trust.

The decision to tip in the distant city is in part a decision about the kinds of character traits one wishes to cultivate. For while modern biologists have established that the capacity to develop various character traits is inherited, no one has successfully challenged the Buddhist conception that indoctrination and practice are required for them to emerge. The direction of causality between character and behavior thus runs both ways. Character influences behavior, of course. But behavior also influences character. Despite our obvious capacities for self-deception and rationalization, few people can maintain a predisposition to behave honestly while at the same time frequently engaging in transparently opportunistic behavior.

The opportunist's goal is to appear honest while availing himself of every prudent opportunity for personal gain. He wants to seem like a good guy to the people who count, but at the same time to refrain from tipping in distant cities. If character traits are observable, however, this may not be possible. In order to *appear* honest, it may be necessary, or at least very helpful, to *be* honest.

In these observations lie the seeds of a very different reason for leaving a tip in the distant restaurant. The motive is not to avoid the possibility of being caught, but to maintain and strengthen the predisposition to behave honestly. My failure to tip in the distant city will make it difficult to sustain the emotions that motivate me to behave honestly on other occasions. It is this change in my emotional makeup, not my failure to tip itself, that other people may apprehend.

Moral philosophers and others have long stressed the adverse social consequences of the unbridled pursuit of self-interest. The utilitarians, for example, urge us to practice restraint because the world will be a better place if everyone does so. For opportunistic persons, however, such appeals have not proved compelling. They reason, with seemingly impeccable logic, that their own behavior will not much affect what others do. Because the state of the world is thus largely independent of how they themselves behave, they conclude that it is best to take what they can and assume others will do likewise. As more and more people adopt this perspective, it becomes increasingly difficult for even basically honest persons not to do so.

Many of my friends, and I too in years past, have complained of feeling like chumps for paying all of our income taxes when so many people evade theirs so brazenly. More recently, however, my work on the commitment model has sharply altered my feelings on this issue. I am still annoyed if a plumber asks me to pay in cash; but now my resentment is tempered by thinking of tax compliance as an investment in maintaining an honest predisposition. Virtue is not only its own reward here; it may also lead to material rewards in other contexts.

Even the mere possibility of such rewards profoundly transforms a person's choice about whether to cultivate an honest predisposition. On traditional views of morality, opportunists have every reason to break the rules (and to teach their children to do likewise) whenever they can profitably do so. The commitment model challenges this view at its very core, which for me is by far its most exciting message. By suggesting an intelligible answer to the pressing question of "what's in it for me?" it encourages even the most hardened cynic to feel genuine regard for others.

Teaching Values

People of earlier times had a keen appreciation of the importance of character development. Moral lessons learned early in life are not easily forgotten, and churches and families spared little effort in seeing to it that children received them.

Moral behavior almost always calls for self-sacrifice, for the interests of others to be put ahead of our own. Slowly but steadily, the willingness to heed this call has eroded under the forces of materialism. Contrary to Adam Smith's clear intention, his invisible hand planted the idea that moral behavior might not be necessary, that the best of all possible worlds might result if people were simply to pursue their own interests. Darwin's survival of the fittest went a step farther, creating the impression that failure to pursue self-interest might even be hazardous to our health. Smith's carrot and Darwin's stick have by now rendered character development an all but completely forgotten theme in many industrialized countries.

In materialist theories, to be moral is to be a chump. To the extent the "chump model" is believed, it has surely encouraged the adoption of opportunistic values.[13] The late British economist Fred Hirsch argued that the capitalist system cannot function without widespread adherence to the values inherent in the Protestant work ethic. He noted that these values, which took centuries to foster, are deteriorating rapidly. The contradiction of capitalism, he concluded, is that its emphasis on individual self-interest tends to erode the very character traits without which it cannot function.

The commitment model casts this contradiction in a new light. Like the chump model, it acknowledges that doing the right or just thing entails costs on each specific occasion; but it stresses that being thus predisposed need not be a losing strategy. Commitment problems abound, and if cooperators can find one another, material advantages are there for the taking. From the perspective offered by the commitment model, the self-denying traits of character required for efficient markets no longer appear in tension with the materialist premises of the marketplace.

The practical importance of this realization is that it might make a difference to someone faced with the choice of what kind of person to become. Attitudes and values are not etched with great specificity at birth. On the contrary, their development is, as noted, largely the task of culture. Most people have the capacity to develop emotional commitments to behave unopportunistically. Unlike the chump model, the commitment model suggests a simple answer to the nagging question of why even an opportunistic person might want to do so.

Teaching moral values was once the nearly exclusive province of organized religion. The church was uniquely well equipped to perform this task because it had a ready answer to the question, "Why shouldn't I cheat when no one is looking?" Indeed, for the religious person, this question does not even arise, for God is *always* looking. The fear of eternal hellfire has obvious power over the temptation to stray. But the threat of damnation appears to have lost much of its punch in recent years. And no alternative institutions have emerged to take over this role of the church.

The decline of religion is not the only important change. Families, even those that want to teach moral values to their children, find themselves increasingly less able to devote the necessary time and energy. Half of all American children now spend some portion of their childhood in single-parent homes. Of those with two parents, it is increasingly the norm for both to work full-time. When the choice is between, on the one hand, having one parent stay home to teach the children moral values (or both stay home part-time) and, on the other, having both work full-time to be able to afford a house in a better school district, most parents feel irresistibly drawn to the latter.

If moral values are important and are not being taught in the home, why not teach them in the public schools? Few subjects excite greater passions than proposals to teach moral values in the public schools. Liberal watchdogs spring into action the moment any item in the curriculum seems to embody a value judgment. For them, the idea of teaching values means that "someone is going to try to stuff *his* moral values down *my* kid's throat." Conservative fundamentalists, for their part, insist that religious doctrine be presented to students with the same status as scientific facts. As they see it, the failure to teach *their* particular slate of values amounts to a public repudiation of them.

On many specific issues, such as abortion, there is little room for the two groups to compromise. Unfortunately, the salience of these issues obscures our very substantial consensus on questions of value. Most people living today in the United States would agree, for example, that people should

- not lie
- not steal

- not cheat
- keep their promises
- follow the golden rule
- have tolerance and respect for diversity

This is not to say there is agreement over hard cases. White lies are often considered acceptable but sometimes hard to define. Even so, there remains striking consensus on most of the concrete examples covered by these simple rules. Why then have *they* not been made part of the curriculum in public schools?

Ironically, part of the difficulty stems from the last item on the list, our respect for diversity. Many judgments about values are of course deeply personal. Even if all but a few of us strongly endorse each item on the list, at least some of those few feel strongly to the contrary. And because of that, many of us feel reluctant to force "our" values on them in a forum like the public schools.

But tolerance, like any of the other virtues, is not absolute. To accommodate the tiny minority who would not be happy to see even this limited slate of values promoted vigorously in the public schools, the rest of us must sacrifice a great deal. If values were merely personal opinions, there might still be ample reason to make this sacrifice. But they are not. When people are taught not to lie and cheat, the world becomes a more attractive place for almost everyone. More important, the gains are not merely general: They will accrue more than proportionately to persons who effectively internalize these values. Thus the people who insist that values not be taught in the public schools are insisting that other people's children—our children—settle for smaller portions of the character traits that will help them make their way in the material world. It is not clear why the community should be willing to accept this cost on behalf of so few.

Teaching values in the public schools has also encountered political opposition because many people believe it blurs the important boundary between church and state. The commitment model stresses, however, that values spring not only from religious teachings, but also from material considerations quite independent of them. In this respect, of course, it is no different from numerous other materialist accounts of moral values. It *is* different from other accounts, though, in stressing that values benefit *individuals*, not just society as a whole. It thus makes clear what other accounts cannot—namely, that the case for teaching moral values in the public schools is, in this sense, much the same as the traditional case for teaching science and math.

Concluding Remarks

On the strength of the evidence, we must say that the self-interest model provides a woefully inadequate description of the way people actually behave. The commitment model is a tentative first step in the construction of a theory of unopportunistic behavior. It challenges the self-interest model's portrayal of human nature in its own terms by accepting the fundamental premise that material incentives ultimately govern behavior. Its point of departure is the observation that persons *directly* motivated to pursue self-interest are often for that very reason incapable of attaining it. They fail because they are unable to solve commitment problems.

These problems can often be solved by persons known to have abandoned the quest for maximum material advantage. The emotions that lead people to behave in seemingly irrational ways can thus indirectly lead to greater material well-being. Viewed in these terms, the commitment model is less a criticism of the self-interest model than a friendly amendment to it. Without abandoning the basic materialist framework, it suggests how the nobler strands of human nature might have emerged and prospered.

It does not seem naive to hope that such an understanding might have beneficial effects on our behavior. After all, the self-interest model, by encouraging us to expect the worst in others, does seem to have brought out the worst in us. Someone who expects always to be cheated has little motive to behave honestly. There is evidence, for example, that economics and business students are much more likely than others to behave opportunistically in social dilemmas.[14] The commitment model may not tell us to expect the best in others, but it does encourage a markedly more optimistic view.

NOTES

Robert H. Frank is Goldwin Smith Professor of Economics, Ethics, and Public Policy at Cornell University. This lecture was prepared for delivery to the Fifth Mind and Life Conference, Dharamsala, India, October 1–5, 1995. It is adapted from his book, *Passions Within Reason: The Strategic Role of the Emotions,* New York: W. W. Norton, 1988.

1. Here I adopt the standard biological definition of altruism, which focuses on the costs of behavior to the actor, not the actor's psychological motive for performing it.

2. *The Strategy of Conflict,* Cambridge, MA: Harvard University Press, 1960.

3. 1960, pp. 43, 44.

4. See Paul Ekman, Wallace Friesen, and Phoebe Ellsworth, *Emotion in the Human Face,* New York: Pergamon, 1972; Paul Ekman, *Darwin and Facial Expression: A Century of Research in Review,* New York: Academic Press, 1973; Ekman, 1973; and Paul Ekman, *Telling Lies,* New York: W. W. Norton, 1985.

5. Ekman, 1985.

6. See, for example, Paul Ekman, Wallace Friesen, and Klaus Scherer, "Body Movements and Voice Pitch in Deceptive Interaction," *Semiotica, 16,* 1976: 23–27.

7. Observable expressions of emotion are of course not the only reliable clues to character. For a discussion of the role of reputation and other factors, see chapter 4 of my *Passions Within Reason.*

8. Paul Ekman, *Telling Lies,* pp. 15, 16.

9. Jerome Kagan, *The Nature of the Child,* New York: Basic Books, 1984, p. xiv.

10. James Abegglen, *Management and Worker,* Tokyo: Sophia University Press, 1973, p. 62.

11. Richard Thaler, "Mental Accounting and Consumer Choice," *Marketing Science,* Summer, 1985.

12. A *New Yorker* cartoon suggested a way of curtailing the waiter's risk. It portrayed a solitary diner in the midst of his meal. On the table was a plate with a few coins on it and a small placard reading, "Your tip so far."

13. Fred Hirsch, *Social Limits to Growth,* Cambridge, MA: Harvard University Press, 1976; Barry Schwartz, *The Battle for Human Nature,* New York: W. W. Norton, 1986.

14. See Robert H. Frank, Thomas D. Gilovich, and Dennis Regan, "Does Studying Economics Inhibit Cooperation?" *Journal of Economic Perspectives, 7,* Spring, 1993: 159–171.

Dialogues, Part II: Pragmatic Extensions and Applications

1. Human nature versus human ethics; or can we derive moral principles from natural principles?
2. What practical methods exist that might enhance compassionate capacity?
3. What is the relationship between compassionate feeling and prosocial action?
4. What role do rational factors play in the cultivation of prosocial compassionate feelings?
5. Is anger always "afflictive" or is it sometimes justified?
6. Is there a "natural" human appetite for violence?
7. Are there gender differences in the inclination toward compassion versus violence?
8. Buddhism without metaphysics; or, is reincarnation relevant?
9. Closing remarks

1. Human Nature versus Human Ethics, or Can We
   Derive Moral Principles from Natural Principles?

DALAI LAMA   One of the things I would like to discuss in this conference is the potential we have for using the understandings we are developing here as the basis for a secular understanding of ethics and morality, one that is based on a right understanding of human nature. Here is
the question I have: Without involving religion, how do we determine
what is the right thing or the wrong thing? I would argue that morality
can be grounded in nature. Something that is morally positive means
something that brings benefit.

ELLIOTT SOBER   Let me speak to that right away, because this is an
issue I feel strongly about. Many scientists and philosophers in the
West, though not all, use the words "natural" and "unnatural" in a deceptive way. They are used to presenting an ethical or moral idea as if it
were a biological idea. For example, some people in Western societies
say that homosexuality is unnatural. What they are really saying is that
they think it is morally wrong. But they are saying it in a deceptive way,
making it sound as if it were some kind of scientific or biological idea.
    When they hear things like this, other philosophers in the West—and
I am one of them—react by demanding clarification of what "natural"
means. We would say: "To claim that something is 'natural' merely
means that it is found in nature. All biology can do is describe what is
found in nature. If someone wants to comment that this is good and
that's bad—that kindness is good and cruelty is bad—that is not a biological statement. It's a statement of morality." It is important not to
confuse biological questions about what is found in nature—including
human nature—with issues of moral value concerning good and bad
conduct. Biology doesn't tell us what's right and what is wrong. These
are separate realms.

GEORGES DREYFUS   I think it is very important to define our terms
here because the cultural connotations of "natural" and its closest
equivalent in Tibetan, *vranshinkin*, are quite different. In the Western
vocabulary, "natural" means part of nature as distinguished from culture. In Tibetan, [*vranshinkin*] doesn't have that connotation yet. It may
be acquiring it slowly, but [*vranshinkin*] means independent from cause,
and it can mean independent from other phenomena. Elliot, you assume
that natural means biological. . .

ELLIOTT SOBER   No, I do not. And I in fact reject the distinction between nature and culture that you are describing here. Look, human beings are one species among many species. Part of what defines our
species is this thing we call culture. Culture is part of nature. Just like
the hill that an ant colony builds is part of what they do to their environment, our culture is part of what we create. I reject the distinction
between nature and culture. They are not dichotomous; rather, the one
is inside the other.

What I mean by "natural" is all that is found in nature. Because I as-
sign that meaning to the word "natural," I think of the potentialities of
kindness and cruelty as both parts of human nature. And I don't understand any other view, frankly.

DALAI LAMA   Well, I am trying here to argue toward what one could
perhaps describe as a naturalistic ethics, a kind of morality grounded in
a biological understanding of human nature. This will perhaps go
against the powerful trend in Western philosophical thinking that holds
to the slogan that "is" and "ought" are two different realms and you
cannot derive "ought" from "is." That view gives the impression that
the world of natural facts is separate from the world of moral values,
and one cannot be derived from the other. Now this clear-cut distinction
is something that I would dispute. For example, one could say that even
from a biological point of view, killing is wrong because. . .

ELLIOTT SOBER   I shouldn't interrupt, I'm sorry, but that's not biology.
I just don't agree.

ANNE HARRINGTON   Elliott, I think there is a practical dilemma that I
am beginning to understand. On the one hand, Your Holiness, you
want to find a way to develop an ethics that transcends the narrowness
that comes from rooting ethics in a particular religious tradition. You
want to universalize ethics. On the other hand, once you pull ethics out
of a particular religious context, where do you find the universal standards for it? How do you avoid moral relativism? How do you avoid
saying that any particular cultural moral system is as good as any other?
Is it possible—I think you are asking—that something like nature could
provide a universal framework for deciding on some basic ethical values? There is a practical imperative that is driving the conversation.

JOSÉ CABEZÓN   Elliott's point is that both caring and killing, for
example, are found in nature. Therefore how can one create a moral

injunction against killing on the basis of nature, when both of these are found in nature?

DALAI LAMA   My point is that, if you examine the biological processes, there's a movement toward growth and fruition, and killing stops it. Not only that, I relate this back to one's own personal, basic desires to exist.

ELLIOTT SOBER   But the description of one's basic desires to exist is a psychological description of what is in one's mind. It takes an additional assumption that those desires are good. That's an ethical assumption, not a biological assumption. I'm going to state a strong position here: Biology as a science does not tell us what is good and what is bad. We can interpret biological facts through our own moral system and make judgments about that. But it does not come purely from the biology.

DALAI LAMA   I don't think there is any major disagreement here. The point is how to ground an ethical morality in a biological understanding of human nature. It is an interpretative process, of course.

ROBERT FRANK   I think biology definitely does teach us something about morality, but not in the sense that what occurs in nature is therefore good. That is the point that Elliott is objecting to, and I agree with his objection.

What biology does teach us is that in evolution often there are conflicts between the interests of the individual and the interests of the group. It can be beneficial for an individual to tell a lie and for his partner also to tell a lie. And yet if they both lie, they each do worse than if they both tell the truth. Nature identifies that conflict between the individual and the group and points out situations where agreements not to lie, for example, can make each person in the group better off than before. So I think the evolutionary theory of emergence through natural selection for the benefit of the individual organism identifies possibilities for everyone to improve. We can each give up narrow advantage for the broader advantage of the group. It's that insight from nature that informs ethics in a deep way and would provide an exciting basis for a nonreligious theory of ethics.

ELLIOTT SOBER   Even as you describe it, Robert, it's questionable whether purely biological statements on their own entail conclusions about right or wrong.

DALAI LAMA   If you take the question of sex, for example, from a biological point of view it has a certain purpose: reproduction.

ELLIOTT SOBER   Which *may* be good. But it's a separate question whether that's a good purpose or a bad purpose, a purpose to be encouraged or thwarted. The bare biological description of sex is neutral on whether it is good or bad.

DALAI LAMA   The purpose of sexuality in biology is reproduction, so male to male or female to female sex, on this basis, is immoral.

ELLIOTT SOBER   Let's consider what the concept of purpose means here.

DALAI LAMA   One can take the example of trees. Why do the trees that bear fruit have flowers? There's a certain biological purpose.

ELLIOTT SOBER   And the purpose of the lion's claws is to kill. What does purpose mean here? Purpose means why these things evolved, why they exist. Perhaps some of them exist for what we would consider destructive ends. Evolution can produce destructive outcomes as well as good outcomes.

THUBTEN JINPA   I personally feel that there is no major disagreement here between His Holiness and Eliott.

ELLIOTT SOBER   I feel like there's a gigantic disagreement. [*Laughter*]

RICHARD DAVIDSON   His Holiness may be thinking of biology in the context of applied ethics. If we learned from biology that the emotion of anger, for example, interfered with those parts of our brain that help us think clearly and if we also found that the experience of anger had negative effects on our heart, then these are biological facts that suggest that anger may not be a healthy emotion. We can then act on that basis. That is one of the ways in which biology can potentially inform ethical choices.

ANNE HARRINGTON   You do have to make one leap of faith. You have to first assume that life is precious. Otherwise, if you stand outside the whole system, everything is equally neutral: we can destroy the planet; we can wipe out human life. But if you are inside the drama, then you can begin to ask: What enhances life? What preserves life and what doesn't? The relationship between that which is natural and that which is moral then becomes more fluid.

ELLIOTT SOBER   I think life is precious, too. But that is not a statement of biology. That's not a discovery of any biologist, nor will it ever be.

ANNE HARRINGTON   That's right, but that's the leap of faith. So, you begin outside of biology with that faith, and then you step inside and you begin to see what you can learn.

DALAI LAMA   My approach—and you can call it a leap of faith if you want—is based on two premises. One is that life is precious. The second is that at the core of human nature there is a need to seek happiness. There is also an understanding of human nature that sees it as fundamentally benevolent at its core. These are the first principles. Everything else is based on them.

ELLIOTT SOBER   Okay, at least one of these premises does not come from biology.

ANNE HARRINGTON   Right, we agree.

ELLIOTT SOBER   So the project includes some biology plus some ethics—namely the assumption that life is precious, which I agree with. It's not that I disagree with that. . . [*Laughter*] But I want to recognize that for what it is. So ethics plus biology gives us more ethics. Great. . . but it's not biology alone.

ERVIN STAUB   But even then we have some difficulty. If life is precious, and if my family and I are attacked by somebody who cannot be stopped by words or kindness, then the preciousness of my children's lives and my own may justify my killing that person in defense. In which case, we may decide that killing is both "natural" and "ethical."

DALAI LAMA   If one were to argue that there is a need for love and affection because it enhances the biological constitution of the body, wouldn't you say that this is a purely biological argument?

ELLIOTT SOBER   What do you mean by "need"? That if you don't get it, you'll be unhappy?

THUBTEN JINPA   Need for proper development, in a functional sense, and without it you have little chance to survive.

ANNE HARRINGTON   Babies will fail to thrive if they are not held—things like that.

ELLIOTT SOBER   If "need" means that if you don't get it you will die, then I agree that it is a biological category. It's another question whether a "need" is the same as a "good." For example, viruses have needs in the sense that if they don't have certain conditions they'll die. But we don't think that the AIDS virus is a good thing that we should help to survive. It has needs—but whether those needs are things that should be frustrated or advanced is a separate question we then address. So, yes, "need" is a biological category when it is understood in this way. But the additional question—whether it is good or bad to satisfy the need— is not a biological question.

ROBERT FRANK   It is in the end a biological question, if you start with the assumption that human life is precious. That is what leads us to con- clude that we should not serve the AIDS virus.

ELLIOTT SOBER   Why assume that just *human* life is precious?

JOSÉ CABEZÓN   What it means to say that human life is precious is also a complex issue. For example, on the question of homosexuality, if reproduction is in itself a good end, that is one imperative that might create a society in which homosexuality is proscribed for the purpose of greater human procreation. On the other hand, there is the question of the preciousness of the life of the gay or lesbian person, and his or her happiness. That may, from another perspective, be also a need that has to be taken into consideration.

ELLIOTT SOBER   Not in the sense of need that was described before, where "need" means that if you don't get it you will die. It's a different concept, if "need" means that if you don't get it you will be unhappy or frustrated or something else.

ANNE HARRINGTON   Although His Holiness also believes, as one of his first principles, that people's happiness is important.

THUBTEN JINPA   I think there's a slight confusion here. We all agree that we have to make the assumption that life is precious. But in many of the arguments the assumption is, when you spell it out, that *human* life is precious. The ethical imperatives that we are talking about here seem to be based on the health of the human being, that what enhances it is good and what goes against it is bad. I think we need to spell out clearly whether the assumption is that life is precious, or that human life is precious.

NANCY EISENBERG   You bring in a whole other set of assumptions with health, too. Is life precious enough that you don't let somebody die if they want to, somebody who is in great pain and is not going to be healthy?

ANNE HARRINGTON   I think Nancy makes an important point, and it raises for me a related thought about what we mean when we say life is precious. Richie and I are involved in a research group studying women who have advanced breast cancer. These women meet once a week for an hour and a half to talk and share their feelings. There is evidence that this may prolong their life, which we would presumably see as something good. I spoke to those women and asked them, "Do you think that this is making you live longer?" They laughed, and said, "We know better. We've seen many of our friends and colleagues die. But that's not the point. We come together because we love each other and because we are like a family here." When I heard that, I began to wonder whether perhaps the biomedical model misses something important in thinking that the only appropriate response to the preciousness of life is to make it last as long as it possibly can. Is there some way of thinking about life being precious that could go beyond thinking about survival? Perhaps the goal driving a claim that life is precious shouldn't just be survival, or the extension of life as a blind, quantitative goal.

DALAI LAMA   Yes, that's the point. I view that human life is precious not because we are human beings saying it, and also not because we have a unique physical constitution. Rather, it is that humans have the capacity not only to love their own species, but also to extend that love toward other species, and to think about the fate and the well-being of the entire life of this planet. We also have the ability to act out of compassion.

ELLIOTT SOBER   If this is your view, that we need to consider a quality of life beyond mere survival, then that further ethical substance cannot be grounded solely in the notion of biological need, assuming that the word "need" means, as you said before, that if you don't get it you die. The concept of "need" in that sense is a very narrow concept, and it doesn't include this idea of quality of life at all. It includes only what is essential for survival, even if surviving means suffering. It's hard to see how a real ethics could be based on such a narrow concept of biological need.

DALAI LAMA   Part of the problem we are struggling with here is one that has occupied so much attention in ancient Indian thought: the limitations of concepts and language when they come face-to-face with describing the complexity of reality. Tibetans have a catch phrase they hide behind when caught in that kind of tricky situation. They say that something is true "from that point of view" or "from this point of view."

Many of the arguments that you have raised are all very true. It's almost impossible to try to capture every aspect of reality in language and concept. Often what we really have to do is just adopt a certain standpoint—choosing whatever is most important, getting the priorities right—and then try to look at it from that perspective.

The concern I have is that, when we base morality on a particular religious philosophy and tradition, it is very effective for some people, but it cannot apply to all human beings. I feel we therefore need to seek some ground that speaks to both believers and nonbelievers, something that says, "We are human beings, we must act this way, not that way." Such right action is not justified by religion, but is purely in our own interests, for our own survival, for our own happiness.

ELLIOTT SOBER   I want to emphasize that the idea of secular morality has very deep and old connections with Western philosophy, from the ancient Greeks all the way to the present. I connect myself with that secular tradition in philosophy, and what I was saying before about morality was not connected with any religion. The kind of idea you are trying to develop here will be understandable as a project in Western philosophy. It is something that people have tried to do and are still interested in doing. It's not alien.

JOSÉ CABEZÓN   If I could play devil's advocate for one moment, I have grave doubts about the possibility of a meaningful secular morality. If we try to reach consensus in the beliefs of 5.7 billion people, we will be left with something that has very little power. So, it would be better to ground one's morality in a strong metaphysics, even if it means a religious metaphysics, and perhaps reach only 100,000 people, than to have a very diffuse morality that might reach a lot of people but will have no power.

DALAI LAMA   The foundation of this universal ethics perhaps is not biology; it is this premise that instinctively we all want to be happy, we all want to avoid suffering. This is really the first principle. But biology can then provide confirmation or justification for it.

ANNE HARRINGTON   So biology, as you see it, is a tool. It's not the foundation.

THUBTEN JINPA   I think José's point is very strong. If you look at history, secular ethics has a very bad record.

ERVIN STAUB   But if you look at history, religious ethics also has a very bad record. [*Laughter*] The greatest number of killings probably have occurred under the guise of religion.

JOSÉ CABEZÓN   Yes, but so has the greatest amount of human spiritual development.

THUBTEN JINPA   At least religious ethics provides a unified vision of life that is easy for ordinary people to relate to. Secular ethics demands too much thinking. The majority of the people don't have the time; nor have they the intellectual aptitude to be able to follow all the arguments. That is the problem with secular ethics.

2. What Practical Methods Exist That Might Enhance Compassionate Capacity?

ERVIN STAUB   The real challenge we're confronting here is the question of how abstract ideas of ethical behavior relate to how people actually behave in the world. In the end, no matter what kind of ethical principles we determine are right, and no matter whether they are based on nature, on biology, on first assumptions, or whatever, people are not going to follow them unless they have certain kinds of life experiences that shape their orientation toward other human beings and toward themselves. And without those, often there may be a disconnect.

RICHARD DAVIDSON   Psychologists who have studied people's attitudes—their belief, for example, that one politician is better than another, or attitudes about homosexuality—have also shown that the behavior a person engages in is not always consistent with what they tell you they believe is right or wrong. We may judge that a particular action is correct or that a choice is good, but our behavior does not necessarily follow. How can we make our thoughts and actions more consistent? If we make an ethical judgment, how then do we translate that judgment into action?

DALAI LAMA   First we want to find a way of explaining these inconsistencies without having to take into account Buddhists' belief in continuous rebirths. In Buddhist psychology, a strong emotional conditioning is not confined to a single lifetime, which explains a paradox such as why a person would think in one way and act in another. The problem here is how to find a way of understanding this without bringing rebirth into the picture.

GEORGES DREYFUS   Though we may not accept the idea of rebirth, it is a fact of human experience that we are conditioned and not acting freely. From a Buddhist point of view, it would be wrong to think of the human mind as a *tabula rasa*; rather, we should think of it as directed by a powerful dynamic. We often don't make free choices, though we could, because a lot of our behavior is impelled by very deep conditioning that we are unable to do anything about.

NANCY EISENBERG   What is meant here by conditioning?

JOSÉ CABEZÓN   Buddhists have the idea that every action we perform in a sense puts a seed in our mental continuum. As a result of having engaged in some action repeatedly in the past, we become more disposed to repeating that action again in the future.

ANNE HARRINGTON   For example, a father doesn't want to strike his son, but the son provokes him. The father has hit him before he even knows it, and he's then very sorry. There is a conflict between what the father consciously wants to be, and what he does.

RICHARD DAVIDSON   In modern neurobiology, there is a basis for that kind of habit learning that is contrasted with cognitive learning. There are certain types of habits that persist even though the thought is in conflict with the habit. They are controlled by different parts of the brain.

DALAI LAMA   There is a three-stage model of human behavior in Buddhist thinking that perhaps may be relevant. The first stage is learning something. This is followed by the stage of intellectual integration of the information. That then is followed by the stage of integration in behavior. Meditation is what really connects them. Meditation is a process where you try to integrate into your personality what you have learned, so there is less of a gap between what you know and how you act. So perhaps meditation is relevant as a solution to our problem here. The principle that is assumed here is that through [meditative] training you can reorient yourself. You can habituate yourself toward a certain disposition. The very word for meditation in Tibetan etymologically has the connotation of "to become familiar" or "to accustom."

ELLIOTT SOBER   Your Holiness, let me challenge a certain part of the picture you are painting. I have two kinds of questions. First of all, there is the question of how much compassion can be improved. Second, there is the question whether the improvability of compassion is something that is true of all people, most people, or some people? Let me offer an example. Consider someone who is severely retarded, whose mental abilities are so diminished that the idea of reflection, meditation, and the various practices that Buddhism has developed for improving the level of compassion simply are not available to this person. Do you nonetheless believe that this person is as improvable in their level of compassion as other people? Is every human being improvable a little bit or a lot, or infinitely improvable?

DALAI LAMA   When we look at humanity on this small planet, there are a lot of problems. Many problems, more than half maybe, actually are manmade problems due to ideology, bad leadership, ecological problems, and so on. One of the root causes is lack of compassion. Therefore, it is extremely important to promote compassion. Compassion is like the prime mover. With that prime mover, then every human action can be constructive.

Can we promote and improve human affection? The answer is yes, because basic human nature is gentle, and affection is the basis for humanity's survival over time. As to the specific question, whether every individual has the same capacity for cultivating and enhancing compassion to the same degree, my position is that it is important that everybody tries. As to the outcome, who can say?

Even in the example that you gave, as a human being the person would have the seed, the potential. But that alone is not enough. You need to use human intelligence and reasoning to enhance that capacity. In the case of a retarded person, perhaps these faculties may not be adequate. Although the person may have the potential, he may lack the necessary tools. But that person would probably still have the capacity to generate some level of compassion or affection spontaneously.

ELLIOTT SOBER   What if this person's retardation is due to very serious brain damage? Where does the seed for the development of capacities lie? Because of the physical problem, I don't understand in what sense this person has the capacity for developing these abilities. It's like my not being able to fly.

DALAI LAMA   Of course, if the situation is so bad that the person can-not differentiate between someone being affectionate and someone being abusive, then it's quite a different situation.

RICHARD DAVIDSON   I'd like to raise one issue about Elliott's com-ment in terms of how much we can improve compassion. I think that with respect to how much we can improve many psychological quali-ties, Western psychology is deeply ignorant. We have not empirically ex-amined the issue at all. I don't think we as scientists have any clue as to how much compassion can be increased if there is extensive training and extensive exposure to models that are exhibiting these qualities. The project that we have been involved in—looking at the mental abili-ties of Tibetan monks—was in part motivated by our intuition that many faculties in our mind, like attention and emotion, are much more changeable than Western psychology believes. This is still an empirical question for which we don't have adequate knowledge.

3. What Is the Relationship between Compassionate Feeling and Prosocial Action?

DALAI LAMA   A distinction is sometimes made in Buddhism between two types of compassion, which may reflect a difference in the tem-perament of the person. Some people take their own self-interest as the primary wish to fulfill, although they may not totally disregard other sentient beings' well-being. When they confront a situation where someone is suffering, they may wish to see that person free of suffering. That's one type of compassion. Other people who confront this situa-tion experience a much more active type of compassion. It is not just a wish to see sentient beings free from suffering, but an immediate need to intervene and actively engage, to try to help. The technical terminol-ogy used is that the former type of compassion is the wish to see others free from suffering; and the latter is the wish to help others be free from suffering.

JOSÉ CABEZÓN   The distinction may be more between sympathy and prosocial behavior rather than between empathy and sympathy.

NANCY EISENBERG   It's an interesting issue that no one on our side has much dealt with: how much sympathy necessitates a motivation to help. I think they are very intimately related. If you experience this other-oriented feeling, you are usually motivated to help, but it's not entirely the same. For instance, if you see someone who has already been helped, you may still feel sympathy but there is no motivation to help.

ERVIN STAUB   In a number of experiments, we found that the feeling of responsibility for others' welfare leads people to help others. On the basis of my work, I felt that the feeling of responsibility, even more than sympathy, makes a person more likely to be moved to help another. Actually this relates to what Anne was saying earlier [about the communication of sympathy as a form of helping action]. In one study, we found that people who had a strong feeling of responsibility were more likely to stop working and just attend when somebody else was in psychological distress. And actually attending in that situation seemed the most helpful response. There is even some evidence that a feeling of responsibility for others' welfare makes it more likely that people will not obey someone who tells them to harm another. That feeling of responsibility is a crucial thing. I am curious about what you think about the place of responsibility in the translation of compassionate feeling into prosocial action.

DALAI LAMA   I base my ideas about responsibility on the fundamental Buddhist ethical message that, in your thoughts and actions, if possible, you should try to help others. If not, at least avoid harming others. It's not asking everybody to leave whatever they are doing and reach out and help others; but it is asking people to have this consideration in whatever they do. They should try to help others, or at least make sure that whatever actions they take have no harmful consequences for others. Even in a case where harm is unavoidable, try to minimize it.

ERVIN STAUB   Is this in addition to feeling compassion?

DALAI LAMA   It is something that needs to come out of compassion. When you have compassion then you can feel the concern. Compassion also includes the sense of respecting others' rights. We said earlier that compassion should not be confused with a pity, which implies a sense of superiority. Rather, in compassion there is an underlying recognition, respect, and sense of concern for the other person. There is no notion of looking down at an unfortunate being.

If my avoidance of harming others is motivated by the consideration that harming others is nonvirtuous and would create negative
potential within myself, that's a self-related, self-oriented consideration; whereas if I consider that I shouldn't harm others because the
other person would suffer and that is bad, that is an other-oriented and
compassionate consideration. And that is definitely going to be a
stronger consideration.

GEORGES DREYFUS   Often in the West, in modern society, when we
think about responsibility, we seem to leave aside completely the proper
emotion that goes with it. Without the proper emotion, the danger is
that we intervene brutally in the life of another. So I think it's very important that the proper emotion has to come together with the sense of
responsibility for others.

ERVIN STAUB   I think that there is a difference between adhering to a
moral role, which you can do without that underlying feeling, and a
feeling of responsibility which has that underlying feeling for the other.

DALAI LAMA   Confucius says in his *Analects* that it's necessary to feed
one's parents, but it has to be done out of a motivation of love. We feed
even horses, so what is to distinguish that sense of responsibility from
the sense of responsibility toward parents, unless the underlying emotion of love is present?

ROBERT FRANK   I think when it's hard enough to get people to do the
right thing, you ought to give them full credit for doing the right thing
for any reason.

   Moreover, as the world evolves, moral questions will occur more and
more in the context of dealings between individuals and large organizations—employers, governments, insurance companies—where naturally stimulated compassion is simply absent. If we cannot develop a
comprehension of the need to behave morally on principle, then what
hope is there for future right conduct? I don't think it's very likely that
people will perform imaginary thought experiments to envision and feel
compassion for the hundreds of thousands of insurance company share-
holders who each lose one-hundredth of a penny when you file a false
insurance claim or a false expense report. It's much more likely that
somebody could learn to behave in accordance with a moral principle.
If that's the best we can do, let's try to do that, praise the person for
doing that, and teach children that they should do that.

4. What Role Do Rational Factors Play in the Cultivation of Prosocial Compassionate Feeling?

DALAI LAMA   This distinction we are looking at between compassion that translates into action and compassion that does not raises a more fundamental issue that strikes me as being very important from the point of view of Western philosophy. There, emotions are often understood as a kind of raw feeling, developed in a mechanistic way. In contrast, here we have the idea that cognitive considerations participate in the development of a richer version of the emotion itself. By cognitive considerations I mean religious and metaphysical considerations about the nature of self, the nature of other, the relationship of self and other. All of these things play into the Buddhist idea of cultivating compassion in a very conscious and cognitive way.

RICHARD DAVIDSON   For Western scientists, that would be part of the knowledge base in our long-term memory. Those are the things that we know and that we draw on in reacting to a new experience. I've previously mentioned the amygdala, a part of the brain that may be responsible for the initial pleasant, unpleasant, or neutral feeling. The emotions that we are talking about clearly involve many different systems in the brain, not just the amygdala. They involve the frontal lobes, which have a lot to do with cognition as well as emotion. These emotions involve goal states: we have a goal to benefit the other. From what we know in modern neuropsychology, the realization of a goal requires the prefrontal cortex that is also critically involved in other kinds of cognitive processes. So, a cognitive involvement with the development of these goal-directed emotional states makes biological sense.

THUBTEN JINPA   I think there is a slight confusion here about the meaning of the term "cognitive": the way it is used in the Western psychological context and the way it is used in the Buddhist context. Although the emotions like sympathy and empathy require a certain degree of cognitive activity, as Elliott said, that would not be understood as cognitive from the Buddhist point of view. When we use the word "cognitive," we are talking about a level where there is not only consciousness, but also self-consciousness.

ELLIOTT SOBER   Does this imply that one takes a theoretical and impersonal perspective? For example, it's not just that I believe that Richie is suffering and therefore I want to help him, but I think in a more abstract and impersonal way about the relationship between ourselves?

[*One translator nods, the other shakes his head. . . . Laughter.*]

GEORGES DREYFUS   I think we're seeing Buddhists trying to read their own distinctions into the Western psychological discussion.

JOSÉ CABEZÓN   I think that's what is required. Most of the discussion that we have had so far has been about the nature of emotion in ordinary people, and how it arises spontaneously. When we talk about different kinds of compassion in Buddhist theory and the way that compassion is cultivated, we are really talking about compassion that is the result of a cognitive process in the Buddhist sense of "cognitive." It is compassion as a result of a higher reasoning process that is cognitively cultivated, but then can lead to certain kinds of spontaneous expressions of compassion.

RICHARD DAVIDSON   And the higher cognitive process is a function of the exposure, training, and teachings that the individual has received.

JOSÉ CABEZÓN   Some of which might be explicable in nonreligious terms. Some might not be.

ELLIOTT SOBER   In the psychological literature, there is a distinction made between helping as a result of emotions such as empathy, sympathy, personal distress, and helping because of a belief in an abstract moral principle. They are treated quite separately. It sounds like the theoretical perspective being described here is similar to this more abstract and impersonal kind of evaluation. Nancy was describing these different emotions as possible causes of prosocial behavior, but she and other psychologists have also worked on other factors, such as having a moral principle. So Western psychology does not think strictly in terms of emotions either. For us, they too are important causes but not the only causes of prosocial behavior.

RICHARD DAVIDSON   It seems that you are describing both the impersonal as well as the emotional, operating together in some complementary way.

DALAI LAMA   To put this very directly, one of the basic Buddhist presuppositions is that reasoning can lead to the enhancement of positive emotions. In other words, we can reason our way into being more compassionate people.

RICHARD DAVIDSON   But Your Holiness, you made the comment earlier that reasoning can't affect our emotions. I would like some clarification on this point because I hear you now saying that reasoning does specifically change emotion.

DALAI LAMA   We were talking about when you are in the grips of anger. When anger is fully developed, at that moment you can't use reason.

GEORGES DREYFUS   It's important to understand that what José said about reasoning is part of a systematic training. It could be described as a kind of meditation.

DALAI LAMA   To take a concrete example: There is a practice in the Buddhist training of the mind where the practitioner is encouraged to adopt a more neutral attitude toward his or her enemy. The idea is not so much to convince oneself that the enemy is not an enemy, or that there is no such thing as enemies and friends; but rather to use that very distinction between enemies and friends, that very recognition of some person as an enemy, as the basis to develop a certain outlook toward the person. Because that person is an enemy, he or she provides me with the opportunity to renounce my intolerance and practice compassion; therefore, that person is precious. It is not so much the tendency to separate self and others that needs to be overcome, it's more the outcome of that tendency that needs to be counteracted.

5. Is Anger Always "Afflictive" or Is It Sometimes Justified?

ROBERT FRANK   In speaking of enemies, I want to ask His Holiness whether emotions like anger are ever appropriate in some circumstances. I think of the case of my son who built a house of sand at the beach. Another boy came and deliberately kicked and broke his house. My son got very angry at this boy and yelled at him. I had no sense that I should tell my son that what he did was wrong. It seemed to me that his response was right under those circumstances. How would a Buddhist teach his own son to behave in such a situation?

DALAI LAMA   Of course, there is anger and anger. Some anger may be more justified than others. One could also argue for an anger out of compassion, an angry reaction that is motivated by compassion in a particular situation. There could also be anger arising out of a sense of justice, as in your case. Buddhists would still try to suggest that anger may not be the best response. There are ways that one can respond to a particular situation, making the point firmly and strongly without giving in to anger. That would be the preferred response.

NANCY EISENBERG   Are you saying it's bad to experience anger or to express it? Is it okay to experience it if you then manage it and cope in a constructive way?

DALAI LAMA   The Buddhist attitude toward anger is quite complicated. The general standpoint is that anger is an emotion that needs to be countered. So, the less you make yourself prone to anger, the better it is. Of course, expressing anger through physical or verbal behavior is more destructive than merely experiencing anger. Also, at the moment when you actually experience anger, one cannot ask you to take control because you are in a fit of strong emotion. That's not the appropriate moment to stop it or put a lid on it, and that's not what the Buddhists are asking. It's quite complicated.

NANCY EISENBERG   You're saying it's both—that you try not to experience it, but if you do experience it you deal constructively?

DALAI LAMA   Yes.

ROBERT FRANK   I accept the value of compassion as you describe it, but I fear that the Buddhist position may rule out anger in cases where I feel we need anger. If one person harms another and a third person sees that and feels angry, the anger may motivate him to help. If he has this obligation to not feel anger, and tries to dismiss anger from his mind, his motivation to help will be weaker. I think we need anger in some circumstances, to do what needs to be done. Is there no concern about that?

DALAI LAMA   It may be possible that a swift reaction, which anger can normally produce, can also be produced without giving in to anger. You may still be able to retain that kind of swiftness and spontaneity through some other factors.

ERVIN STAUB   There is actually some interesting research showing that people who respond with anger don't go to help the person that was harmed when they see somebody attacked. Instead, they go to attack the person who harmed that person. So they don't act altruistically; they act out of their anger.

RICHARD DAVIDSON   There is also evidence that anger even acts to harm the person who is angry. Your Holiness may be interested in some very interesting new research. In the United States there are many people who get heart transplants. The heart that is placed in the person's body has to be very healthy; it's typically from a young person. It has been found that those recipients who have more hostility and anger develop disease in the new heart that they receive from the transplant. Scar tissue forms much more quickly in the new healthy heart in these individuals than in those who are less angry and show less hostility. So even with a new heart, a disposition toward anger is very toxic.

DALAI LAMA   [*Laughing*] It is a supporting argument. But I'm very curious: Is there a counterargument here?

RICHARD DAVIDSON   No, it is very much supportive.

6. Is There a "Natural" Human Appetite for Violence?

ADAM ENGLE   I'd like to relate these questions we're asking about anger to something that may or may not be related. We have been exploring the premise that Western science, in its studies of human nature, has focused more on antisocial, violent activities, whereas Eastern science offers a more balanced picture that includes careful attention to altruism and compassion. How do these different understandings make a difference in the real world? In my own field of business, and in the greater part of society, I think about the apparent increased appetite on the part of consumers for entertainment that is more violent than altruistic—not only theatrical entertainment but also in newspapers and other media. The news business seems to get higher ratings reporting violence than reporting good works. I wonder whether in native Buddhist cultures there is that same appetite for violent entertainment, or whether altruism and compassion sell better.

DALAI LAMA   We are all the same human beings. Many monks like a good boxing match.

NANCY EISENBERG   How do we make sense of that appetite for violence? Given everything else that we're saying, where does that fit?

DALAI LAMA   My normal standpoint on this is that compassion and affection are, in some sense, our natural state of being, so violence and aggression come almost as a surprise. It is out of the norm, so it becomes news. Good news is not news.

ANNE HARRINGTON   Is it only the element of surprise, even if we seek it out over and over?

DALAI LAMA   Admittedly, it is also colorful. Maybe that's the reason.

ANNE HARRINGTON   So the thought here is that we don't find altruism as exciting and colorful as violence. It does not makes us feel as excited when someone commits an altruistic act as when someone kills another person in a film. If that's true of human nature everywhere, Tibetan as well as Western, that's an important piece of information.

MICHAEL SAUTMAN   It's much more male-oriented though, I think.

ANNE HARRINGTON   I would also say that. I hate those kinds of films.

ERVIN STAUB   I also think that these things can become culturally conditioned. Society becomes more and more intense, the pace faster and faster, and with difficulties of life added, also. There can be more aggression and hostility within people, and therefore people respond more to hostility outside. Whether we like it or not, aggression may also be a function of culture. I can imagine a culture in which people would get deep satisfaction by watching acts of great kindness toward others.

ROBERT FRANK   I agree that culture really matters, and the amount of violence that we experience varies from one society to another, but I think there is still something basic in human nature that responds to violence. It's true that violent films are packaged in sophisticated ways that attract attention, but we see this interest in violence even when that is not present. In America, when two young boys get into a fight on the school ground, all activity stops and everyone watches very intently. I taught in a Nepalese school, and when two boys fought in the school yard, all activity stopped and everyone watched. The cultures are very different, but the attention to violence was the same in the two cases as far as I could tell.

DALAI LAMA   One factor that seems pretty evidently environmentally conditioned is our reliance on weapons to express violence. Given that our physical structure is not very strong, in order to survive human beings started using tools, spears, knives, and so forth, up to atom bombs.

Also, because of our use of tools, when we engage in acts of violence the damage is much more striking than if we just used our hands. When the destructive powers of our weapons increase, then of course the outcome of such violent acts is much more horrifying.

ANNE HARRINGTON   The ethnologist Konrad Lorenz talks about the fact that because we are, as you say, weak and puny, we did not evolve internal mechanisms to check aggression. Big aggressive animals have checks built into them so that aggression never goes too far. There are rituals: for example, an animal will roll over and expose its throat to stop the violence. But we never needed such checks because we couldn't hurt each other too much, until we got too smart. When we got smart, we were able to develop weapons, but we still didn't have the internal checks that would have evolved if we had not been so puny. Lorenz makes a comparison between us and doves, which are symbols of peace in our culture.

Do you know what happens when you put two doves in a cage? They peck each other to death, because they have no internal checks. We are like doves that have evolved weapons—clubs and knives and guns and now atom bombs—and we have nothing built into ourselves, Lorenz says, to stop us from using them.

ERVIN STAUB   I also think differences in individual biography affect how drawn we are to these things. Children who are badly treated, who experience hostility and aggression at home, watch more violent television. They watch more television in general, which would result in more exposure to violent television, but I think there is some indication that they are more interested in violent television. The violence on television may fit more with their experience of the world. Even in families that function well, often children are raised by what Nancy describes as "power exertion"—adults using their power as adults to exert influence on the child—rather than with love and caring. This might also contribute to an interest in violence—violent films and violent television— by enabling an identification with the aggressor who expresses some of our feeling of pain, but has power.

ROBERT FRANK   To that point, maybe it's useful to suggest that I think it's not just violence that we see in these films. Usually these films also portray a drama of good versus evil. There are forces of evil that do injury to the forces of good, and then usually someone triumphs against evil. In other words, the films that people want to see have a very interesting common thread. There are good people and bad people in the film. Bad people do bad things to the good people in the film. The good people suffer injury. They are patient; they try to resist the impulse to retaliate. Finally they reach a point where they can resist no longer, and they retaliate. And the audience is very happy when that happens.

Gangs of men go to soccer games in England and deliberately insult the opposing teams' spectators. They throw bottles and rocks at them. Then the opposing teams' spectators throw things at them, and they become outraged. It creates an appetite for justice, and a big fight happens. They go to games with the hope of seeing this drama unfold. So I think we have to understand the relationship between what we might call a thirst for violence, and a thirst for justice. We need a broader framework than one that simply says that people like violence.

ANNE HARRINGTON   When we successfully overcome danger in a battle between good and evil, that may be when we feel most alive. And maybe one of our needs as human beings is to connect to that feeling of "aliveness," feel our hearts beat faster, to feel how precious our life is. Watching a violent film of this sort might be one way to satisfy that need to feel life very intensely. However, it may not be the only way. Some people go on roller coasters at amusement parks. I've been interested in a Christian group in the United States called Pentecostalists. The Pentecostalists claim to be quite successful in recruiting people who were previously violent, involved with gangs and drugs. Now it turns out that part of the church service involves a very ecstatic, intense, trancelike experience. But the price for being able to have this experience—one could say—involves agreeing to curb the tendency to seek excitment in the form of violence. So perhaps it isn't exactly the violence itself but the kick we get from coming out the other end of a violent experience that gives us what we really seek.

ELLIOTT SOBER   Are we also sure that being attentive to something and being attracted to something is the same thing? We may focus on and attend to things that we don't like because they are dangerous to us. Because of evolution, we are especially attentive to dangerous things, just for the reason that they are dangerous. It wasn't so important in our evolutionary history to attend to things that are not dangerous. So when a violent television program engages the attention of the person watching, one has to determine whether it is engaging attention only, or it involves approval and internalizing of negative values.

ANNE HARRINGTON   But people do seek this stuff out, they go to the movies. We need to be able to account for an appetite that the film industry is apparently serving.

ALEXANDER NORMAN   When I was in the British army, I was stationed in Germany. The favorite thing to do on a Friday and Saturday night was to go down to a German bar and start fights. We had a lot of difficulty preventing our soldiers from going. They loved it; it was just something they seemed to enjoy doing. I wonder whether it was really the violence they liked, or whether we got addicted to the excitement as a fairly straightforward physiological response.

RICHARD DAVIDSON   I would like to suggest another alternative. We walk around with a lot of background mental activity that is often of a painful nature. People tend to engage in activity that leads to a diminishing of this background mental activity. There is a psychological concept called "flow," which refers to the feeling we get when we lose our sense of self and merge with the activity in which we are engaged. At that time the background mental chatter diminishes. Children may watch television to block or diminish the intrusions of negative chit-chat in the background. For many children, this is the only means they have available to reduce that kind of mental activity. If healthier, more beneficial substitutes were available, our preference for television might diminish. In the West many adults do crossword puzzles for the same reasons.

DALAI LAMA   There is a similar thing in Tibetan poetry, where you have to write verses so that you can read them backwards and forwards.

RICHARD DAVIDSON   I wonder, if we had opportunities to exercise our attention in very mindful ways in our daily life, would we require less of these other means of commanding attention? Would we be less likely to derive benefit from watching violent movies? Is there some relation between the cultivation of certain qualities of attention and mindfulness, and our propensity to watch these kinds of films?

7. Are There Gender Differences in the Inclination
   toward Compassion versus Violence?

ANNE HARRINGTON   Maybe this would be an interesting moment to re-ask a question—we touched on it in our discussion about violence—

as to whether there are any gender differences in the tendency toward compassionate behavior on the one side, and violent behavior on the other. Generally, our first impulse would be to ask the question in biological terms: women's brains versus men's brains, female evolutionary history versus male evolutionary history. But perhaps there's an alternative way to understand why—if there is one—there might be a gender difference. In our culture, if we identify compassion, as I think we sometimes do, with stereotypically "female" qualities like gentleness and vulnerability, and we identify anger with stereotypically "macho" qualities like strength and courage, then this has consequences. It could mean many women would feel more freedom in a culture like ours to behave in compassionate ways than men. Men may be threatened in their masculinity by compassionate behavior in ways that women are not. So the question of gender differences becomes a question of a value system that allows the sexes different opportunities to be compassionate.

If our concern is to help people become more compassionate and less angry, we need to understand what anger and compassion "mean" to people—what values they convey beyond themselves. If violence is valorized in our culture as something manly, related to courage and action, that is important. In a peculiar way, it then becomes a positive value in our culture, and compassion could be seen as rather negative—as weak, as female.

In the United States, nurses who are engaged in the compassionate dimension of medicine are not paid as much as surgeons engaged in the more macho aspects of medicine, although of course both are on some level involved in caring professions. But the compassionate expressions of this profession are not as valued as other action-oriented expressions. We need to understand that anger and compassion are not simply emotions: they carry inside them cultural values, that have a "gendered" nature.

DALAI LAMA   This male-dominated value system is still a residue of much earlier times, when human intelligence and reasoning faculties were not fully developed. These distinctions were made when superiority and inferiority were very much based on the size of the body and on physical strength. In history, you will find that in the old days, kings were made to look really big, with broad shoulders, even if they were not physically big. If you compare this with the animal realm, it is the powerful and the strong who dominate.

ANNE HARRINGTON   Yes, but my point was not biological.

DALAI LAMA   I still feel that it is important to see if there is a biologically based difference between male and female in terms of their disposition toward compassion, anger, and hostility. According to Buddhist psychology, there can't be any fundamental difference. Buddhism does speak about the difference in the intensity of emotions at different ages, or depending on the constitution of the body. So there may be some slight differences between men and women in terms of their disposition toward particular types. But fundamentally there cannot be any real difference.

It is possible from an evolutionary standpoint that women are more disposed toward caring and compassion because it is the female that normally conceives and nurtures the infant for a long period of time, whereas men pretty much plant the seed.

I always try to relate the patterns of human behavior to animals. If you look at the animal realm, you see that there are some species of birds in which the male and female remain together, sharing the responsibility for care until the offspring are grown up and fully independent. And then you see other animals like dogs where the male doesn't have any responsibility. But in all species, the female nurtures the offspring and takes care of it. So maybe there's something.

ELLIOTT SOBER   There are all kinds of patterns. There are some species in which the females abandon the young and the males care for them. Many species of fish and seahorses do this.

DALAI LAMA   This is fair. The female has already worked by conceiving and keeping the eggs and giving birth. Once she has given birth, it is the male's responsibility. [Laughter]

ROBERT LIVINGSTON   Lizards, on the other hand, lay the egg and leave it to its own resources. There's no female or male contribution to the young lizard.

DALAI LAMA   It is the same for butterflies. From a very early stage they are completely on their own. It is very sad.

NANCY EISENBERG   In the human case, there actually are data on huge differences in the perception of males and females concerning their own sympathy and compassion. And it's interesting. Females *see* themselves as much more compassionate: that's the self-image. However, when you look at other kinds of data, for instance, facial expressions in reaction to others in distress, there is a very small difference, at best, favoring females. And on physiological measures, we have found absolutely no evidence of differences so far.

ELLIOTT SOBER   What about behavior in experiments on helping? Do women help more than men?

NANCY EISENBERG   That depends; it's very complex. We just did a major meta-analysis on children. Meta-analysis is a statistical technique where you combine the findings of many studies and see what they all say together.

There is a really interesting pattern across the tasks that were studied. In general, girls are a bit more helpful, generous, and so forth, but it depends on the task. For instance, in instrumental helping, which is a more masculine activity, there is a much smaller difference. In adults, the evidence in general shows males actually being more helpful, because most of the studies have been done on behavior related to instrumental helping. An example of instrumental helping is helping someone when their car has broken down, or approaching a stranger to help them. In this case, it might be risky for a woman to approach a stranger. So it really depends on the task. Men score higher on instrumental helping but, from what little data we have, females probably score higher on comforting and that kind of helping.

One thing that's important to say about these differences is that they probably aren't organic. They're probably cultural, and perception of competence plays a role. If you feel competent, you can help. It's clear that girls are encouraged to do certain kinds of tasks and males are encouraged to do others.

ROBERT FRANK   On this same point, and also picking up Anne's point from before, there's some very powerful evidence of a kind of difference between male and female compassion in the labor market. We know that people like morally satisfying jobs. If there were two jobs, one more morally satisfying than the other and they both paid the same salary, most people would prefer the morally satisfying job. As a result, the morally satisfying jobs pay less. For example, the publicity director for a cigarette company gets paid more than the publicity director for a charity. We can explain a great deal of the difference in what people earn by how morally satisfying their jobs are.

More interestingly, all of the wage difference between men and women in a large sample of college students was explained by the gender pattern in choices of moral versus nonmoral jobs. The women were much more likely to choose morally satisfying jobs and therefore get paid less. And when the men chose morally satisfying jobs, they got paid less, just the same as the women. It was a very powerful demonstration that to the extent that people have a choice about their jobs, women valued the moral dimension more than men.

DALAI LAMA   Homage to the women. But are there also data from cross-cultural studies relevant to these issues, and what kinds of patterns do they show?

NANCY EISENBERG   There are just one or two here and there. The most interesting one was the one done by the anthropologist Whiting. There were several things found. We already mentioned that children who were assigned important responsibilities for others showed more helpfulness. Another finding was that the women in these cultures played more important roles in the family and elsewhere. The society itself was less complexly layered, with less diversification in occupations. There were gender differences: Older girls particularly were the most prosocial, and they were the ones caring for younger siblings. A few socialization studies have been done in Europe, with similar findings. Generally, the findings have been consistent.

ERVIN STAUB   In one study of aggression, anthropologists looked cross-culturally at the difference in aggressiveness between boys and girls. They found that in each society they looked at, boys were more aggressive than girls. But because there were big differences between societies, girls in some societies were more aggressive than boys in other societies. I see aggression and altruism in many ways as opposites.

DALAI LAMA   Is this difference between societies confined to a particular age group? Do these differences appear right from the beginning or when they reach a certain age? In your talk and also in Nancy's, you spoke about a child's behavior at different ages or grade levels.

ERVIN STAUB   In these studies, researchers didn't look at the very youngest children. They think, as Nancy and I do, that these differences are the result of culture and the way the society operates. They do look at several age groups, though I don't remember the range exactly. But what I described about the relative aggressiveness of boys and girls in different societies holds across different age groups.

NANCY EISENBERG   In Whiting's study on altruism that I mentioned, I'm pretty sure that the sex difference was greater for the older kids than the younger.

DALAI LAMA   At a conference I attended, an anthropologist talked about matriarchal Polynesian societies. Have there been any studies done on that culture to see if the girls tend to be more aggressive? That definitely would indicate that there is cultural influence.

ERVIN STAUB   I don't know of any such study. But there has been a lot of research in the United States on the verbal behavior of men and women in groups. It used to be assumed that men were much more verbally assertive, and that women were verbally submissive and talked a different way. The new research indicates that it very much depends on the position and status of the men and women. Women who are in more important positions behave the way men usually were found to behave.

NANCY EISENBERG   On the cross-cultural issue, there is some research showing that conceptions of what is helpful may differ somewhat. In Western societies like the United States, Europe, and in the Jewish part of Israel, spontaneously offered prosocial behaviors are more valued than helping behaviors in response to requests. But among Arab children in the area around Israel, responding to requests is more valued than just helping without a request. There are also a number of studies on the differences of conceptions of morality between Hindus in India and children and adults in the United States. For instance, interpersonal responsibilities are much more a part of morality and morality is seen as less of a personal decision in the Hindu population than in the United States.

RICHARD DAVIDSON   In our discussion at mealtime, we were reflecting on how there are certain human characteristics, like language, which require exposure to a community in order for them to emerge. Similarly, a characteristic like compassion is like a seed, as Your Holiness described it, which then requires cultivation from a community. We began to consider the prospect that we may be spiritually feral, like a feral child that is deprived of a normal environment. We may be spiritually feral in that we have been deprived of spiritual nourishment in our everyday life. If we were exposed from a very early age to a community that exhibited these characteristics, it is certainly possible that these qualities would be expressed in a stronger way than they are now in the West.

DALAI LAMA We have had such a good, detailed discussion about how we can instill values through various techniques in the upbringing of a child, and the importance of an appropriate environment. Why can't we disseminate this to the wider public, so families can start adopting these practices and rear their children according to these principles? It is through this transformation in the upbringing of children, at the family level, at the community level, at the national level, that we can create a different generation.

If ten families, a hundred families, a thousand families, a million families, sincerely implemented more caring and affection in their way of life, then these children would pass this on to many more when they grow up, marry, and teach their own children. Not only within the family but a similar approach should also be implemented in the schools and academic institutions. That is the way to change humanity.

8. Buddhism without Metaphysics; or, Is Reincarnation Relevant?

ADAM ENGLE Your Holiness, I know you are concerned about secularizing and universalizing our conversation about compassion and its cultivation, and I have the deepest respect for your motivations. At the same time, we have learned that the early environment of children is important in determining their capacity for compassion and altruism. This leads me to think it might be important to look at what happens in Buddhist cultures when children are raised with an understanding of reincarnation and karma. If we could see that Buddhist cultures are more altruistic and compassionate than Western cultures, and that this is partly because of teachings on reincarnation and karma, perhaps we could look into other psychological elements of those teachings, and even see ways to secularize their underlying message. For example, Your Holiness said that lack of personal responsibility and short-sightedness are fundamental problems. Reincarnation and karma seem to address those issues: They make you more personally responsible and help you to take the long view.

MICHAEL SAUTMAN Adam, I think you are making an assumption that there is more compassion in Buddhist cultures. If you look at Cambodia, Vietnam, China, in many countries based on Buddhist cultures, great atrocities have taken place.

RICHARD DAVIDSON   Your Holiness, in our discussions at mealtime over the course of this week, the issues of karma and reincarnation have also arisen in connection with altruism and compassion. For Western scientists, those are not familiar concepts and they raise many questions. I wonder if you can speak to that, so we can better understand the role of these concepts in Buddhist doctrine and how you think they may influence the spontaneous expression of altruism and compassion, as well as the cultivation of compassion in meditation practice.

DALAI LAMA   Much of the discussion in the Buddhist teachings on techniques for enhancing our compassionate disposition, and also our understanding of compassion, are very much based on Buddhist doctrines such as the theory of rebirth and the nature of karma, as well as on the notion of perfectibility—the possibility of attaining spiritual perfection. Part of that, of course, is the fundamental Buddhist tenet that all sentient beings possess the potential for enlightenment. All of these, in addition to the Buddhist understanding of the nonsubstantial and interdependent nature of reality, inform the various techniques that you find in the Buddhist teachings for cultivating compassion. But that does not mean that it is impossible to cultivate compassion without these doctrines as a basis. I personally feel it is possible to develop a practical system in the framework of a single lifetime that cultivates compassion and altruistic behavior.

Here in this discussion, the speakers are all coming from different backgrounds and representing different disciplines. But it seems there is a consensus emerging that compassion is something that can be cultivated and enhanced, and something that is very fundamental to human nature. But the minute you bring in metaphysical notions like rebirth, it will have less impact on the majority of the people, although a lot of us here personally may agree about the importance of such doctrines.

RICHARD DAVIDSON   I agree. But leaving aside the metaphysical issue there is a psychological consequence to the belief in rebirth, I think, which is that people feel more interdependent, more connected to everybody else. For the large majority who do not believe in rebirth, is there anything else that you could offer to enhance this feeling of connectedness?

DALAI LAMA   Well, one area where we could develop this conviction more and have a better understanding of interdependence is through understanding the very complex nature of the modern economy, not only nationally but globally. Also I think the issue of ecology is important here. The realities here show us how we are connected, how we have to work together.

One of the values that gets in the way of developing this sense of interconnectedness with others is the idea of national sovereignty. In my own case, because the Tibetan nation has passed through a difficult period, we need some kind of patriotism in order to carry on the struggle. But at the same time we are also part of humanity. We cannot forget about the ultimate goal or the basic thinking that all of humanity is the same. This is what I call a sense of global responsibility. However, in order to develop a genuine sense of global responsibility, first each individual community should have a sense of security. It is very difficult for a community who themselves face a threat to develop that kind of global responsibility. So, you see, there is no contradiction. Contradictions arise when one goes to extremes in disregarding the rights of others.

ANNE HARRINGTON   What I am hearing Your Holiness say is that there have been times when rebirth seemed plausible to enough people that it would stand as a belief that also advanced important human goals, and therefore was valuable. But if, in today's world, rebirth is no longer plausible to the majority of people, it is best to put it aside and find a more plausible belief that advances the same primary human goals. This thought took me back to the understanding of knowledge that I raised at the beginning of this conference: In some sense, human values and our idea of the kind of life we want to live are primary, and we then search for plausible truths that advance those goals as a secondary effort. This does not mean we make the world up. But it may make the relationship between our moral positions and our understanding of science a more dialogical process, rather than a process of looking to science for authority and then adopting it in accordance. We know what sort of people we want to become. We know what sort of world we want to create, and we need to both find and challenge ourselves with truths that advance human life and not hinder it.

DALAI LAMA   When I spoke about the ineffectiveness of appealing to Buddhist doctrines like rebirth, I was talking about the non-Buddhist general public. For the Buddhists, rebirth is still a very powerful and important belief. My main audience is the majority of nonbelievers.

Also, I am sensitive to the implication that I am trying to propagate Buddhist ideas. That's not good. One of my main concerns now is genuine harmony among different religious traditions. In some cases, the work of missionaries undermines this. I have a slightly critical view about this, especially after my visit to Mongolia. Mongolia is a Buddhist country where a lot of missionaries came, which I felt was not very good. From our side, we have no interest in missionary work and conversion. Therefore, I am a little bit sensitive about this: I do not want to bring religious ideas into the public sphere.

Still sometimes when I look at modern scientific analysis, whether of cosmology or particularly of our behavior and emotions and different temperaments, I am struck by the diversity. For a Buddhist, once you believe in rebirth, it becomes easier to account for variations because you can talk about habits and dispositions being carried over through successive lifetimes. In the current scientific paradigm, you have to account for every aspect of these differences within the frame of a single lifetime, through environmental conditions and differences in upbringing. Sometimes I feel that it really makes the task much more complex and difficult. Buddhism is no match for science when it comes to the discussion of the nature of physical reality. But I feel that sometime in the future our concept of science will expand so it will be able to embrace the inner sciences that Buddhism has been committed to as well. When people say "science" then, it will not be confined to the objective physical domain alone. And this may change lots of things.

9. Closing Remarks

RICHARD DAVIDSON   Let me take this opportunity to express my very deep gratitude on behalf of all of the participants for your time and generosity. It has personally been a privilege and an honor for me to be the scientific coordinator for this meeting. We've had many stimulating exchanges and I believe that each of us, as we go back into our respective academic disciplines, has been very significantly touched by our participation in this meeting. It is my firm conviction that this process will facilitate change in our disciplines in a way that will promote altruism, compassion, and ethics more forcefully. I also believe that we've all been touched personally as well as academically by the opportunity to interact with Your Holiness. We are very deeply grateful and give you our heartfelt thanks.

DALAI LAMA   I would also like to express my deep thanks to all of you for putting so much effort, out of great commitment, into explaining the various points from your own respective disciplines.

Although there are a number of people around us, when the individual speakers were making their presentations, most of the time they were looking straight into my eyes. So it also makes me feel that I ought to be more responsible. I would like to express my deep thanks for your showing so much concern to me personally.

If I'm allowed to make a critical comment here, there is one thing I would like to say. Sometimes as a Buddhist when I look at much of the research that you have conducted, it seems that scientists first set clear parameters and then make a decision that whatever explanation they are seeking must be found in science. My hope is that one of these days there will no longer be any need for these parameters, this fence. People will be much more open and flexible, looking at any event or phenomenon from many different angles and perspectives freely.

So thank you. That's all. As Tibetans, we always consider that when we make a friendship, it remains until the last day. That is our tradition. Thank you.

Appendix: About the Mind and Life Institute

The Mind and Life dialogues between His Holiness the Dalai Lama and Western scientists were brought to life through a collaboration between R. Adam Engle, a North American businessman, and Dr. Francisco J. Varela, a Chilean-born neuroscientist living and working in Paris. In 1983, both men independently had the initiative to create a series of cross-cultural meetings between His Holiness and Western scientists.

Engle, a Buddhist practitioner since 1974, had become aware of His Holiness's long-standing and keen interest in science, and His desire to both deepen His understanding of Western science and to share his understanding of Eastern contemplative science with Westerners. In 1983, Engle began work on this project, and in the autumn of 1984, Engle and Michael Sautman met with His Holiness's younger brother, Tendzin Choegyal (Ngari Rinpoche), in Los Angeles and presented their plan to create a week-long cross-cultural scientific meeting. Rinpoche graciously offered to take the matter up with His Holiness. Within days, Rinpoche reported that His Holiness would very much like to participate in such a discussion and authorized plans for a first meeting.

Varela, also a Buddhist practitioner since 1974, had met His Holiness at an international meeting in 1983, the Alpbach Symposia on Consciousness. Their communication was immediate. His Holiness was keenly interested in science but had little opportunity for discussion with brain scientists who had some understanding of Tibetan Buddhism. This encounter led to a series of informal discussions over the next few years;

through these discussions, His Holiness expressed the desire to have more extensive, planned time for mutual discussion and inquiry.

In the spring of 1985, Dr. Joan Halifax, then the director of the Ojai Foundation, and a friend of Varela, became aware that Engle and Sautman were moving forward with their meeting plans. She contacted them on Varela's behalf and suggested that they all work together to organize the first meeting collaboratively. The four gathered at the Ojai Foundation in October of 1985 and agreed to go forward jointly. They decided to focus on the scientific disciplines that address mind and life, since these disciplines might provide the most fruitful interface with the Buddhist tradition. That insight provided the name of the project and, in time, of the Mind and Life Institute itself.

It took two more years of work and communication with the Private Office of His Holiness before the first meeting was held in Dharamsala in October 1987. During this time, Engle and Varela collaborated closely to find a useful structure for the meeting. Varela, acting as scientific coordinator, was primarily responsible for the scientific content of the meeting, issuing invitations to scientists and editing a volume from transcripts of the meeting. Engle, acting as general coordinator, was responsible for fundraising, relations with His Holiness and His office, and all other aspects of the project. This division of responsibility between general and scientific coordinators has been part of the organizational strategy for all subsequent meetings. While Dr. Varela has not been the scientific coordinator of all the subsequent meetings, he has remained a guiding force in the Mind and Life Institute, which was formally incorporated in 1990 with Engle as its Chairman.

A word is in order here concerning these conferences' unique character. The bridges that can mutually enrich traditional Buddhist thought and modern life science are notoriously difficult to build. Varela had a first taste of these difficulties while helping to establish a science program at Naropa Institute, a liberal arts institution created by Tibetan meditation master Chogyam Trungpa as a meeting ground between Western traditions and contemplative studies. In 1979 the program received a grant from the Sloan Foundation to organize what was probably the very first conference of its kind: "Comparative Approaches to Cognition: Western and Buddhist." Some twenty-five academics from prominent North American institutions convened. Their disciplines included mainstream philosophy, cognitive science (neurosciences, experimental psychology, linguistics, artificial intelligence) and, of course, Buddhist studies. The gathering's difficulties served as a hard lesson on the organizational care and finesse that a successful cross-cultural dialogue requires.

Thus in 1987, wishing to avoid some of the pitfalls encountered during the Naropa experience, several operating principles were adopted that have contributed significantly to the success of the Mind and Life series. These include the following:

- Choosing open-minded and well-respected scientists who ideally have some familiarity with Buddhism
- Creating fully participatory meetings where His Holiness is briefed on general scientific background from a nonpartisan perspective before discussion is opened
- Employing gifted translators like Dr. Thupten Jinpa, Dr. Alan Wallace, and Dr. José Cabezón, who are comfortable with scientific vocabulary in both Tibetan and English
- Finally, creating a private, protected space where relaxed and spontaneous discussion can proceed away from the Western media's watchful eye

The first Mind and Life Conference took place in October of 1987 in Dharamsala. The meeting focused on the basic groundwork of modern cognitive science, the most natural starting point for a dialogue between the Buddhist tradition and modern science. The curriculum for the first conference introduced broad themes from cognitive science, including scientific method, neurobiology, cognitive psychology, artificial intelligence, brain development, and evolution. In attendance were Jeremy Hayward (physics and philosophy of science), Robert Livingston (neuroscience and medicine), Eleonor Rosch (cognitive science), and Newcomb Greenleaf (computer science). At our concluding session, the Dalai Lama asked us to continue the dialogue with biennial conferences. Mind and Life I was published as *Gentle Bridges: Conversations with the Dalai Lama on the Sciences of Mind*, edited by Jeremy Hayward and Francisco Varela (Boston: Shambala Publications, 1992). The volume has been translated into French, Spanish, Portuguese, German, Japanese, Chinese, and Thai.

Mind and Life II took place in October 1989 in Newport Beach, California, with Robert Livingston as the scientific coordinator. The conference focused on neuroscience and the mind/body relationship. Participants included Patricia Smith Churchland (philosophy), Antonio R. Damasio (neurology), J. Allan Hobson (psychiatry), Lewis L. Judd (psychopharmacology), and Larry R. Squire (psychiatry). Coinciding fortuitously with the announcement of the award of the Nobel Peace Prize to His Holiness, the two-day meeting was atypical for the Mind and Life Conferences both in its brevity and its Western venue. It has been published as *Consciousness at the Crossroads: Conversations with the Dalai Lama on Brain Science and Buddhism* (Ithaca: Snow Lion Publications, 1999).

Mind and Life III was held in Dharamsala in 1990. Daniel Goleman (psychology) served as scientific coordinator. This meeting focused on the relationship between emotions and health. Participants included Dan Brown (experimental psychology), Jon Kabat-Zinn (medicine), Clifford Saron (neuroscience), Lee Yearly (philosophy), and Francisco Varela (immunology and neuroscience). Mind and Life III was published as *Healing Emotions: Conversations with the Dalai Lama on Mindfulness, Emotions, and Health*, edited by Daniel Goleman (Boston: Shambala Publications, 1997). That volume has been translated into French, Spanish, Portuguese, German, Japanese, Chinese, Dutch, Italian, and Polish.

During Mind and Life III a new mode of exploration emerged: participants initiated a research project to investigate the neurobiological effects of meditation on long-term meditators. To facilitate such research, the Mind and Life network was created to connect other scientists interested in both Eastern contemplative experience and Western science. With seed money from the Hershey family Foundation, the Mind and Life Institute was born. The Fetzer Institute funded two years of network expenses and the initial stages of the research project. Research continues on various topics such as the effect of meditation on emotional processes, attention, and their neural substrates.

We met for the fourth Mind and Life Conference in Dharamsala in October 1992, with Francisco Varela again acting as scientific coordinator. The dialogue focused on the areas of sleep, dreams, and the process of dying. Participants were Charles Taylor (philosophy), Jerome Engle (medicine), Joan Halifax (anthropology, death and dying), Jayne Gackenbach (psychology of lucid dreaming), and Joyce McDougall (psychoanalysis). The account of this conference is now available as *Sleeping, Dreaming and Dying: An Exploration of Consciousness with the Dalai Lama*, edited by Francisco J. Varela (Boston: Wisdom Publications, 1997). That volume has been translated into French, Spanish, German, Japanese, and Chinese.

After Mind and Life V, which took place in 1995, (the subject of this volume), Mind and Life VI opened a new area of exploration beyond the previous focus on life science. That meeting took place in Dharamsala in

October 1997, with Arthur Zajonc (physics) as the scientific coordinator. The topic was The New Physics and Cosmology. The participants, in addition to Dr. Zajonc and His Holiness, were David Finkelstein (physics), George Greenstein (astronomy), Piet Hut (astrophysics), Tu Weiming (philosophy), and Anton Zeilinger (quantum physics). The volume covering this meeting is in preparation.

The dialogue on quantum physics was continued at a smaller meeting held at Anton Zeilinger's laboratories at the Institut für Experimentalphysic in Innsbruck, Austria, in June 1998. Present were His Holiness, Drs. Zeilinger and Zajonc, and interpreters Wallace and Jinpa. That meeting was written up for a cover story in the January 1999 issue of *GEO* magazine of Germany.

In March 2000, our next meeting will be held in Dharamsala, with Daniel Goleman as scientific coordinator. The discussion will return to cognitive sciences, with a focus on destructive emotions.

ACKNOWLEDGMENTS   Over the years, the Mind and Life Conferences have been supported by the generosity of several individuals and organizations.

Barry and Connie Hershey of the Hershey Family Foundation have been our most loyal and steadfast patrons since 1990. Not only has their generous support guaranteed the continuity of the conferences, but also it has breathed life into the Mind and Life Institute itself.

The Institute has also received generous financial support from the Fetzer Institute, The Nathan Cummings Foundation, Mr. Branco Weiss, Mr. Adam Engle, Michael Sautman, Mr. and Mrs. R. Thomas Northcote, Ms. Christine Austin, Mr. Dennis Perlman, Mr. Donald Gevirts, Ms. Michele Grennon, Dr. Howard Cutler, and Joe and Mary Ellyn Sensenbrenner. On behalf of His Holiness the Dalai Lama and all the other participants over the years, we thank all of these individuals and organizations. Your generosity has had a profound impact on the lives of many people.

We would also like to thank a number of people for their assistance in making the work of the Institute itself a success. Many of these people have assisted the Institute since its inception. We thank and acknowledge His Holiness the Dalai Lama; Tenzin Geyche Tethong and the other wonderful people of the Private Office of His Holiness; Ngari Rinpoche and Rinchen Khandro, together with the staff of Kashmir Cottage; all the scientists and other participants; scientific coordinators; our extraordinary interpreters; Maazda Travel in the United States and Middle Path Travel in India; Pier Luigi Luisi; Elaine Jackson; Zara Houshmand; Dr. Thubten Jinpa, Dr. Alan Wallace, and Dr. Jose Cabezón; Clifford Saron; Alan Kelly; Peter Jepson; Pat Rockland; Thubten Chodron; Laurel Chiten; Shambala Publications; Wisdom Publications; and Snow Lion Publications.

The Mind and Life Institute was created in 1990 as a 501(c) 3 public charity to support the Mind and Life dialogues and to promote cross-cultural scientific research and understanding.

Mailing address: P.O. Box 808, Boulder Creek, CA 95006
Website: www.mindandlife.org
Email: info@mindandlife.org

Index

Baker, Russell, 182–83
bargaining, 188–89, 201
BAS. *See* Behavioral Activation
   Scale
beauty, 69
behavior, 222–23
Behavioral Activation Scale
   (BAS), 118, 120
Behavioral Inhibition Scale (BIS),
   118
behavioral predispositions,
   190–94, 205
Bhagsu Mountain, 3, 6
Big Bang, 97
biology, 214, 216–19, 221
biomedicine, 83
BIS. *See* Behavioral Inhibition
   Scale
blink magnitude, 119
bodhisattvas, 43, 96
body language, 192
bombing, 202
Bosnia, 174
brain, 228
   Dalai Lama on, 123
   damage, 112–13
   and emotion, 110–24
   and meditation, 6, 123
   prefrontal cortex, 110–15
   See also mind
breast-feeding, 71, 99
Brentano, F., 35
Brown, Dan, 250
Buddhism
   as benign religion, 132
   compassion in, 42–43, 132–33,
      134, 242
   lack of word for emotion in,
      31–32
   meditation in, 5, 6, 7, 98,
      107–8, 139, 223
   model of human behavior,
      223

and "natural state" of humans,
   22
positive and negative mental
   factors, 39–41
reincarnation and karma in,
   242–45
role of emotion in, 9, 41–44
and self-interest, 195–96
spiritual endeavor in, 84
state of nothingness in, 133
and suffering, 19
via positiva, 133
view of mind, 4, 34–38, 96, 97,
   223
and Western science, 19
See also cross-cultural research;
   Dalai Lama
Burundi, 174
butterflies, 194–95, 238
bystanders, 165–66, 173

Cabezón, José, 4, 10, 12
caita, 37, 38
cancer, 74, 220
capitalism, 207
Chamberlain, Neville, 194
chance, 67
character, 205, 207
characteristics, of organisms, 48
charity, 24
children
   caring and nonviolent, 175–78
   and conflict in family, 154–55
   Dalai Lama on, 70–71, 73, 77,
      156, 242
   difference between sympathy
      and personal distress,
      136–37
   empathy-related responding,
      139–50
   gender differences, 240–41
   helping behavior, 167–68, 176,
      239

learning by doing, 154,
176
modeling of behavior, 152
need for structure and guidance, 176
nondisciplinary verbalizations
for, 153
parental care, 58–59, 70–71,
152
parental disciplinary practices,
142–48, 151–52
parental love, 58, 63, 77
parent-child relationship and
vicarious responding,
141–43
prefrontal asymmetry, 122
raised in Buddhism, 242
reinforcement for prosocial
behavior, 153–54
socialization of sympathy versus socialization of prosocial
behavior, 150–55
sympathetic reactions, 100
teaching moral values, 207,
208–9
televison viewing, 234, 236
and violence, 234
Christianity, 22
"chump model," 207
Churchland, Patricia Smith, 249
circles of compassion, 47, 58–63
citta, 37, 38
clarity, 35–36, 37
cocaine, 115
cognition, 33, 35–38, 228–29
commitment, 186–90, 196
commitment model, 196–200,
202, 203, 205–10
communication, 11
community of nations, 174
comparative fitness, 60–61
compassion
of bodhisattvas, 43

in Buddhism, 42–43, 132–33,
134, 242
capacity for, 222–25, 242
circle of, 47, 58–62
Dalai Lama on, 68–70, 73–75,
77–79, 90, 98, 102, 224–26,
229, 243
as emotion, 31–45
extended, 61–63, 64
as fragile, 90–91
gender differences in inclination toward, 236–42
and happiness, 97–100
in human nature, 20–26,
42–43, 70, 85–89
as "knowing eye," 26–29
limited, 61–62
in meditation, 15, 98
neglect by biobehavioral
sciences, 82–84
origin of, 95
and positive affect, 107–25
as producer of biological benefits, 94
as product of evolution, 96
and prosocial action,
225–27
recognition of in others,
100–103
role of rational factors in
prosocial, 228–30
science of versus compassionate science, 18–30
Tibetan monks on, 14–15
competition, 51, 61, 77, 88
altruism in competitive environments, 182–211
as "natural," 91–94
conditioning, 223
conflicts of interest, 59
Confucius, 227
consciousness, 37–38, 96, 97, 99,
107

joy, 74, 86
Judaism, 22
Judd, Lewis L., 249
justice, 69

Kabat-Zinn, Jon, 123, 250
Kagan, Jerome, 196
karma, 242, 243
karuna (compassion), 133, 139
kindness, 46–47, 86
kin selection model, 185
knowledge, 19, 84, 85

leadership, 92
learning, 143, 223
life, 217–20
liking system, 112
linguistic processing, 4
Livingston, Robert, 249
lizard, 238
Lorenz, Konrad, 234
love, 69, 72, 77, 86, 87–88, 175, 218
loving-kindness, 42
lying, 69, 194, 195, 209, 216

MAD. *See* Mutually Assured Destruction
Maharishi Mahesh Yogi, 17n.5
Mahayana Buddhism, 95–96
marriage, 95–96, 189
Marxism, 70
materialism, 36, 207, 209
McClelland, David, 94
McDougall, Joyce, 250
McGuire, Michael, 92
meditation
  and brain activity, 6, 123
  Buddhist, 5, 6, 7, 98, 107–8, 139, 223
  compassion in, 15, 98
  early studies on, 5–6
  long-term effects of, 4, 6

unusual mental powers associated with, 4–5
meditative quiescence, 7–8
Meehl, Paul, 117
men, 236–42
mental factors, 37–43
mental illness, 26
mental imagery. *See* visualization
mental retardation, 224
mental state, 37–38
mental typologies, 31–45
mesolimbic dopaminergic pathway, 115
meta-analysis, 239
metta (kindness), 133, 135
military/strategic planning, 202
mimicry, 194–96
mind, 12, 34
  Buddhist view of, 4, 34–38, 96
  continuum of, 96, 223
  Plato on, 33
  training, 3–17
Mind and Life Institute, 4, 6, 247–51
mind-body dualism, 36
missionaries, 245
Modern Synthesis, 53
modifications, 48
Monarch butterfly, 194–95
monasteries, 69
Mongolia, 245
monks, 3–4, 6, 10–16, 17n.9, 90
morality
  Dalai Lama on, 66, 68, 77, 80, 214–16, 221
  Darwin on, 52–53, 60
  derivation of from natural principles, 214–22
  and emotional predispositions, 197–98, 203
  helping for reasons of, 169, 229

prefrontal cortex (PFC), 110–15, 228
prefrontal electrical asymmetries, 117–22
pregoal attainment positive affect, 111–12, 114
principal-agent problem, 199–201
procaine, 115
prosocial actions
  and compassion, 225–27
  and empathy-related respond-ing, 134–49
  modeling of, 152
  parental emphasis on, 154
  reinforcement for, 153–54
  socialization of versus social-ization of sympathy, 150–55
prosocial compassionate feeling, 228–30
prosocial value orientation, 168–69
psychological egoism, 47
psychology, 82–84

quality of life, 220

Rand Corporation, 202
rank, 92–94
rats, 122
reality, 20, 171, 221
reason, 76, 85, 229–30
reasonable inference, 197
rebirth. *See* reincarnation
reciprocal altruism, 185
reciprocity, 169
recognition, 38
reincarnation, 12, 223, 242–45
relaxation, 7
religion, 22, 68, 132, 134, 208
reproduction, 217, 219
Republic (Plato), 33
reputation, 185

responsibility, 166–70, 226, 227
reward, 153
rhesus monkey, 120–21
Rinpoche, Ngari, 247
Rosch, Eleonor, 249
rules, 177
Rwanda, 174

sadness, 15
Sāṃkhya metaphysics, 36, 45n.9
Saron, Clifford, 4, 250
satiation, 111
Sautman, Michael, 247, 248
scapegoating, 171–72
Schelling, Thomas, 186–87
scholarship, 85
schools, 208–9
science
  and Buddhism, 19–20
  and compassion, 18–30
  Dalai Lama on, 245
  knowledge of as neutral, 84–85
  and suffering, 19–20
  See also cross-cultural research
seahorse, 238
secular morality, 221, 222
self-interest, 98, 169, 186–89, 192, 193, 195–96, 205–7
self-interest model, 183–85, 196, 199–202, 210
selfishness, 21, 53–58, 77, 78, 195
self-sacrifice, 21
serotonin, 92
sex, 217
shamatha. See meditative quies-cence
shirking, in workplace, 199–201
Simpson, Gregory, 4
slavery, 70

weapons, 233–34
Weiming, Tu, 251
Weinberg, Steven, 20
Weisskopf, Victor, 18
welfare, 24
Wiesel, Elie, 22
Williams, G.C., 53, 54
wisdom, 42
witnesses, 166
women, 236–42

workplace
  morally satisfying jobs, 239–40
  shirking on job, 199–201
  wage and price setting, 201–2
World War II, 202

Yearly, Lee, 250

Zajonc, Arthur, 251
Zeilinger, Anton, 251

Lightning Source UK Ltd.
Milton Keynes UK
22 March 2011

169661UK00007B/26/A